SOME
ANSWERED
QUESTIONS

SOME ANSWERED QUESTIONS

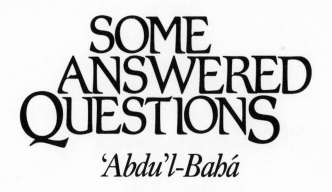

'Abdu'l-Bahá

Collected and translated
from the Persian
by
Laura Clifford Barney

BAHÁ'Í PUBLISHING TRUST
WILMETTE, ILLINOIS 60091

Library of Congress Cataloging in Publication Data

Abdul Baha, 1844–1921.
  Some answered questions.

  Includes bibliographical references and index.
  1. Bahaism—Doctrines. I. Barney, Laura Clifford.
II. Title.
BP360.A3813 1981   297'.892   81-2467
ISBN 0-87743-162-0   AACR2
ISBN 0-87743-163-9 (pbk.)

The first edition of *Some Answered Questions* was published
in 1908 by Kegan Paul, Trench, Trubner & Co. Ltd.
The first U.S. edition was published in 1918,
subsequent editions appearing in
1930, 1954, and 1981.

Design by John Solarz

Printed in the United States of America

CONTENTS

Part 2

SOME CHRISTIAN SUBJECTS

Part 3

ON THE POWERS AND CONDITIONS OF THE MANIFESTATIONS OF GOD

Part 4

ON THE ORIGIN, POWERS AND
CONDITIONS OF MAN

Part 5

MISCELLANEOUS SUBJECTS

PUBLISHER'S FOREWORD TO 1981 EDITION

CAN we know God? Is there a God? Can religious teaching be reconciled with scientific knowledge? What does it mean to be human? These are questions that once were considered exclusively the province of philosophers and theologians. But no more. In our time they are public domain. Our distressed and bewildered civilization, cut loose from the beliefs and values that sustained it for centuries, totters on the brink of self-destruction. We, the individuals in it, experience loss of the meaning and purpose in life that our ancestors took for granted. Today these questions beg for answers.

Some Answered Questions addresses, in a charming, succinct, and logical manner, not only questions about God and the relationship between science and religion but a wide range of questions certain to be of interest to the soul in search of religious truth as well as to the inquisitive, scientific mind. The answers come from 'Abdu'l-Bahá, son of the Prophet-Founder of the Bahá'í Faith, a new and independent world religion with followers in virtually every country. The answers were compiled from a series of talks He gave at table during 1904, 1905, and 1906. In each of the five sections of the book 'Abdu'l-Bahá expounds questions ranging from the metaphysical to the matter-of-fact. On the one hand, He reaches into the philosophical realm to discuss topics such as immortality, predestination, free will, and the erroneous doctrine of reincarnation—always treading the mystical path with practical feet. On the other hand, He speaks to questions concerning the organization of human society—questions such as the problem of strikes, the treatment of criminals, and the proper relations between capital and labor—infusing these ordinarily secular matters with spiritual significance.

In the opening section of *Some Answered Questions* 'Abdu'l-Bahá uses both logical and traditional proofs to establish the existence of God and the necessity of Divine Educators or Manifestations of God. He devotes several talks to the lives and accomplishments of some of these Divine Manifestations, including Abraham, Moses, Christ, Muḥammad, the Báb, and Bahá'u'lláh, seeing each as a successive link in God's unfolding plan for mankind's education. Thus He sheds new light on religious history and on the nature of religion itself. 'Abdu'l-Bahá returns to the theme of Manifestations of God in the third section of the book, where He elucidates in greater detail the character, station, and powers of the unique Beings chosen to act as God's spokesmen.

In the second section of *Some Answered Questions* 'Abdu'l-Bahá presents the Bahá'í point of view on a number of knotty Christian subjects. He gives particular attention to the issue of the "return" or Second Coming of Christ. He also examines the birth of Christ, the Resurrection, baptism, the meaning of the eucharist, the miracles of Christ, and the Trinity in a manner that readers schooled in traditional Christian doctrine are sure to find startlingly fresh and illuminating.

In the fourth section of the book 'Abdu'l-Bahá considers the origin, powers, and conditions of man. The Bahá'í affirmation of an underlying harmony and agreement between science and religion comes alive in His explanation of the origin and development of the human species. The book's fifth and final section is devoted to miscellaneous subjects, including discussions of the grounds of human knowledge and of pantheism.

Some Answered Questions, in style and structure, is unlike

'Abdu'l-Bahá's other works. His *Will and Testament*, written in three sections, provides the authority for the Administrative Order of the Bahá'í Faith and ensures its integrity and unity. *The Secret of Divine Civilization* is a treatise on the general state of modern civilization. *A Traveler's Narrative* chronicles the early history of the Bábí and Bahá'í Faiths. *Memorials of the Faithful* contains 'Abdu'l-Bahá's remembrances of seventy-nine early Bahá'ís, all bound by their love for Bahá'u'lláh. Only *Some Answered Questions*, shaped as it is from questions put to Him over meals, affords the reader essays on a variety of themes— each of which can be read either at one sitting as an individual topic for study and reflection, or as part of a whole that emerges from the collection of talks. Most of the talks are short. All bear the marks of conversation. All use lucid, concrete illustrations to clarify difficult topics. Humor relieves the serious. At every turn a "brilliant simplicity," "persuasiveness," and "force" illuminate the fundamentals and the fine points of Bahá'í belief.

The Bahá'í Faith was founded by Mírzá Ḥusayn 'Alí (1817–1892), known as Bahá'u'lláh, the "Glory of God." The Bahá'í Faith's origins are intimately linked with the Bábí Faith, founded in Persia (Írán) in 1844 by Mírzá 'Alí-Muḥammad (1819–1850), known as the Báb, or "Gate." The Báb announced that He was not only the founder of an independent religion, but the herald of a new and far greater prophet or messenger of God, Who would usher in an age of peace for all mankind. In 1863 Bahá'u'lláh declared that He was the One prophesied by the Báb.

Bahá'u'lláh's teachings quickly brought Him into conflict with the Persian government and the Muslim clergy, and He was exiled from Írán to various places within the Ottoman Empire. In 1868 He was sent as a prisoner to the fortress city of 'Akká in the Holy Land, in the vicinity of which He passed away in 1892. In His will

He appointed 'Abdu'l-Bahá (1844–1921), His eldest son, to succeed Him in leading the Bahá'í community and in interpreting the Bahá'í writings. 'Abdu'l-Bahá in turn appointed His eldest grandson, Shoghi Effendi (1897–1957), as His successor, the Guardian of the Cause and authorized interpreter of the Bahá'í teachings. Today the affairs of the Bahá'í world community are administered by The Universal House of Justice, the supreme elected council of the Bahá'í Faith.

The central teachings of the Bahá'í Faith are the oneness of God, the oneness of religion, and the oneness of mankind. The fundamental principles proclaimed by Bahá'u'lláh are that religious truth is not absolute but relative; that Divine Revelation is a continuous and progressive process; that all the great religions of the world are divine in origin; and that their missions represent successive stages in the spiritual evolution of human society. Since Bahá'u'lláh teaches that the purpose of religion is the promotion of concord and unity and that religion is the foremost agency for the achievement of peace and orderly progress in society, the Bahá'í writings provide the outline of institutions necessary for the establishment of peace and world order. These include a world federation or commonwealth, with executive, legislative, and judiciary arms; an international auxiliary language; a world economy; a mechanism for world intercommunication; and a universal system of currency, weights, and measures.

The Bahá'í writings also provide specific guidance that helps Bahá'ís (followers of Bahá'u'lláh) fulfill the basic purpose of human life—knowing and worshiping God and "carrying forward an ever-advancing civilization"—while they strive to bring about the unity of mankind, world peace, and world order. For example, the Bahá'í writings call for the fostering of a good character and the development of spiritual qualities such as honesty, trustworthiness, compassion, and justice. These are achieved through prayer, meditation, and work done in the spirit of service to humanity—all expressions, for Bahá'ís, of the worship of God. In the pursuance of the Bahá'í principle of the organic oneness of humanity, the Bahá'í writings call for the eradication of prejudices of race, creed, class, nationality, and sex. They call for the systematic elimination of all forms of superstition hampering human progress and the achievement of a balance between the material and spiritual aspects of life, both of which rest on an understanding of the principles of an unfettered search for truth and of the harmony of science and religion as two facets of truth. They encourage the development of the unique talents and abilities of every individual, through the pursuit of knowledge and the acquisition of skills, for the practice of a trade or profession is required not only for personal satisfaction but also for the enrichment of society as a whole. They call for the full participation of both men and women in all aspects of community life, including the elective and administrative processes and decision-making, in implementation of the Bahá'í principle of equal opportunities, rights, and privileges for both sexes. They call for the fostering of the principle of universal compulsory education.

Some Answered Questions has appeared in a number of editions since it was first published in London in 1908. It continues to be one of the most popular and eagerly sought after works in the growing literature of the Bahá'í Faith. More important, the book has assumed a significant place in the sacred literature of the Faith, being one of the very few compilations of 'Abdu'l-Bahá's utterances authenticated by 'Abdu'l-Bahá Himself. This new edition once more makes readily available a priceless resource for the student of the Bahá'í teachings and for the seeking soul.

PUBLISHER'S FOREWORD TO 1964 EDITION

In view of questions that have sometimes arisen concerning *Some Answered Questions* and how it came to be written, Laura Clifford Barney, the interlocutor who obtained the answers from 'Abdu'l-Bahá, has made known to the publishers the following facts:

THE talks between 'Abdu'l-Bahá and Laura Clifford Barney took place during the difficult years, 1904–1906, when He was confined to the city of 'Akká by the Turkish government and permitted to receive only a few visitors. At the time He was under constant threat of removal to a distant desert confinement.

As interlocutor, Miss Barney arranged for one of 'Abdu'l-Bahá's sons-in-law, or for one of the three distinguished Persians of His secretariat of that period, to be present during the talks to insure accuracy in recording His replies to the questions asked Him. 'Abdu'l-Bahá later read the transcriptions, sometimes changing a word or a line with His reed pen. They were later translated into English by Miss Barney. The original Persian texts are today a part of the Bahá'í archives of Haifa. For additional commentary on this work, refer to Shoghi Effendi's statements in *God Passes By*, pages 107, 260, 268, 305 and 383.

'Abdu'l-Bahá was finally freed in 1908 after the revolution in the Ottoman Empire and the overthrow of the Sultán. A few years later He traveled to Egypt, Europe and North America, welcoming persons of all religious faiths and classes, meeting outstanding personalities, and speaking before groups in temples, universities, religious centers and missions, as well as before friendly home gatherings.

AUTHOR'S PREFACE TO FIRST EDITION

"I HAVE given to you my tired moments," were the words of 'Abdu'l-Bahá as He rose from table after answering one of my questions.

As it was on this day, so it continued; between the hours of work, His fatigue would find relief in renewed activity; occasionally He was able to speak at length; but often, even though the subject might require more time, He would be called away after a few moments; again, days and even weeks would pass, in which He had no opportunity of instructing me. But I could well be patient, for I had always before me the greater lesson—the lesson of His personal life.

During my several visits to 'Akká, these answers were written down in Persian while 'Abdu'l-Bahá spoke, not with a view to publication, but simply that I might have them for future study. At first they had to be adapted to the verbal translation of the interpreter; and later, when I had acquired a slight knowledge of Persian, to my limited vocabulary. This accounts for repetition of figures and phrases, for no one has a more extensive command of felicitous expressions than 'Abdu'l-Bahá. In these lessons He is the teacher adapting Himself to His pupil, and not the orator or poet.

This book presents only certain aspects of the Bahá'í Faith, which is universal in its message and has for each questioner the answer suited to his special development and needs.

In my case the teachings were made simple, to correspond to my rudimentary knowledge, and are therefore in no way complete and exhaustive, as the Table of Contents may suggest—the Table of Contents having been added merely to indicate the subjects treated of. But I believe that what has been so valuable to me may be of use to others, since all men, notwithstanding their differences, are united in their search for reality; and I have therefore asked 'Abdu'l-Bahá's permission to publish these talks.

Originally they were not given in any special order, but have now been roughly classified for the convenience of the reader. The Persian text has been closely followed, at times even to the detriment of the English, a few alterations being made in the translation merely where the literal rendering seemed too involved and obscure; and the interpolated words, required to make the meaning clearer, have not been indicated in any way in order to avoid the too frequent interruption of the thought by technical or explanatory signs. Also many of the Persian and Arabic names have been written in their simplest form without strictly adhering to a scientific system which would be confusing to the average reader.

LAURA CLIFFORD BARNEY

Part One

ON THE INFLUENCE OF THE PROPHETS
IN THE EVOLUTION OF
HUMANITY

1

NATURE IS GOVERNED BY ONE
UNIVERSAL LAW

NATURE is that condition, that reality, which in appearance consists in life and death, or, in other words, in the composition and decomposition of all things.

This Nature is subjected to an absolute organization, to determined laws, to a complete order and a finished design, from which it will never depart—to such a degree, indeed, that if you look carefully and with keen sight, from the smallest invisible atom up to such large bodies of the world of existence as the globe of the sun or the other great stars and luminous spheres, whether you regard their arrangement, their composition, their form or their movement, you will find that all are in the highest degree of organization and are under one law from which they will never depart.

But when you look at Nature itself, you see that it has no intelligence, no will. For instance, the nature of fire is to burn; it burns without will or intelligence. The nature of water is fluidity; it flows without will or intelligence. The nature of the sun is radiance; it shines without will or intelligence. The nature of vapor is to ascend; it ascends without will or intelligence. Thus it is clear that the natural movements of all things are compelled; there are no voluntary movements except those of animals and, above all, those of man. Man is able to resist and to oppose Nature because he discovers the constitution of things, and through this he commands the forces of Nature; all the inventions he has made are due to his discovery of the con-

stitution of things. For example, he invented the tele-
graph, which is the means of communication between the
East and the West. It is evident, then, that man rules over
Nature.

Now, when you behold in existence such organizations, arrangements and laws, can you say that all these
are the effect of Nature, though Nature has neither intelligence nor perception? If not, it becomes evident that this
Nature, which has neither perception nor intelligence, is
in the grasp of Almighty God, Who is the Ruler of the
world of Nature; whatever He wishes, He causes Nature
to manifest.

One of the things which has appeared in the world of
existence, and which is one of the requirements of Nature,
is human life. Considered from this point of view man is
the branch; nature is the root. Then can the will and the
intelligence, and the perfections which exist in the branch,
be absent in the root?

It is said that Nature in its own essence is in the grasp of
the power of God, Who is the Eternal Almighty One: He
holds Nature within accurate regulations and laws, and
rules over it.[1]

1. On the idea of God, cf. "The Divinity Can Only Be Comprehended through the Divine Manifestations," p. 146; and "Man's
Knowledge of God," p. 220.

The reader will there see that the Bahá'í Faith has not an an-
thropomorphic conception of God, and that if it employs a customary
terminology, it is careful to explain its symbolic meaning.

2

PROOFS AND EVIDENCES OF THE EXISTENCE OF GOD

ONE of the proofs and demonstrations of the existence of God is the fact that man did not create himself: nay, his creator and designer is another than himself.

It is certain and indisputable that the creator of man is not like man because a powerless creature cannot create another being. The maker, the creator, has to possess all perfections in order that he may create.

Can the creation be perfect and the creator imperfect? Can a picture be a masterpiece and the painter imperfect in his art? For it is his art and his creation. Moreover, the picture cannot be like the painter; otherwise, the painting would have created itself. However perfect the picture may be, in comparison with the painter it is in the utmost degree of imperfection.

The contingent world is the source of imperfections: God is the origin of perfections. The imperfections of the contingent world are in themselves a proof of the perfections of God.

For example, when you look at man, you see that he is weak. This very weakness of the creature is a proof of the power of the Eternal Almighty One, because, if there were no power, weakness could not be imagined. Then the weakness of the creature is a proof of the power of God; for if there were no power, there could be no weakness; so from this weakness it becomes evident that there is power in the world. Again, in the contingent world there is poverty; then necessarily wealth exists, since poverty is

apparent in the world. In the contingent world there is
ignorance; necessarily knowledge exists, because ignorance is found; for if there were no knowledge, neither
would there be ignorance. Ignorance is the nonexistence
of knowledge, and if there were no existence, nonexistence could not be realized.

It is certain that the whole contingent world is subjected to a law and rule which it can never disobey; even
man is forced to submit to death, to sleep and to other
conditions—that is to say, man in certain particulars is
governed, and necessarily this state of being governed im-
plies the existence of a governor. Because a characteristic
of contingent beings is dependency, and this dependency
is an essential necessity, therefore, there must be an independent being whose independence is essential.

In the same way it is understood from the man who is
sick that there must be one who is in health; for if there
were no health, his sickness could not be proved.

Therefore, it becomes evident that there is an Eternal
Almighty One, Who is the possessor of all perfections, be-
cause unless He possessed all perfections He would be like
His creation.

Throughout the world of existence it is the same; the
smallest created thing proves that there is a creator. For
instance, this piece of bread proves that it has a maker.

Praise be to God! the least change produced in the form
of the smallest thing proves the existence of a creator: then
can this great universe, which is endless, be self-created
and come into existence from the action of matter and the
elements? How self-evidently wrong is such a supposition!

These obvious arguments are adduced for weak souls;
but if the inner perception be open, a hundred thousand
clear proofs become visible. Thus, when man feels the in-
dwelling spirit, he is in no need of arguments for its existence; but for those who are deprived of the bounty of the
spirit, it is necessary to establish external arguments.

3

THE NEED OF AN EDUCATOR

WHEN we consider existence, we see that the mineral, vegetable, animal and human worlds are all in need of an educator.

If the earth is not cultivated, it becomes a jungle where useless weeds grow; but if a cultivator comes and tills the ground, it produces crops which nourish living creatures. It is evident, therefore, that the soil needs the cultivation of the farmer. Consider the trees: if they remain without a cultivator, they will be fruitless, and without fruit they are useless; but if they receive the care of a gardener, these same barren trees become fruitful, and through cultivation, fertilization and engrafting the trees which had bitter fruits yield sweet fruits. These are rational proofs; in this age the peoples of the world need the arguments of reason.

The same is true with respect to animals: notice that when the animal is trained it becomes domestic, and also that man, if he is left without education, becomes bestial, and, moreover, if left under the rule of nature, becomes lower than an animal, whereas if he is educated he becomes an angel. For the greater number of animals do not devour their own kind, but men, in the Sudan, in the central regions of Africa, kill and eat each other.

Now reflect that it is education that brings the East and the West under the authority of man; it is education that produces wonderful industries; it is education that spreads great sciences and arts; it is education that makes manifest new discoveries and institutions. If there were no educator, there would be no such things as comforts, civilization or humanity. If a man be left alone in a wilderness where he sees none of his own kind, he will undoubtedly become a mere brute; it is then clear that an educator is needed.

But education is of three kinds: material, human and spiritual. Material education is concerned with the progress and development of the body, through gaining its sustenance, its material comfort and ease. This education is common to animals and man.

Human education signifies civilization and progress—that is to say, government, administration, charitable works, trades, arts and handicrafts, sciences, great inventions and discoveries and elaborate institutions, which are the activities essential to man as distinguished from the animal.

Divine education is that of the Kingdom of God: it consists in acquiring divine perfections, and this is true education; for in this state man becomes the focus of divine blessings, the manifestation of the words, "Let Us make man in Our image, and after Our likeness."[1] This is the goal of the world of humanity.

Now we need an educator who will be at the same time a material, human and spiritual educator, and whose authority will be effective in all conditions. So if anyone should say, "I possess perfect comprehension and intelligence, and I have no need of such an educator," he would be denying that which is clear and evident, as though a child should say, "I have no need of education; I will act according to my reason and intelligence, and so I shall attain the perfections of existence"; or as though the blind should say, "I am in no need of sight, because many other blind people exist without difficulty."

Then it is plain and evident that man needs an educator, and this educator must be unquestionably and indubitably perfect in all respects and distinguished above all men. Otherwise, if he should be like the rest of humanity, he

1. Cf. Gen. 1:26.

could not be their educator, more particularly because he must be at the same time their material and human as well as their spiritual educator—that is to say, he must teach men to organize and carry out physical matters, and to form a social order in order to establish cooperation and mutual aid in living so that material affairs may be organized and regulated for any circumstances that may occur. In the same way he must establish human education—that is to say, he must educate intelligence and thought in such a way that they may attain complete development, so that knowledge and science may increase, and the reality of things, the mysteries of beings and the properties of existence may be discovered; that, day by day, instructions, inventions and institutions may be improved; and from things perceptible to the senses conclusions as to intellectual things may be deduced.

He must also impart spiritual education, so that intelligence and comprehension may penetrate the metaphysical world, and may receive benefit from the sanctifying breeze of the Holy Spirit, and may enter into relationship with the Supreme Concourse. He must so educate the human reality that it may become the center of the divine appearance, to such a degree that the attributes and the names of God shall be resplendent in the mirror of the reality of man, and the holy verse "We will make man in Our image and likeness" shall be realized.[1]

It is clear that human power is not able to fill such a great office, and that reason alone could not undertake the responsibility of so great a mission. How can one solitary person without help and without support lay the foundations of such a noble construction? He must depend on the help of the spiritual and divine power to be able to undertake this mission. One Holy Soul gives life to the world of humanity, changes the aspect of the terrestrial globe, causes intelligence to progress, vivifies souls, lays the basis

1. Cf. Gen. 1:26.

of a new life, establishes new foundations, organizes the world, brings nations and religions under the shadow of one standard, delivers man from the world of imperfections and vices, and inspires him with the desire and need of natural and acquired perfections. Certainly nothing short of a divine power could accomplish so great a work. We ought to consider this with justice, for this is the office of justice.

A Cause which all the governments and peoples of the world, with all their powers and armies, cannot promulgate and spread, one Holy Soul can promote without help or support! Can this be done by human power? No, in the name of God! For example, Christ, alone and solitary, upraised the standard of peace and righteousness, a work which all the victorious governments with all their hosts are unable to accomplish. Consider what was the fate of so many and diverse empires and peoples: the Roman Empire, France, Germany, Russia, England, etc.; all were gathered together under the same tent—that is to say, the appearance of Christ brought about a union among these diverse nations, some of whom, under the influence of Christianity, became so united that they sacrificed their lives and property for one another. After the time of Constantine, who was the protagonist of Christianity, divisions broke out among them. The point is this, that Christ united these nations but after a while governments became the cause of discord. What I mean is that Christ sustained a Cause that all the kings of the earth could not establish! He united the various religions and modified ancient customs. Consider what great differences existed between Romans, Greeks, Syrians, Egyptians, Phoenicians, Israelites and other peoples of Europe. Christ removed these differences and became the cause of love between these communities. Although after some time governments destroyed this union, the work of Christ was accomplished.

Therefore, the Universal Educator must be at the same time a physical, human and spiritual educator; and He must possess a supernatural power, so that He may hold the position of a divine teacher. If He does not show forth such a holy power, He will not be able to educate, for if He be imperfect, how can He give a perfect education? If He be ignorant, how can He make others wise? If He be unjust, how can He make others just? If He be earthly, how can He make others heavenly?

Now we must consider justly: did these Divine Manifestations Who have appeared possess all these qualifications or not?[1] If They had not these qualifications and these perfections, They were not real Educators.

Therefore, it must be our task to prove to the thoughtful by reasonable arguments the prophethood of Moses, of Christ and of the other Divine Manifestations. And the proofs and evidences which we give are not based on traditional but on rational arguments.

It has now been proved by rational arguments that the world of existence is in the utmost need of an educator, and that its education must be achieved by divine power. There is no doubt that this holy power is revelation, and that the world must be educated through this power which is above human power.

---

1. Divine Manifestations are the founders of religions. Cf. "Two Classes of Prophets," p. 164.

4

ABRAHAM

ONE of those Who possessed this power and was assisted
by it was Abraham. And the proof of it was that He was
born in Mesopotamia, and of a family who were ignorant
of the Oneness of God. He opposed His own nation and
people, and even His own family, by rejecting all their
gods. Alone and without help He resisted a powerful
tribe, a task which is neither simple nor easy. It is as if in
this day someone were to go to a Christian people who are
attached to the Bible, and deny Christ; or in the Papal
Court—God forbid!—if such a one were in the most
powerful manner to blaspheme against Christ and oppose
the people.

These people believed not in one God but in many
gods, to whom they ascribed miracles; therefore, they all
arose against Him, and no one supported Him except Lot,
His brother's son, and one or two other people of no importance. At last, reduced to the utmost distress by the
opposition of His enemies, He was obliged to leave His
native land. In reality they banished Him in order that He
might be crushed and destroyed, and that no trace of Him
might be left.

Abraham then came into the region of the Holy Land.
His enemies considered that His exile would lead to His
destruction and ruin, as it seemed impossible that a man
banished from His native land, deprived of His rights and
oppressed on all sides—even though He were a king
—could escape extermination. But Abraham stood fast and
showed forth extraordinary firmness—and God made this

exile to be to His eternal honor until He established the
Unity of God in the midst of a polytheistic generation.
This exile became the cause of the progress of the descendants of Abraham, and the Holy Land was given to them.
As a result the teachings of Abraham were spread abroad,
a Jacob appeared among His posterity, and a Joseph who
became ruler in Egypt. In consequence of His exile a
Moses and a being like Christ were manifested from His
posterity, and Hagar was found from whom Ishmael was
born, one of whose descendants was Muḥammad. In consequence of His exile the Báb appeared from His
posterity, [1] and the Prophets of Israel were numbered
among the descendants of Abraham. And so it will continue for ever and ever. Finally, in consequence of His
exile the whole of Europe and most of Asia came under the
protecting shadow of the God of Israel. See what a power
it is that enabled a Man Who was a fugitive from His
country to found such a family, to establish such a faith,
and to promulgate such teachings. Can anyone say that all
this occurred accidentally? We must be just: was this Man
an Educator or not?

Since the exile of Abraham from Ur to Aleppo in Syria
produced this result, we must consider what will be the
effect of the exile of Bahá'u'lláh in His several removes
from Ṭihrán to Baghdád, from thence to Constantinople,
to Rumelia and to the Holy Land.

See what a perfect Educator Abraham was!

---

1. The Báb's descent was from Muḥammad.

5

MOSES

Moses was for a long time a shepherd in the wilderness. Regarded outwardly, He was a Man brought up in a tyrannical household, and was known among men as One Who had committed a murder and become a shepherd. By the government and the people of Pharaoh He was much hated and detested.

It was such a Man as this that freed a great nation from the chains of captivity, made them contented, brought them out from Egypt, and led them to the Holy Land.

This people from the depths of degradation were lifted up to the height of glory. They were captive; they became free. They were the most ignorant of peoples; they became the most wise. As the result of the institutions that Moses gave them, they attained a position which entitled them to honor among all nations, and their fame spread to all lands, to such a degree indeed that among surrounding nations if one wished to praise a man one said, "Surely he is an Israelite." Moses established laws and ordinances; these gave life to the people of Israel, and led them to the highest possible degree of civilization at that period.

To such a development did they attain that the philosophers of Greece would come and acquire knowledge from the learned men of Israel. Such an one was Socrates, who visited Syria, and took from the children of Israel the teachings of the Unity of God and of the immortality of the soul. After his return to Greece, he promulgated these teachings. Later the people of Greece rose in opposition to him, accused him of impiety, arraigned him before the Areopagus, and condemned him to death by poison.

Now, how could a Man Who was a stammerer, Who had been brought up in the house of Pharaoh, Who was known among men as a murderer, Who through fear had for a long time remained in concealment, and Who had become a shepherd, establish so great a Cause, when the wisest philosophers on earth have not displayed one thousandth part of this influence? This is indeed a prodigy.

A Man Who had a stammering tongue, Who could not even converse correctly, succeeded in sustaining this great Cause! If He had not been assisted by divine power, He would never have been able to carry out this great work. These facts are undeniable. Materialist philosophers, Greek thinkers, the great men of Rome became famous in the world, each one of them having specialized in one branch of learning only. Thus Galen and Hippocrates became celebrated in medicine, Aristotle in logic and reasoning, and Plato in ethics and theology. How is it that a shepherd could acquire all of this knowledge? It is beyond doubt that He must have been assisted by an omnipotent power.

Consider also what trials and difficulties arise for people. To prevent an act of cruelty, Moses struck down an Egyptian and afterward became known among men as a murderer, more notably because the man He had killed was of the ruling nation. Then He fled, and it was after that that He was raised to the rank of a Prophet!

In spite of His evil repute, how wonderfully He was guided by a supernatural power in establishing His great institutions and laws!

6

CHRIST

AFTERWARD Christ came, saying, "I am born of the Holy Spirit." Though it is now easy for the Christians to believe this assertion, at that time it was very difficult. According to the text of the Gospel the Pharisees said, "Is not this the son of Joseph of Nazareth Whom we know? How can He say, therefore, I came down from heaven?"[1]

Briefly, this Man, Who, apparently, and in the eyes of all, was lowly, arose with such great power that He abolished a religion that had lasted fifteen hundred years, at a time when the slightest deviation from it exposed the offender to danger or to death. Moreover, in the days of Christ the morals of the whole world and the condition of the Israelites had become completely confused and corrupted, and Israel had fallen into a state of the utmost degradation, misery and bondage. At one time they had been taken captive by the Chaldeans and Persians; at another time they were reduced to slavery to the Assyrians; then they became the subjects and vassals of the Greeks; and finally they were ruled over and despised by the Romans.

This young Man, Christ, by the help of a supernatural power, abrogated the ancient Mosaic Law, reformed the general morals, and once again laid the foundation of eternal glory for the Israelites. Moreover, He brought to humanity the glad tidings of universal peace, and spread abroad teachings which were not for Israel alone but were for the general happiness of the whole human race.

1. Cf. John 6:42.

Those who first strove to do away with Him were the Israelites, His own kindred. To all outward appearances they overcame Him and brought Him into direst distress. At last they crowned Him with the crown of thorns and crucified Him. But Christ, while apparently in the deepest misery and affliction, proclaimed, "This Sun will be resplendent, this Light will shine, My grace will surround the world, and all My enemies will be brought low." And as He said, so it was; for all the kings of the earth have not been able to withstand Him. Nay, all their standards have been overthrown, while the banner of that Oppressed One has been raised to the zenith.

But this is opposed to all the rules of human reason. Then it becomes clear and evident that this Glorious Being was a true Educator of the world of humanity, and that He was helped and confirmed by divine power.

7

MUḤAMMAD

Now we come to Muḥammad. Americans and Europeans have heard a number of stories about the Prophet which they have thought to be true, although the narrators were either ignorant or antagonistic: most of them were clergy; others were ignorant Muslims who repeated unfounded traditions about Muḥammad which they ignorantly believed to be to His praise.

Thus some benighted Muslims made His polygamy the pivot of their praises and held it to be a wonder, regarding it as a miracle; and European historians, for the most part, rely on the tales of these ignorant people.

For example, a foolish man said to a clergyman that the true proof of greatness is bravery and the shedding of blood, and that in one day on the field of battle a follower of Muḥammad had cut off the heads of one hundred men! This misled the clergyman to infer that killing is considered the way to prove one's faith to Muḥammad, while this is merely imaginary. The military expeditions of Muḥammad, on the contrary, were always defensive actions: a proof of this is that during thirteen years, in Mecca, He and His followers endured the most violent persecutions. At this period they were the target for the arrows of hatred: some of His companions were killed and their property confiscated; others fled to foreign lands. Muḥammad Himself, after the most extreme persecutions by the Qurayshites, who finally resolved to kill Him, fled to Medina in the middle of the night. Yet even then His enemies did not cease their persecutions, but pursued Him to Medina, and His disciples even to Abyssinia.

These Arab tribes were in the lowest depths of savagery and barbarism, and in comparison with them the savages of Africa and wild Indians of America were as advanced as a Plato. The savages of America do not bury their children alive as these Arabs did their daughters, glorying in it as being an honorable thing to do.[1] Thus many of the men would threaten their wives, saying, "If a daughter is born to you, I will kill you." Even down to the present time the Arabs dread having daughters. Further, a man was permitted to take a thousand women, and most husbands had more than ten wives in their household. When these tribes made war, the one which was victorious would take the women and children of the vanquished tribe captive and treat them as slaves.

When a man who had ten wives died, the sons of these women rushed at each other's mothers; and if one of the sons threw his mantle over the head of his father's wife and cried out, "This woman is my lawful property," at once the unfortunate woman became his prisoner and slave. He could do whatever he wished with her. He could kill her, imprison her in a well, or beat, curse and torture her until death released her. According to the Arab habits and customs, he was her master. It is evident that malignity, jealousy, hatred and enmity must have existed between the wives and children of a household, and it is, therefore, needless to enlarge upon the subject. Again, consider what was the condition and life of these oppressed women! Moreover, the means by which these Arab tribes lived consisted in pillage and robbery, so that they were perpetually engaged in fighting and war, killing one another, plundering and devastating each other's property,

---

1. The Banú-Tamím, one of the most barbarous Arab tribes, practiced this odious custom.

and capturing women and children, whom they would sell to strangers. How often it happened that the daughters and sons of a prince, who spent their day in comfort and luxury, found themselves, when night fell, reduced to shame, poverty and captivity. Yesterday they were princes, today they are captives; yesterday they were great ladies, today they are slaves.

Muḥammad received the Divine Revelation among these tribes, and after enduring thirteen years of persecution from them, He fled.[1] But this people did not cease to oppress; they united to exterminate Him and all His followers. It was under such circumstances that Muḥammad was forced to take up arms. This is the truth: we are not bigoted and do not wish to defend Him, but we are just, and we say what is just. Look at it with justice. If Christ Himself had been placed in such circumstances among such tyrannical and barbarous tribes, and if for thirteen years He with His disciples had endured all these trials with patience, culminating in flight from His native land—if in spite of this these lawless tribes continued to pursue Him, to slaughter the men, to pillage their property, and to capture their women and children—what would have been Christ's conduct with regard to them? If this oppression had fallen only upon Himself, He would have forgiven them, and such an act of forgiveness would have been most praiseworthy; but if He had seen that these cruel and bloodthirsty murderers wished to kill, to pillage and to injure all these oppressed ones, and to take captive the women and children, it is certain that He would have protected them and would have resisted the tyrants. What objection, then, can be taken to Muḥammad's action? Is it this, that He did not, with His followers, and their women and children, submit to these savage tribes? To free these tribes from their bloodthirstiness was the greatest kindness, and to coerce and restrain them was

1. To Medina.

a true mercy. They were like a man holding in his hand a cup of poison, which, when about to drink, a friend breaks and thus saves him. If Christ had been placed in similar circumstances, it is certain that with a conquering power He would have delivered the men, women and children from the claws of these bloodthirsty wolves.

Muḥammad never fought against the Christians; on the contrary, He treated them kindly and gave them perfect freedom. A community of Christian people lived at Najrán and were under His care and protection. Muḥammad said, "If anyone infringes their rights, I Myself will be his enemy, and in the presence of God I will bring a charge against him." In the edicts which He promulgated it is clearly stated that the lives, properties and honor of the Christians and Jews are under the protection of God; and that if a Muḥammadan married a Christian woman, the husband must not prevent her from going to church, nor oblige her to veil herself; and that if she died, he must place her remains in the care of the Christian clergy. Should the Christians desire to build a church, Islám ought to help them. In case of war between Islám and her enemies, the Christians should be exempted from the obligation of fighting, unless they desired of their own free will to do so in defense of Islám, because they were under its protection. But as a compensation for this immunity, they should pay yearly a small sum of money. In short, there are seven detailed edicts on these subjects, some copies of which are still extant at Jerusalem. This is an established fact and is not dependent on my affirmation. The edict of the second Caliph[1] still exists in the custody of the orthodox Patriarch of Jerusalem, and of this there is no doubt.[2]

Nevertheless, after a certain time, and through the

1. Of 'Umar.
2. Cf. Jurjí Zaydán's *Umayyads and Abbasids*, trans. D. S. Margoliouth.

transgression of both the Muḥammadans and the Christians, hatred and enmity arose between them. Beyond this fact, all the narrations of the Muslims, Christians and others are simply fabrications, which have their origin in fanaticism, or ignorance, or emanate from intense hostility.

For example, the Muslims say that Muḥammad cleft the moon, and that it fell on the mountain of Mecca: they think that the moon is a small body which Muḥammad divided into two parts and threw one part on this mountain, and the other part on another mountain.

Such stories are pure fanaticism. Also the traditions which the clergy quote, and the incidents with which they find fault, are all exaggerated, if not entirely without foundation.

Briefly, Muḥammad appeared in the desert of Ḥijáz in the Arabian Peninsula, which was a desolate, sterile wilderness, sandy and uninhabited. Some parts, like Mecca and Medina, are extremely hot; the people are nomads with the manners and customs of the dwellers in the desert, and are entirely destitute of education and science. Muḥammad Himself was illiterate, and the Qur'án was originally written upon the bladebones of sheep, or on palm leaves. These details indicate the condition of the people to whom Muḥammad was sent. The first question which He put to them was, "Why do you not accept the Pentateuch and the Gospel, and why do you not believe in Christ and in Moses?" This saying presented difficulties to them, and they argued, "Our forefathers did not believe in the Pentateuch and the Gospel; tell us, why was this?" He answered, "They were misled; you ought to reject those who do not believe in the Pentateuch and the Gospel, even though they are your fathers and your ancestors."

In such a country, and amidst such barbarous tribes, an illiterate Man produced a book in which, in a perfect and eloquent style, He explained the divine attributes and perfections, the prophethood of the Messengers of God, the divine laws, and some scientific facts.

Thus, you know that before the observations of modern times—that is to say, during the first centuries and down to the fifteenth century of the Christian era—all the mathematicians of the world agreed that the earth was the center of the universe, and that the sun moved. The famous astronomer who was the protagonist of the new theory discovered the movement of the earth and the immobility of the sun.[1] Until his time all the astronomers and philosophers of the world followed the Ptolemaic system, and whoever said anything against it was considered ignorant. Though Pythagoras, and Plato during the latter part of his life, adopted the theory that the annual movement of the sun around the zodiac does not proceed from the sun, but rather from the movement of the earth around the sun, this theory had been entirely forgotten, and the Ptolemaic system was accepted by all mathematicians. But there are some verses revealed in the Qur'án contrary to the theory of the Ptolemaic system. One of them is "The sun moves in a fixed place," which shows the fixity of the sun, and its movement around an axis.[2] Again, in another verse, "And each star moves in its own heaven."[3] Thus is explained the movement of the sun, of the moon, of the earth, and of other bodies. When the Qur'án appeared, all the mathematicians ridiculed these statements and attributed the theory to ignorance. Even the doctors of Islám, when they saw that these verses were contrary to the accepted Ptolemaic system, were obliged to explain them away.

It was not until after the fifteenth century of the Christian era, nearly nine hundred years after Muḥammad, that a famous astronomer made new observations and important discoveries by the aid of the telescope, which he had

1. Copernicus.
2. Cf. Qur'án 36:37.
3. Cf. Qur'án 36:38.

invented.[1] The rotation of the earth, the fixity of the sun, and also its movement around an axis, were discovered. It became evident that the verses of the Qur'án agreed with existing facts, and that the Ptolemaic system was imaginary.

In short, many Oriental peoples have been reared for thirteen centuries under the shadow of the religion of Muḥammad. During the Middle Ages, while Europe was in the lowest depths of barbarism, the Arab peoples were superior to the other nations of the earth in learning, in the arts, mathematics, civilization, government and other sciences. The Enlightener and Educator of these Arab tribes, and the Founder of the civilization and perfections of humanity among these different races, was an illiterate Man, Muḥammad. Was this illustrious Man a thorough Educator or not? A just judgment is necessary.

1. Galileo.

8

THE BÁB

As for the Báb—may my soul be His sacrifice!—at a youthful age, that is to say, when He had reached the twenty-fifth year of His blessed life, He stood forth to proclaim His Cause.[1] It was universally admitted by the Shí'ites that He had never studied in any school and had not acquired knowledge from any teacher; all the people of Shíráz bear witness to this. Nevertheless, He suddenly appeared before the people, endowed with the most complete erudition. Although He was but a merchant, He confounded all the 'ulamá of Persia.[2] All alone, in a way which is beyond imagination, He upheld the Cause among the Persians, who are renowned for their religious fanaticism. This illustrious Soul arose with such power that He shook the supports of the religion, of the morals, the conditions, the habits and the customs of Persia, and instituted new rules, new laws and a new religion. Though the great personages of the State, nearly all the clergy, and the public men arose to destroy and annihilate Him, He alone withstood them and moved the whole of Persia.

Many 'ulamá and public men, as well as other people, joyfully sacrificed their lives in His Cause, and hastened to the plain of martyrdom.

1. The Báb is here designated by His title Ḥaḍrat-i-A'lá, His Supreme Highness; but for the convenience of the reader we shall continue to designate Him by the name under which He is known throughout Europe—i.e., the Báb.
2. Doctors of the religion of Islám.

The government, the nation, the doctors of divinity and the great personages desired to extinguish His light, but they could not do so. At last His moon arose, His star shone forth, His foundations became firmly established, and His dawning-place became brilliant. He imparted divine education to an unenlightened multitude and produced marvelous results on the thoughts, morals, customs and conditions of the Persians. He announced the glad tidings of the manifestation of the Sun of Bahá to His followers and prepared them to believe.

The appearance of such wonderful signs and great results; the effects produced upon the minds of the people, and upon the prevailing ideas; the establishment of the foundations of progress; and the organization of the principles of success and prosperity by a young merchant, constitute the greatest proof that He was a perfect Educator. A just person will never hesitate to believe this.

9

BAHÁ'U'LLÁH

BAHÁ'U'LLÁH[1] appeared at a time when the Persian Empire was immersed in profound obscurantism and ignorance and lost in the blindest fanaticism.

In the European histories, no doubt, you have read detailed accounts of the morals, customs and ideas of the Persians during the last centuries. It is useless to repeat them. Briefly, we will say that Persia had fallen so low that to all foreign travelers it was a matter of regret that this country, which in former times had been so glorious and highly civilized, had now become so decayed, ruined and upset, and that its population had lost its dignity.

It was at this time that Bahá'u'lláh appeared. His father was one of the viziers, not one of the 'ulamá. As all the people of Persia know, He had never studied in any school, nor had He associated with the 'ulamá or the men of learning. The early part of His life was passed in the greatest happiness. His companions and associates were Persians of the highest rank, but not learned men.

As soon as the Báb became manifested, Bahá'u'lláh said, "This great Man is the Lord of the righteous, and faith in Him is incumbent upon all." And He arose to assist the Báb and gave many proofs and positive evidences of His truth, in spite of the fact that the 'ulamá of the state

1. Jamál-i-Mubárak, the Blessed Beauty, the title which is here given to Bahá'u'lláh. He is also called Jamál-i-Qidam, the Preexistent, or Ancient Beauty. But we shall designate Him as Bahá'u'lláh, the title by which He is known in the West.

27

religion had constrained the Persian government to oppose and resist Him and had further issued decrees or-
dering the massacre, pillage, persecution and expulsion of
His followers. In all the provinces they began to kill, to
burn, to pillage the converts and even to assault the
women and children. Regardless of this, Bahá'u'lláh arose
to proclaim the word of the Báb with the greatest firmness
and energy. Not for one moment was He in concealment;
He mixed openly with His enemies. He was occupied in
showing forth evidences and proofs and was recognized as
the Herald of the Word of God. In many changes and
chances He endured the greatest misfortunes, and at every
moment He ran the risk of being martyred.

He was put into chains and confined in an underground
prison. His vast property and inheritance were pillaged
and confiscated. He was exiled four times from land to
land and found rest only in the "Greatest Prison."[1]

In spite of all this He never ceased for one instant His
proclamation of the greatness of the Cause of God. He
manifested such virtue, knowledge and perfections that
He became a wonder to all the people of Persia. So much
so that in Ṭihrán, Baghdád, Constantinople, Rumelia,
and even in 'Akká, every one of the learned and scientific
men who entered His presence, whether friend or enemy,
never failed to receive the most sufficient and convincing
answer to whatever question was propounded. All frequently acknowledged that He was alone and unique in all
perfections.

It often happened that in Baghdád certain Muḥammadan 'ulamá, Jewish rabbis and Christians met together
with some European scholars, in a blessed reunion: each
one had some question to propose, and although they were

1. Exiled first to Baghdád, then to Constantinople, then to Adrianople, He was imprisoned in 'Akká (Acre), "the Greatest Prison," in
1869.

possessed of varying degrees of culture, they each heard a sufficient and convincing reply, and retired satisfied. Even the Persian 'ulamá who were at Karbilá and Najaf chose a wise man whom they sent on a mission to Him; his name was Mullá Ḥasan 'Amú. He came into the Holy Presence, and proposed a number of questions on behalf of the 'ulamá, to which Bahá'u'lláh replied. Then Ḥasan 'Amú said, "The 'ulamá recognize without hesitation and confess the knowledge and virtue of Bahá'u'lláh, and they are unanimously convinced that in all learning he has no peer or equal; and it is also evident that he has never studied or acquired this learning; but still the 'ulamá say, 'We are not contented with this; we do not acknowledge the reality of his mission by virtue of his wisdom and righteousness. Therefore, we ask him to show us a miracle in order to satisfy and tranquilize our hearts.'"

Bahá'u'lláh replied, "Although you have no right to ask this, for God should test His creatures, and they should not test God, still I allow and accept this request. But the Cause of God is not a theatrical display that is presented every hour, of which some new diversion may be asked for every day. If it were thus, the Cause of God would become mere child's play.

"The 'ulamás must, therefore, assemble, and, with one accord, choose one miracle, and write that, after the performance of this miracle they will no longer entertain doubts about Me, and that all will acknowledge and confess the truth of My Cause. Let them seal this paper, and bring it to Me. This must be the accepted criterion: if the miracle is performed, no doubt will remain for them; and if not, We shall be convicted of imposture." The learned man, Ḥasan 'Amú, rose and replied, "There is no more to be said"; he then kissed the knee of the Blessed One although he was not a believer, and went. He gathered the 'ulamá and gave them the sacred message. They consulted

together and said, "This man is an enchanter; perhaps he
will perform an enchantment, and then we shall have
nothing more to say." Acting on this belief, they did not
dare to push the matter further.[1]

This man, Ḥasan 'Amú, mentioned this fact at many
meetings. After leaving Karbilá he went to Kirmánsháh
and Ṭihrán and spread a detailed account of it every-
where, laying emphasis on the fear and the withdrawal of
the 'ulamá.

Briefly, all His adversaries in the Orient acknowledged
His greatness, grandeur, knowledge and virtue; and
though they were His enemies, they always spoke of Him
as "the renowned Bahá'u'lláh."

At the time when this great Light suddenly arose upon
the horizon of Persia, all the people, the ministers, the
'ulamá and men of other classes rose against Him, pursu-
ing Him with the greatest animosity, and proclaiming
"that this man wishes to suppress and destroy the religion,
the law, the nation and the empire." The same was said of
Christ. But Bahá'u'lláh alone and without support resisted
them all, without ever showing the least weakness. At last
they said, "As long as this man is in Persia, there will be no
peace and tranquillity; we must banish him, so that Persia
may return to a state of quietude."

They proceeded to use violence toward Him to oblige
Him to ask for permission to leave Persia, thinking that by
this means the light of His truth would be extinguished,
but the result was quite the contrary. The Cause became
magnified, and its flame more intense. At first it spread
throughout Persia only, but the exile of Bahá'u'lláh caused
the diffusion of the Cause throughout other countries.

---

1. The penetrating judgment of Bahá'u'lláh upon this occasion
overcame the malignity of His enemies, who, it was certain, would
never agree in choosing what miracle to ask for.

Afterward His enemies said, "'Iráq-i-'Arab[1] is not far enough from Persia; we must send him to a more distant kingdom." This is why the Persian government determined to send Bahá'u'lláh from 'Iráq to Constantinople. Again the event proved that the Cause was not in the least weakened. Once more they said, "Constantinople is a place of passage and of sojourn for various races and peoples; among them are many Persians." For this reason the Persians had Him further exiled to Rumelia; but, when there, the flame became more powerful, and the Cause more exalted. At last the Persians said, "Not one of these places is safe from his influence; we must send him to some place where he will be reduced to powerlessness, and where his family and followers will have to submit to the direst afflictions." So they chose the prison of 'Akká, which is reserved especially for murderers, thieves and highway robbers, and in truth they classed Him with such people. But the power of God became manifested: His word was promulgated, and the greatness of Bahá'u'lláh then became evident, for it was from this prison and under such humiliating circumstances that He caused Persia to advance from one state into another state. He overcame all His enemies and proved to them that they could not resist the Cause. His holy teachings penetrated all regions, and His Cause was established.

Indeed, in all parts of Persia His enemies arose against Him with the greatest hatred, imprisoning, killing and beating His converts, and burning and razing to the ground thousands of dwellings, striving by every means to exterminate and crush the Cause. In spite of all this, from the prison of murderers, highway robbers and thieves, it became exalted. His teachings were spread abroad, and His exhortations affected many of those who had been the

1. 'Iráq; as opposed to that district of Írán known then as 'Iráq-i-A'ẓam and now called Arák.

most full of hatred, and made them firm believers. Even the Persian government itself became awakened and regretted that which had arisen through the fault of the 'ulamá.

When Bahá'u'lláh came to this prison in the Holy Land, the wise men realized that the glad tidings which God gave through the tongue of the Prophets two or three thousand years before were again manifested, and that God was faithful to His promise; for to some of the Prophets He had revealed and given the good news that "the Lord of Hosts should be manifested in the Holy Land." All these promises were fulfilled; and it is difficult to understand how Bahá'u'lláh could have been obliged to leave Persia, and to pitch His tent in this Holy Land, but for the persecution of His enemies, His banishment and exile. His enemies intended that His imprisonment should completely destroy and annihilate the blessed Cause, but this prison was in reality of the greatest assistance and became the means of its development. The divine renown of Bahá'u'lláh reached the East and the West, and the rays of the Sun of Truth illuminated all the world. Praise be to God! though He was a prisoner, His tent was raised on Mount Carmel, and He moved abroad with the greatest majesty. Every person, friend or stranger, who came into His presence used to say, "This is a prince, not a captive."

Upon His arrival in prison[1] He addressed an epistle to Napoleon,[2] which He sent through the French ambassador. The gist of it was, "Ask what is Our crime, and why We are confined in this prison and this dungeon." Napoleon made no reply. Then a second epistle was issued, which is contained in the Súriy-i-Haykal.[3] The epitome of it is: "Oh Napoleon, as thou hast not listened to My proclamation, and as thou hast not answered it, thy

1. Adrianople.
2. Napoleon III.
3. One of Bahá'u'lláh's works written after His declaration.

dominion will before long be taken away from thee, and thou wilt be utterly destroyed." This epistle was sent to Napoleon by post, through the care of Cesar Ketaphakou,[1] as was known to all the companions of His exile. The text of this warning reached the whole of Persia, for it was at that time that the Kitáb-i-Haykal was spread in Persia, and this epistle was among the contents of this book. This happened in A.D. 1869, and as this Súriy-i-Haykal was circulated in Persia and India and was in the hands of all believers, they were waiting to see what would come to pass. Not long after, in A.D. 1870, the war between Germany and France broke out; and though no one at that time expected the victory of Germany, Napoleon was defeated and dishonored; he surrendered to his enemies, and his glory was changed into deep abasement.

Tablets[2] were also sent to other kings, and among them was the letter to H. M. Náṣiri'd-Dín Sháh. In that epistle Bahá'u'lláh said, "Have Me summoned, gather the 'ulamá, and ask for proofs and arguments, so that the truth and falsehood may become known." H. M. Náṣiri'd-Dín Sháh sent the blessed epistle to the 'ulamá and proposed to them that they should undertake this mission, but they dared not do so. Then he asked seven of the most celebrated among them to write an answer to the challenge. After some time they returned the blessed letter, saying, "This man is the opposer of religion and the enemy of the Sháh." His majesty the Sháh of Persia was much vexed, and said, "This is a question for proofs and arguments, and of truth or falsehood: what has it to do with enmity to the government? Alas! how much we respected these 'ulamá, who cannot even reply to this epistle."

Briefly, all that was recorded in the Tablets to the Kings is being fulfilled: if from the year A.D. 1870 we compare

1. Son of a French Consul in Syria with whom Bahá'u'lláh had friendly relations.
2. Name given to the epistles of Bahá'u'lláh.

the events that have occurred, we will find everything that has happened has appeared as predicted; only a few remain which will afterward become manifested.

So also foreign peoples, and other sects who were not believers, attributed many wonderful things to Bahá'u'lláh. Some believed that He was a saint,[1] and some even wrote treatises about Him. One of them, Siyyid Dávúdí, a Sunnite savant of Baghdád, wrote a short treatise in which he related certain supernatural acts of Bahá'u'lláh. Even now, in all parts of the East, there are some people who, though they do not believe in His manifestation, nevertheless believe Him to be a saint and relate miracles attributed to Him.

To sum up, both His antagonists and His partisans, as well as all those who were received in the sacred spot, acknowledged and bore witness to the greatness of Bahá'u'lláh. Though they did not believe in Him, still they acknowledged His grandeur, and as soon as they entered the sacred spot, the presence of Bahá'u'lláh produced such an effect on most of them that they could not utter a word. How many times it happened that one of His most bitter enemies would resolve within himself, "I will say such and such things when I reach His presence, and I will dispute and argue thus with Him," but when he entered the Holy Presence, he would become amazed and confounded, and remain speechless.

Bahá'u'lláh had never studied Arabic; He had not had a tutor or teacher, nor had He entered a school. Nevertheless, the eloquence and elegance of His blessed expositions in Arabic, as well as His Arabic writings, caused astonishment and stupefaction to the most accomplished Arabic scholars, and all recognized and declared that He was incomparable and unequaled.

If we carefully examine the text of the Torah, we see that the Divine Manifestation never said to those who de-

1. Valí.

nied Him, "Whatever miracle you desire, I am ready to perform, and I will submit to whatever test you propose." But in the Epistle to the <u>Sh</u>áh, Bahá'u'lláh said clearly, "Gather the 'ulamá, and summon Me, that the evidences and proofs may be established."[1]

For fifty years Bahá'u'lláh faced His enemies like a mountain: all wished to annihilate Him and sought His destruction. A thousand times they planned to crucify and destroy Him, and during these fifty years He was in constant danger.

In this day Persia is in such a state of decadence and ruin that all intelligent men, whether Persians or foreigners, who realize the true state of affairs, recognize that its progress, its civilization and its reconstruction depend upon the promulgation of the teachings and the development of the principles of this great Personage.

Christ, in His blessed day, in reality only educated eleven men: the greatest of them was Peter, who, nevertheless, when he was tested, thrice denied Christ. In spite of this, the Cause of Christ subsequently permeated the world. At the present day Bahá'u'lláh has educated thousands of souls who, while under the menace of the sword, raised to the highest heaven the cry of "Yá Bahá'u'l-Abhá";[2] and in the fire of tests, their faces became illuminated like gold. Then reflect what will take place in the future.

Finally, we must be just and acknowledge what an Educator this Glorious Being was, what marvelous signs were manifested by Him, and what power and might have been realized in the world through Him.

---

1. Cf. p. 30, n. 1. In giving such importance to this example of the good sense of Bahá'u'lláh, 'Abdu'l-Bahá means to emphasize the uselessness of miracles as a proof of the truth of the Manifestations of God. Cf. "Miracles," p. 100.

2. A cry used as a declaration of faith by the Bahá'ís, literally, "Oh Thou the Glory of Glories!"

10

TRADITIONAL PROOFS EXEMPLIFIED
FROM THE BOOK OF DANIEL

TODAY, at table, let us speak for a little of proofs. If you had come to this blessed place in the days of the manifestation of the evident Light,[1] if you had attained to the court of His presence, and had witnessed His luminous beauty, you would have understood that His teachings and perfection were not in need of further evidence.

Only through the honor of entering His presence, many souls became confirmed believers; they had no need of other proofs. Even those people who rejected and hated Him bitterly, when they had met Him, would testify to the grandeur of Bahá'u'lláh, saying, "This is a magnificent man, but what a pity that he makes such a claim! Otherwise, all that he says is acceptable."

But now, as that Light of Reality has set, all are in need of proofs; so we have undertaken to demonstrate rational proofs of the truth of His claim. We will cite another which alone is sufficient for all who are just, and which no one can deny. It is that this illustrious Being uplifted His Cause in the "Greatest Prison";[2] from this Prison His light was shed abroad, His fame conquered the world, and the proclamation of His glory reached the East and West. Until our time no such thing has ever occurred.

If there be justice, this will be acknowledged; but there are some people who, even if all the proofs in the world be adduced before them, still will not judge justly!

1. Bahá'u'lláh.
2. 'Akká.

Thus nations and states with all their strength could not resist Him. Verily, single and alone, imprisoned and oppressed, He accomplished whatever He desired.

I do not wish to mention the miracles of Bahá'u'lláh, for it may perhaps be said that these are traditions, liable both to truth and to error, like the accounts of the miracles of Christ in the Gospel, which come to us from the apostles, and not from anyone else, and are denied by the Jews. Though if I wish to mention the supernatural acts of Bahá'u'lláh, they are numerous; they are acknowledged in the Orient, and even by some non-Bahá'ís. But these narratives are not decisive proofs and evidences to all; the hearer might perhaps say that this account may not be in accordance with what occurred, for it is known that other sects recount miracles performed by their founders. For instance, the followers of Brahmanism relate miracles. From what evidence may we know that those are false and that these are true? If these are fables, the others also are fables; if these are generally accepted, so also the others are generally accepted. Consequently, these accounts are not satisfactory proofs. Yes, miracles are proofs for the eyewitness only, and even he may regard them not as a miracle but as an enchantment. Extraordinary feats have also been related of some conjurors.

Briefly, my meaning is that many wonderful things were done by Bahá'u'lláh, but we do not recount them, as they do not constitute proofs and evidences for all the peoples of the earth, and they are not decisive proofs even for those who see them: they may think that they are merely enchantments.

Also, most of the miracles of the Prophets which are mentioned have an inner significance. For instance, in the Gospel it is written that at the martyrdom of Christ darkness prevailed, and the earth quaked, and the veil of the Temple was rent in twain from the top to the bottom, and the dead came forth from their graves. If these events had happened, they would indeed have been awesome, and would certainly have been recorded in the history of the times. They would have become the cause of much troublings of heart. Either the soldiers would have taken down Christ from the cross, or they would have fled. These events are not related in any history; therefore, it is evident they ought not to be taken literally, but as having an inner significance.[1]

Our purpose is not to deny such miracles; our only meaning is that they do not constitute decisive proofs, and that they have an inner significance.

Accordingly, today, at table, we will refer to the explanation of the traditional proofs which are in the Holy Books. Until now, all that we have spoken of are rational proofs.

The state in which one should be to seriously search for the truth is the condition of the thirsty, burning soul desiring the water of life, of the fish struggling to reach the sea, of the sufferer seeking for the true doctor to obtain the divine cure, of the lost caravan endeavoring to find the right road, of the lost and wandering ship striving to reach the shore of salvation.

Therefore, the seeker must be endowed with certain qualities. First of all, he must be just and severed from all else save God; his heart must be entirely turned to the supreme horizon; he must be free from the bondage of self and passion, for all these are obstacles. Furthermore, he must be able to endure all hardships. He must be absolutely pure and sanctified, and free from the love or the hatred of the inhabitants of the world. Why? because the fact of his love for any person or thing might prevent him from recognizing the truth in another, and, in the same way, hatred for anything might be a hindrance in discerning truth. This is the condition of seeking, and the

1. Cf. "Miracles," p. 100.

seeker must have these qualities and attributes. Until he reaches this condition, it is not possible for him to attain to the Sun of Reality.

Let us now return to our subject.

All the peoples of the world are awaiting two Manifestations, Who must be contemporaneous; all wait for the fulfillment of this promise. In the Bible the Jews have the promise of the Lord of Hosts and the Messiah; in the Gospel the return of Christ and Elijah is promised.

In the religion of Muḥammad there is the promise of the Mihdí and the Messiah, and it is the same with the Zoroastrian and the other religions, but if we relate these matters in detail, it would take too long. The essential fact is that all are promised two Manifestations, Who will come, one following on the other. It has been prophesied that in the time of these two Manifestations the earth will be transformed, the world of existence will be renewed, and beings will be clothed in new garments. Justice and truth will encompass the world; enmity and hatred will disappear; all causes of division among peoples, races and nations will vanish; and the cause of union, harmony and concord will appear. The negligent will awake, the blind will see, the deaf will hear, the dumb will speak, the sick will be cured, the dead will arise. War will give place to peace, enmity will be conquered by love, the causes of dispute and wrangling will be entirely removed, and true felicity will be attained. The world will become the mirror of the Heavenly Kingdom; humanity will be the Throne of Divinity. All nations will become one; all religions will be unified; all individual men will become of one family and of one kindred. All the regions of the earth will become one; the superstitions caused by races, countries, individuals, languages and politics will disappear; and all men will attain to life eternal, under the shadow of the Lord of Hosts.

Now we must prove from the Holy Books that these two Manifestations have come, and we must divine the meaning of the words of the Prophets, for we wish for proofs drawn from the Holy Books.

A few days ago, at table, we put forth rational proofs establishing the truth of these two Manifestations.

To conclude: in the Book of Daniel, from the rebuilding of Jerusalem to the martyrdom of Christ, seventy weeks are appointed; for by the martyrdom of Christ the sacrifice is accomplished and the altar destroyed.[1] This is a prophecy of the manifestation of Christ. These seventy weeks begin with the restoration and the rebuilding of Jerusalem, concerning which four edicts were issued by three kings.

The first was issued by Cyrus in the year 536 B.C.; this is recorded in the first chapter of the Book of Ezra. The second edict, with reference to the rebuilding of Jerusalem, is that of Darius of Persia in the year 519 B.C.; this is recorded in the sixth chapter of Ezra. The third is that of Artaxerxes in the seventh year of his reign—that is, in 457 B.C.; this is recorded in the seventh chapter of Ezra. The fourth is that of Artaxerxes in the year 444 B.C.; this is recorded in the second chapter of Nehemiah.

But Daniel refers especially to the third edict which was issued in the year 457 B.C. Seventy weeks make four hundred and ninety days. Each day, according to the text of the Holy Book, is a year. For in the Bible it is said: "The day of the Lord is one year."[2] Therefore, four hundred and ninety days are four hundred and ninety years. The third edict of Artaxerxes was issued four hundred and fifty-seven years before the birth of Christ, and Christ when He was martyred and ascended was thirty-three years of age. When you add thirty-three to four hundred

1. See Dan. 9:24.
2. Cf. Num. 14:34.

and fifty-seven, the result is four hundred and ninety, which is the time announced by Daniel for the manifestation of Christ.

But in the twenty-fifth verse of the ninth chapter of the Book of Daniel this is expressed in another manner, as seven weeks and sixty-two weeks; and apparently this differs from the first saying. Many have remained perplexed at these differences, trying to reconcile these two statements. How can seventy weeks be right in one place, and sixty-two weeks and seven weeks in another? These two sayings do not accord.

But Daniel mentions two dates. One of these dates begins with the command of Artaxerxes to Ezra to rebuild Jerusalem: this is the seventy weeks which came to an end with the ascension of Christ, when by His martyrdom the sacrifice and oblation ceased.

The second period, which is found in the twenty-sixth verse, means that after the termination of the rebuilding of Jerusalem until the ascension of Christ, there will be sixty-two weeks: the seven weeks are the duration of the rebuilding of Jerusalem, which took forty-nine years. When you add these seven weeks to the sixty-two weeks, it makes sixty-nine weeks, and in the last week (69–70) the ascension of Christ took place. These seventy weeks are thus completed, and there is no contradiction.

Now that the manifestation of Christ has been proved by the prophecies of Daniel, let us prove the manifestations of Bahá'u'lláh and of the Báb. Up to the present we have only mentioned rational proofs; now we shall speak of traditional proofs.

In the eighth chapter of the Book of Daniel, verse thirteen, it is said: "Then I heard one saint speaking, and another saint said unto that certain saint which spake, How long shall be the vision concerning the daily sacrifice, and the transgression of desolation, to give both the sanctuary

and the host to be trodden under foot?" Then he answered
(v. 14): "Unto two thousand and three hundred days; then
shall the sanctuary be cleansed"; (v. 17) "But he said unto
me. . . . at the time of the end shall be the vision." That is
to say, how long will this misfortune, this ruin, this
abasement and degradation last? meaning, when will be
the dawn of the Manifestation? Then he answered, "Two
thousand and three hundred days; then shall the sanctuary
be cleansed." Briefly, the purport of this passage is that he
appoints two thousand three hundred years, for in the text
of the Bible each day is a year. Then from the date of the
issuing of the edict of Artaxerxes to rebuild Jerusalem
until the day of the birth of Christ there are 456 years, and
from the birth of Christ until the day of the manifestation
of the Báb there are 1844 years. When you add 456 years
to this number it makes 2300 years. That is to say, the
fulfillment of the vision of Daniel took place in the year
A.D. 1844, and this is the year of the Báb's manifestation
according to the actual text of the Book of Daniel. Consider
how clearly he determines the year of manifestation; there
could be no clearer prophecy for a manifestation than this.

In Matthew, chapter 24, verse 3, Christ clearly says
that what Daniel meant by this prophecy was the date of
the manifestation, and this is the verse: "As He sat upon
the mount of Olives, the disciples came unto Him pri-
vately, saying, Tell us, when shall these things be? and
what shall be the sign of Thy coming, and of the end of the
world?" One of the explanations He gave them in reply
was this (v. 15): "When ye therefore shall see the abomination of desolation, spoken of by Daniel the prophet,
stand in the holy place, (whoso readeth, let him understand)." In this answer He referred them to the eighth
chapter of the Book of Daniel, saying that everyone who
reads it will understand that it is this time that is spoken of.
Consider how clearly the manifestation of the Báb is spo-

ken of in the Old Testament and in the Gospel.

To conclude, let us now explain the date of the manifestation of Bahá'u'lláh from the Bible. The date of Bahá'u'lláh is calculated according to lunar years from the mission and the Hejira of Muḥammad; for in the religion of Muḥammad the lunar year is in use, as also it is the lunar year which is employed concerning all commands of worship.

In Daniel, chapter 12, verse 6, it is said: "And one said to the man clothed in linen, which was upon the waters of the river, How long shall it be to the end of these wonders? And I heard the man clothed in linen, which was upon the waters of the river, when he held up his right hand and his left hand unto heaven, and sware by Him that liveth for ever that it shall be for a time, times, and a half; and that when He shall have accomplished to scatter the power of the holy people, all these things shall be finished."[1]

As I have already explained the signification of one day, it is not necessary to explain it further; but we will say briefly that each day of the Father counts as a year, and in each year there are twelve months. Thus three years and a half make forty-two months, and forty-two months are twelve hundred and sixty days. The Báb, the precursor of Bahá'u'lláh, appeared in the year 1260 from the Hejira of Muḥammad, by the reckoning of Islám.

Afterward, in verse 11, it is said: "And from the time that the daily sacrifice shall be taken away, and the abomination that maketh desolation be set up, there shall be a thousand two hundred and ninety days. Blessed is he that waiteth, and cometh to the thousand three hundred and five and thirty days."[2]

The beginning of this lunar reckoning is from the day of the proclamation of the prophethood of Muḥammad in the

1. Cf. Dan. 12:6–7.
2. The reference appears in verses 11 and 12.

country of Ḥijáz; and that was three years after His mission, because in the beginning the prophethood of Muḥammad was kept secret, and no one knew it save Khadíjah and Ibn Nawfal.[1] After three years it was announced. And Bahá'u'lláh, in the year 1290 from the proclamation of the mission of Muḥammad, caused His manifestation to be known.[2]

1. Varaqat-Ibn-Nawfal, Khadíjah's cousin.
2. The year 1290 from the proclamation of the mission of Muḥammad was the year 1280 of the Hejira, or 1863–64 of our era. It was at this epoch (April 1863) that Bahá'u'lláh, on leaving Baghdád for Constantinople, declared to those who surrounded Him that He was the Manifestation announced by the Báb.

It is this declaration which the Bahá'ís celebrate by the Feast of Riḍván, this name being that of the garden at the entrance of the city, where Bahá'u'lláh stayed during twelve days, and where He made the declaration.

11

COMMENTARY ON THE ELEVENTH CHAPTER OF THE REVELATION OF ST. JOHN

In the beginning of the eleventh chapter of the Revelation of St. John it is said:

"And there was given me a reed like unto a rod: and the angel stood, saying, Rise, and measure the temple of God, and the altar, and them that worship therein.

"But the court which is without the temple leave out, and measure it not; for it is given unto the Gentiles: and the holy city shall they tread under foot forty and two months."

This reed is a Perfect Man Who is likened to a reed, and the manner of its likeness is this: when the interior of a reed is empty and free from all matter, it will produce beautiful melodies; and as the sound and melodies do not come from the reed, but from the flute player who blows upon it, so the sanctified heart of that blessed Being is free and emptied from all save God, pure and exempt from the attachments of all human conditions, and is the companion of the Divine Spirit. Whatever He utters is not from Himself, but from the real flute player, and it is a divine inspiration. That is why He is likened to a reed; and that reed is like a rod—that is to say, it is the helper of every impotent one, and the support of human beings. It is the rod of the Divine Shepherd by which He guards His flock and leads them about the pastures of the Kingdom.

Then it is said: "The angel stood, saying, Rise, and measure the temple of God, and the altar, and them that worship therein"—that is to say, compare and measure: measuring is the discovery of proportion. Thus the angel said: compare the temple of God and the altar and them that are praying therein—that is to say, investigate what is their true condition and discover in what degree and state they are, and what conditions, perfections, behavior and attributes they possess; and make yourself cognizant of the mysteries of those holy souls who dwell in the Holy of Holies in purity and sanctity.

"But the court which is without the temple leave out, and measure it not; for it is given unto the Gentiles."

In the beginning of the seventh century after Christ, when Jerusalem was conquered, the Holy of Holies was outwardly preserved—that is to say, the house which Solomon built; but outside the Holy of Holies the outer court was taken and given to the Gentiles. "And the holy city shall they tread under foot forty and two months"—that is to say, the Gentiles shall govern and control Jerusalem forty and two months, signifying twelve hundred and sixty days; and as each day signifies a year, by this reckoning it becomes twelve hundred and sixty years, which is the duration of the cycle of the Qur'án. For in the texts of the Holy Book, each day is a year; as it is said in the fourth chapter of Ezekiel, verse 6: "Thou shalt bear the iniquity of the house of Judah forty days: I have appointed thee each day for a year."

This prophesies the duration of the Dispensation of Islám when Jerusalem was trodden under foot, which means that it lost its glory—but the Holy of Holies was preserved, guarded and respected—until the year 1260. This twelve hundred and sixty years is a prophecy of the manifestation of the Báb, the "Gate" of Bahá'u'lláh, which took place in the year 1260 of the Hejira of Muḥammad, and as the period of twelve hundred and sixty years has expired, Jerusalem, the Holy City, is now beginning to become prosperous, populous and flourishing. Anyone who saw Jerusalem sixty years ago, and who sees it now, will recognize how populous and flourishing it has become, and how it is again honored.

This is the outward meaning of these verses of the Revelation of St. John; but they have another explanation and a symbolic sense, which is as follows: the Law of God is divided into two parts. One is the fundamental basis which comprises all spiritual things—that is to say, it refers to the spiritual virtues and divine qualities; this does not change nor alter: it is the Holy of Holies, which is the essence of the Law of Adam, Noah, Abraham, Moses, Christ, Muḥammad, the Báb and Bahá'u'lláh, and which lasts and is established in all the prophetic cycles. It will never be abrogated, for it is spiritual and not material truth; it is faith, knowledge, certitude, justice, piety, righteousness, trustworthiness, love of God, benevolence, purity, detachment, humility, meekness, patience and constancy. It shows mercy to the poor, defends the oppressed, gives to the wretched and uplifts the fallen.

These divine qualities, these eternal commandments, will never be abolished; nay, they will last and remain established for ever and ever. These virtues of humanity will be renewed in each of the different cycles; for at the end of every cycle the spiritual Law of God—that is to say, the human virtues—disappears, and only the form subsists.

Thus among the Jews, at the end of the cycle of Moses, which coincides with the Christian manifestation, the Law of God disappeared, only a form without spirit remaining. The Holy of Holies departed from among them, but the outer court of Jerusalem—which is the expression used for the form of the religion—fell into the hands of the Gentiles. In the same way, the fundamental principles of the religion of Christ, which are the greatest virtues of humanity, have disappeared; and its form has remained in the hands of the clergy and the priests. Likewise, the foundation of the religion of Muḥammad has disappeared, but its form remains in the hands of the official 'ulamá.

These foundations of the Religion of God, which are spiritual and which are the virtues of humanity, cannot be abrogated; they are irremovable and eternal, and are renewed in the cycle of every Prophet.

The second part of the Religion of God, which refers to the material world, and which comprises fasting, prayer, forms of worship, marriage and divorce, the abolition of slavery, legal processes, transactions, indemnities for murder, violence, theft and injuries—this part of the Law of God, which refers to material things, is modified and altered in each prophetic cycle in accordance with the necessities of the times.

Briefly, what is meant by the term Holy of Holies is that spiritual Law which will never be modified, altered or abrogated; and the Holy City means the material Law which may be abrogated; and this material Law, which is described as the Holy City, was to be trodden under foot for twelve hundred and sixty years.

"And I will give power unto my two witnesses, and they shall prophesy a thousand two hundred and three-score days, clothed in sackcloth."[1] These two witnesses are Muḥammad the Messenger of God, and 'Alí, son of Abú Ṭálib.

In the Qur'án it is said that God addressed Muḥammad, the Messenger of God, saying: "We made You a Witness, a Herald of good news, and a Warner"—that is to say, We have established Thee as the witness, the giver of good tidings, and as One bringing the wrath of God.[2] The meaning of "a witness" is one by whose testimony things may be verified. The commands of these two witnesses were to be performed for twelve hundred and sixty days, each day signifying a year. Now, Muḥammad was the

1. Rev. 11:3.
2. This sentence is the Persian translation of the Arabic text of the Qur'án which has been quoted.

root, and 'Alí the branch, like Moses and Joshua. It is said they "are clothed in sackcloth," meaning that they, apparently, were to be clothed in old raiment, not in new raiment; in other words, in the beginning they would possess no splendor in the eyes of the people, nor would their Cause appear new; for Muḥammad's spiritual Law corresponds to that of Christ in the Gospel, and most of His laws relating to material things correspond to those of the Pentateuch. This is the meaning of the old raiment.

Then it is said: "These are the two olive trees, and the two candlesticks standing before the God of the earth."[1] These two souls are likened to olive trees because at that time all lamps were lighted by olive oil. The meaning is two persons from whom that spirit of the wisdom of God, which is the cause of the illumination of the world, appears. These lights of God were to radiate and shine; therefore, they are likened to two candlesticks: the candlestick is the abode of the light, and from it the light shines forth. In the same way the light of guidance would shine and radiate from these illumined souls.

Then it is said: "They are standing before God," meaning that they are standing in the service of God, and educating the creatures of God, such as the barbarous nomad Arab tribes of the Arabian peninsula, whom they educated in such a way that in those days they reached the highest degree of civilization, and their fame and renown became worldwide.

"And if any man would hurt them, fire proceedeth out of their mouth, and devoureth their enemies."[2] That is to say, that no one would be able to withstand them, that if a person wished to belittle their teachings and their law, he would be surrounded and exterminated by this same law which proceedeth out of their mouth; and everyone who attempted to injure, to antagonize and to hate them would

1. Rev. 11:4.
2. Cf. Rev. 11:5.

be destroyed by a command which would come out of their mouth. And thus it happened: all their enemies were vanquished, put to flight and annihilated. In this most evident way God assisted them.

Afterward it is said: "These have power to shut heaven, that it rain not in the days of their prophecy,"[1] meaning that in that cycle they would be like kings. The law and teachings of Muḥammad, and the explanations and commentaries of 'Alí, are a heavenly bounty; if they wish to give this bounty, they have power to do so. If they do not wish it, the rain will not fall: in this connection rain stands for bounty.

Then it is said: "They have power over water to turn it to blood,"[2] meaning that the prophethood of Muḥammad was the same as that of Moses, and that the power of 'Alí was the same as that of Joshua: if they wished, they could turn the water of the Nile into blood, so far as the Egyptians and those who denied them were concerned—that is to say, that that which was the cause of their life, through their ignorance and pride, became the cause of their death. So the kingdom, wealth and power of Pharaoh and his people, which were the causes of the life of the nation, became, through their opposition, denial and pride, the cause of death, destruction, dispersion, degradation and poverty. Hence these two witnesses have power to destroy the nations.

Then it is said: "And smite the earth with all plagues, as often as they will,"[2] meaning that they also would have the power and the material force necessary to educate the wicked and those who are oppressors and tyrants, for to these two witnesses God granted both outward and inward power, that they might educate and correct the ferocious, bloodthirsty, tyrannical nomad Arabs, who were like beasts of prey.

1. Rev. 11:6.
2. Cf. Rev. 11:6.

"And when they shall have finished their testimony"[1] means when they should have performed that which they are commanded, and should have delivered the divine message, promoting the Law of God and propagating the heavenly teachings, to the intent that the signs of spiritual life might be manifest in souls, and the light of the virtues of the world of humanity might shine forth, until complete development should be brought about among the nomad tribes.

"The beast that ascendeth out of the bottomless pit shall war against them, and shall overcome them, and kill them":[2] this beast means the Umayyads who attacked them from the pit of error, and who rose against the religion of Muḥammad and against the reality of 'Alí—in other words, the love of God.

It is said, "The beast made war against these two witnesses"[2]—that is to say, a spiritual war, meaning that the beast would act in entire opposition to the teachings, customs and institutions of these two witnesses, to such an extent that the virtues and perfections which were diffused by the power of those two witnesses among the peoples and tribes would be entirely dispelled, and the animal nature and carnal desires would conquer. Therefore, this beast making war against them would gain the victory—meaning that the darkness of error coming from this beast was to have ascendency over the horizons of the world, and kill those two witnesses—in other words, that it would destroy the spiritual life which they spread abroad in the midst of the nation, and entirely remove the divine laws and teachings, treading under foot the Religion of God. Nothing would thereafter remain but a lifeless body without spirit.

"And their dead bodies shall lie in the street of the great city, which spiritually is called Sodom and Egypt, where

1. Rev. 11:7.
2. Cf. Rev. 11:7.

also our Lord was crucified."[1] "Their bodies" means the Religion of God, and "the street" means in public view. The meaning of "Sodom and Egypt," the place "where also our Lord was crucified," is this region of Syria, and especially Jerusalem, where the Umayyads then had their dominions; and it was here that the Religion of God and the divine teachings first disappeared, and a body without spirit remained. "Their bodies" represents the Religion of God, which remained like a dead body without spirit.

"And they of the people and kindreds and tongues and nations shall see their dead bodies three days and a half, and shall not suffer their dead bodies to be put in graves."[2]

As it was before explained, in the terminology of the Holy Books three days and a half signify three years and a half, and three years and a half are forty and two months, and forty and two months twelve hundred and sixty days; and as each day by the text of the Holy Book signifies one year, the meaning is that for twelve hundred and sixty years, which is the cycle of the Qur'án, the nations, tribes and peoples would look at their bodies—that is to say, that they would make a spectacle of the Religion of God: though they would not act in accordance with it, still, they would not suffer their bodies—meaning the Religion of God—to be put in the grave. That is to say, that in appearance they would cling to the Religion of God and not allow it to completely disappear from their midst, nor the body of it to be entirely destroyed and annihilated. Nay, in reality they would leave it, while outwardly preserving its name and remembrance.

Those "kindreds, people and nations" signify those who are gathered under the shadow of the Qur'án, not permitting the Cause and Law of God to be, in outward appearance, entirely destroyed and annihilated—for

1. Rev. 11:8.
2. Rev. 11:9.

there are prayer and fasting among them—but the fundamental principles of the Religion of God, which are morals and conduct, with the knowledge of divine mysteries, have disappeared; the light of the virtues of the world of humanity, which is the result of the love and knowledge of God, is extinguished; and the darkness of tyranny, oppression, satanic passions and desires has become victorious. The body of the Law of God, like a corpse, has been exposed to public view for twelve hundred and sixty days, each day being counted as a year, and this period is the cycle of Muḥammad.

The people forfeited all that these two persons had established, which was the foundation of the Law of God, and destroyed the virtues of the world of humanity, which are the divine gifts and the spirit of this religion, to such a degree that truthfulness, justice, love, union, purity, sanctity, detachment and all the divine qualities departed from among them. In the religion only prayers and fasting persisted; this condition lasted for twelve hundred and sixty years, which is the duration of the cycle of the Furqán.[1] It was as if these two persons were dead, and their bodies were remaining without spirit.

"And they that dwell upon the earth shall rejoice over them, and make merry, and shall send gifts to one another, because these two prophets tormented them that dwelt on the earth."[2] "Those who dwelt upon the earth" means the other nations and races, such as the peoples of Europe and distant Asia, who, when they saw that the character of Islám was entirely changed, the Law of God forsaken—that virtues, zeal and honor had departed from among them, and that their qualities were changed—became happy, and rejoiced that corruption of morals had infected the people of Islám, and that they would in consequence

1. Another name for the Qur'án, signifying the Distinction.
2. Cf. Rev. 11:10.

be overcome by other nations. So this thing has come to pass. Witness this people which had attained the summit of power, how degraded and downtrodden it is now.

The other nations "shall send gifts to one another," meaning that they should help each other, for "these two prophets tormented them that dwelt upon the earth"— that is, they overcame the other nations and peoples of the world and conquered them.

"And after three days and a half the spirit of life from God entered into them, and they stood upon their feet; and great fear fell upon them that saw them."[1] Three days and a half, as we before explained, is twelve hundred and sixty years. Those two persons whose bodies were lying spiritless are the teachings and the law that Muḥammad established and ʿAlí promoted, from which, however, the reality had departed and only the form remained. The spirit came again into them means that those foundations and teachings were again established. In other words, the spirituality of the Religion of God had been changed into materiality, and virtues into vices; the love of God had been changed into hatred, enlightenment into darkness, divine qualities into satanic ones, justice into tyranny, mercy into enmity, sincerity into hypocrisy, guidance into error, and purity into sensuality. Then after three days and a half, which by the terminology of the Holy Books is twelve hundred and sixty years, these divine teachings, heavenly virtues, perfections and spiritual bounties were again renewed by the appearance of the Báb and the devotion of Jináb-i-Quddús.[2]

The holy breezes were diffused, the light of truth shone forth, the season of the life-giving spring came, and the morn of guidance dawned. These two lifeless bodies again

1. Cf. Rev. 11:11.
2. Ḥájí Mullá Muḥammad-ʿAlíy-i-Bárfurúshí, one of the chief disciples of the Báb and one of the nineteen Letters of the Living.

became living, and these two great ones—one the Founder and the other the promoter—arose and were like two candlesticks, for they illumined the world with the light of truth.

"And they heard a great voice from heaven saying unto them, Come up hither. And they ascended up to heaven,"[1] meaning that from the invisible heaven they heard the voice of God, saying: You have performed all that was proper and fitting in delivering the teachings and glad tidings; you have given My message to the people and raised the call of God, and have accomplished your duty. Now, like Christ, you must sacrifice your life for the Well-Beloved, and be martyrs. And that Sun of Reality, and that Moon of Guidance,[2] both, like Christ, set on the horizon of the greatest martyrdom and ascended to the Kingdom of God.

"And their enemies beheld them,"[3] meaning that many of their enemies, after witnessing their martyrdom, realized the sublimity of their station and the exaltation of their virtue, and testified to their greatness and perfection.

"And the same hour there was a great earthquake, and the tenth part of the city fell, and in the earthquake were slain of men seven thousand."[4]

This earthquake occurred in Shíráz after the martyrdom of the Báb. The city was in a turmoil, and many people were destroyed. Great agitation also took place through diseases, cholera, dearth, scarcity, famine and afflictions, the like of which had never been known.

"And the remnant was affrighted and gave glory to the God of heaven."[4]

When the earthquake took place in Fárs, all the remnant

1. Rev. 11:12.
2. The Báb and Jináb-i-Quddús.
3. Rev. 11:12.
4. Cf. Rev. 11:13.

```

lamented and cried day and night, and were occupied in glorifying and praying to God. They were so troubled and affrighted that they had no sleep nor rest at night.

"The second woe is past; and, behold, the third woe cometh quickly."[1] The first woe is the appearance of the Prophet, Muḥammad, the son of 'Abdu'lláh—peace be upon Him! The second woe is that of the Báb—to Him be glory and praise! The third woe is the great day of the manifestation of the Lord of Hosts and the radiance of the Beauty of the Promised One. The explanation of this subject, woe, is mentioned in the thirtieth chapter of Ezekiel, where it is said: "The word of the Lord came again unto me, saying, Son of man, prophesy and say, Thus saith the Lord God; Howl ye, Woe worth the day! For the day is near, even the day of the Lord is near."[2]

Therefore, it is certain that the day of woe is the day of the Lord; for in that day woe is for the neglectful, woe is for the sinners, woe is for the ignorant. That is why it is said, "The second woe is past; behold the third woe cometh quickly!" This third woe is the day of the manifestation of Bahá'u'lláh, the day of God; and it is near to the day of the appearance of the Báb.

"And the seventh angel sounded; and there were great voices in heaven, saying, The kingdoms of this world are become the kingdoms of our Lord, and of His Christ; and He shall reign for ever and ever."[3]

The seventh angel is a man qualified with heavenly attributes, who will arise with heavenly qualities and character. Voices will be raised, so that the appearance of the Divine Manifestation will be proclaimed and diffused. In the day of the manifestation of the Lord of Hosts, and at the epoch of the divine cycle of the Omnipotent which is promised and mentioned in all the books and writings of

1. Rev. 11:14.
2. Ez. 30:1–3.
3. Rev. 11:15.
```

the Prophets—in that day of God, the Spiritual and Divine Kingdom will be established, and the world will be renewed; a new spirit will be breathed into the body of creation; the season of the divine spring will come; the clouds of mercy will rain; the sun of reality will shine; the life-giving breeze will blow; the world of humanity will wear a new garment; the surface of the earth will be a sublime paradise; mankind will be educated; wars, disputes, quarrels and malignity will disappear; and truthfulness, righteousness, peace and the worship of God will appear; union, love and brotherhood will surround the world; and God will rule for evermore—meaning that the Spiritual and Everlasting Kingdom will be established. Such is the day of God. For all the days which have come and gone were the days of Abraham, Moses and Christ, or of the other Prophets; but this day is the day of God, for the Sun of Reality will arise in it with the utmost warmth and splendor.

"And the four and twenty elders, which sat before God on their seats, fell upon their faces, and worshipped God.

"Saying, We give Thee thanks, O Lord God Almighty, Which art, and wast, and art to come; because Thou hast taken to Thee Thy great power, and hast reigned."[1]

In each cycle the guardians and holy souls have been twelve. So Jacob had twelve sons; in the time of Moses there were twelve heads or chiefs of the tribes; in the time of Christ there were twelve Apostles; and in the time of Muḥammad there were twelve Imáms. But in this glorious manifestation there are twenty-four, double the number of all the others, for the greatness of this manifestation requires it. These holy souls are in the presence of God seated on their own thrones, meaning that they reign eternally.

These twenty-four great persons, though they are seated on the thrones of everlasting rule, yet are worship-

1. Rev. 11:16–17.

ers of the appearance of the universal Manifestation, and they are humble and submissive, saying, "We give thanks to Thee, O Lord God Almighty, Which art, and wast, and art to come, because Thou hast taken to Thee Thy great power and hast reigned"—that is to say, Thou wilt issue all Thy teachings, Thou wilt gather all the people of the earth under Thy shadow, and Thou wilt bring all men under the shadow of one tent. Although it is the Eternal Kingdom of God, and He always had, and has, a Kingdom, the Kingdom here means the manifestation of Himself;[1] and He will issue all the laws and teachings which are the spirit of the world of humanity and everlasting life. And that universal Manifestation will subdue the world by spiritual power, not by war and combat; He will do it with peace and tranquillity, not by the sword and arms; He will establish this Heavenly Kingdom by true love, and not by the power of war. He will promote these divine teachings by kindness and righteousness, and not by weapons and harshness. He will so educate the nations and people that, notwithstanding their various conditions, their different customs and characters, and their diverse religions and races, they will, as it is said in the Bible, like the wolf and the lamb, the leopard, the kid, the sucking child and the serpent, become comrades, friends and companions. The contentions of races, the differences of religions, and the barriers between nations will be completely removed, and all will attain perfect union and reconciliation under the shadow of the Blessed Tree.

"And the nations were angry," for Thy teachings opposed the passions of the other peoples; "and Thy wrath is come"[2]—that is to say, all will be afflicted by evident loss; because they do not follow Thy precepts, counsels and teachings, they will be deprived of Thy everlasting bounty, and veiled from the light of the Sun of Reality.

1. i.e., His most complete manifestation.
2. Rev. 11:18.

"And the time of the dead, that they should be judged" means that the time has come that the dead[1]—that is to say, those who are deprived of the spirit of the love of God and have not a share of the sanctified eternal life—will be judged with justice, meaning they will arise to receive that which they deserve. He will make the reality of their secrets evident, showing what a low degree they occupy in the world of existence, and that in reality they are under the rule of death.

"That Thou shouldst give reward unto Thy servants the prophets, and the saints, and them that fear Thy name, small and great"[2]—that is to say, He will distinguish the righteous by endless bounty, making them shine on the horizon of eternal honor, like the stars of heaven. He will assist them by endowing them with behavior and actions which are the light of the world of humanity, the cause of guidance, and the means of everlasting life in the Divine Kingdom.

"And shouldst destroy them which destroy the earth"[1] means that He will entirely deprive the neglectful; for the blindness of the blind will be manifest, and the vision of the seers will be evident; the ignorance and want of knowledge of the people of error will be recognized, and the knowledge and wisdom of the people under guidance will be apparent; consequently, the destroyers will be destroyed.

"And the temple of God was opened in heaven"[3] means that the divine Jerusalem is found, and the Holy of Holies has become visible. The Holy of Holies, according to the terminology of the people of wisdom, is the essence of the Divine Law, and the heavenly and true teachings of the Lord, which have not been changed in the cycle of any Prophet, as it was before explained. The sanctuary of

1. Rev. 11:18.
2. Cf. Rev. 11:18.
3. Rev. 11:19.

Jerusalem is likened to the reality of the Law of God, which is the Holy of Holies; and all the laws, conventions, rites and material regulations are the city of Jerusalem—this is why it is called the heavenly Jerusalem. Briefly, as in this cycle the Sun of Reality will make the light of God shine with the utmost splendor, therefore, the essence of the teachings of God will be realized in the world of existence, and the darkness of ignorance and want of knowledge will be dispelled. The world will become a new world, and enlightenment will prevail. So the Holy of Holies will appear.

"And the temple of God was opened in heaven"[1] means also that by the diffusion of the divine teachings, the appearance of these heavenly mysteries, and the rising of the Sun of Reality, the doors of success and prosperity will be opened in all directions, and the signs of goodness and heavenly benedictions will be made plain.

"And there was seen in His temple the ark of His Testament"[1]—that is to say, the Book of His Testament will appear in His Jerusalem, the Epistle of the Covenant[2] will be established, and the meaning of the Testament and of the Covenant will become evident. The renown of God will overspread the East and West, and the proclamation of the Cause of God will fill the world. The violators of the Covenant will be degraded and dispersed, and the faithful cherished and glorified, for they cling to the Book of the Testament and are firm and steadfast in the Covenant.

"And there were lightnings, and voices, and thunderings, and an earthquake, and great hail,"[1] meaning that after the appearance of the Book of the Testament there will be a great storm, and the lightnings of the anger and the wrath of God will flash, the noise of the thunder of the

1. Rev. 11:19.
2. One of the works of Bahá'u'lláh, in which He expressly points to 'Abdu'l-Bahá as being the One to Whom all must turn after His death.

violation of the Covenant will resound, the earthquake of doubts will take place, the hail of torments will beat upon the violators of the Covenant, and even those who profess belief will fall into trials and temptations.

12

COMMENTARY ON THE ELEVENTH
CHAPTER OF ISAIAH

In Isaiah, chapter 11, verses 1 to 10, it is said: "And there shall come forth a rod out of the stem of Jesse, and a Branch shall grow out of his roots: And the spirit of the Lord shall rest upon him, the spirit of wisdom and understanding, the spirit of counsel and might, the spirit of knowledge and of the fear of the Lord; And shall make him of quick understanding in the fear of the Lord: and he shall not judge after the sight of his eyes, neither reprove after the hearing of his ears: But with righteousness shall he judge the poor, and reprove with equity for the meek of the earth: and he shall smite the earth with the rod of his mouth, and with the breath of his lips shall he slay the wicked. And righteousness shall be the girdle of his loins, and faithfulness the girdle of his reins. The wolf also shall dwell with the lamb, and the leopard shall lie down with the kid; and the calf and the young lion and the fatling together; and a little child shall lead them. And the cow and the bear shall feed; their young ones shall lie down together: and the lion shall eat straw like the ox. And the sucking child shall play on the hole of the asp, and the weaned child shall put his hand on the cockatrice' den. They shall not hurt nor destroy in all My holy mountain: for the earth shall be full of the knowledge of the Lord, as the waters cover the sea."

This rod out of the stem of Jesse might be correctly applied to Christ, for Joseph was of the descendants of

Jesse, the father of David; but as Christ found existence through the Spirit of God, He called Himself the Son of God. If He had not done so, this description would refer to Him. Besides this, the events which he indicated as coming to pass in the days of that rod, if interpreted symbolically, were in part fulfilled in the day of Christ, but not all; and if not interpreted, then decidedly none of these signs happened. For example, the leopard and the lamb, the lion and the calf, the child and the asp, are metaphors and symbols for various nations, peoples, antagonistic sects and hostile races, who are as opposite and inimical as the wolf and lamb. We say that by the breath of the spirit of Christ they found concord and harmony, they were vivified, and they associated together.

But "they shall not hurt nor destroy in all My holy mountain: for the earth shall be full of the knowledge of the Lord, as the waters cover the sea." These conditions did not prevail in the time of the manifestation of Christ; for until today various and antagonistic nations exist in the world: very few acknowledge the God of Israel, and the greater number are without the knowledge of God. In the same way, universal peace did not come into existence in the time of Christ—that is to say, between the antagonistic and hostile nations there was neither peace nor concord, disputes and disagreements did not cease, and reconciliation and sincerity did not appear. So, even at this day, among the Christian sects and nations themselves, enmity, hatred and the most violent hostility are met with.

But these verses apply word for word to Bahá'u'lláh. Likewise in this marvelous cycle the earth will be transformed, and the world of humanity arrayed in tranquillity and beauty. Disputes, quarrels and murders will be replaced by peace, truth and concord; among the nations, peoples, races and countries, love and amity will appear. Cooperation and union will be established, and finally war will be entirely suppressed. When the laws of the Most Holy Book are enforced, contentions and disputes will find a final sentence of absolute justice before a general tribunal of the nations and kingdoms, and the difficulties that appear will be solved. The five continents of the world will form but one, the numerous nations will become one, the surface of the earth will become one land, and mankind will be a single community. The relations between the countries—the mingling, union and friendship of the peoples and communities—will reach to such a degree that the human race will be like one family and kindred. The light of heavenly love will shine, and the darkness of enmity and hatred will be dispelled from the world. Universal peace will raise its tent in the center of the earth, and the blessed Tree of Life will grow and spread to such an extent that it will overshadow the East and the West. Strong and weak, rich and poor, antagonistic sects and hostile nations—which are like the wolf and the lamb, the leopard and kid, the lion and the calf—will act toward each other with the most complete love, friendship, justice and equity. The world will be filled with science, with the knowledge of the reality of the mysteries of beings, and with the knowledge of God.

Now consider, in this great century which is the cycle of Bahá'u'lláh, what progress science and knowledge have made, how many secrets of existence have been discovered, how many great inventions have been brought to light and are day by day multiplying in number. Before long, material science and learning, as well as the knowledge of God, will make such progress and will show forth such wonders that the beholders will be amazed. Then the mystery of this verse in Isaiah, "For the earth shall be full of the knowledge of the Lord," will be completely evident.

Reflect also that in the short time since Bahá'u'lláh has appeared, people from all countries, nations and races have entered under the shadow of this Cause. Christians, Jews, Zoroastrians, Buddhists, Hindus and Persians all associate together with the greatest friendship and love, as if indeed these people had been related and connected together, they and theirs, for a thousand years; for they are like father and child, mother and daughter, sister and brother. This is one of the meanings of the companionship of the wolf and the lamb, the leopard and the kid, and the lion and the calf.

One of the great events which is to occur in the Day of the manifestation of that Incomparable Branch (Bahá'u'lláh) is the hoisting of the Standard of God among all nations. By this is meant that all nations and kindreds will be gathered together under the shadow of this Divine Banner, which is no other than the Lordly Branch itself, and will become a single nation. Religious and sectarian antagonism, the hostility of races and peoples, and differences among nations, will be eliminated. All men will adhere to one religion, will have one common faith, will be blended into one race, and become a single people. All will dwell in one common fatherland, which is the planet itself. Universal peace and concord will be realized between all the nations, and that Incomparable Branch will gather together all Israel, signifying that in this cycle Israel will be gathered in the Holy Land, and that the Jewish people who are scattered to the East and West, South and North, will be assembled together.

Now see: these events did not take place in the Christian cycle, for the nations did not come under the One Standard which is the Divine Branch. But in this cycle of the Lord of Hosts all the nations and peoples will enter under the shadow of this Flag. In the same way, Israel, scattered all over the world, was not reassembled in the Holy Land in the Christian cycle; but in the beginning of the cycle of Bahá'u'lláh this divine promise, as is clearly stated in all the Books of the Prophets, has begun to be manifest. You can see that from all the parts of the world tribes of Jews are coming to the Holy Land; they live in villages and lands which they make their own, and day by day they are increasing to such an extent that all Palestine will become their home.

13

COMMENTARY ON THE TWELFTH CHAPTER OF THE REVELATION OF ST. JOHN

WE have before explained that what is most frequently meant by the Holy City, the Jerusalem of God, which is mentioned in the Holy Book, is the Law of God. It is compared sometimes to a bride, and sometimes to Jerusalem, and again to the new heaven and earth. So in chapter 21, verses 1, 2 and 3 of the Revelation of St. John, it is said: "And I saw a new heaven and a new earth: for the first heaven and the first earth were passed away; and there was no more sea. And I John saw the holy city, new Jerusalem, coming down from God out of heaven, prepared as a bride adorned for her husband. And I heard a great voice out of heaven saying, Behold, the tabernacle of God is with men, and He will dwell with them, and they shall be His people, and God Himself shall be with them, and be their God."

Notice how clear and evident it is that the first heaven and earth signify the former Law. For it is said that the first heaven and earth have passed away and there is no more sea—that is to say, that the earth is the place of judgment, and on this earth of judgment there is no sea, meaning that the teachings and the Law of God will entirely spread over the earth, and all men will enter the Cause of God, and the earth will be completely inhabited by believers; therefore, there will be no more sea, for the dwelling place and abode of man is the dry land. In other words, at that epoch the field of that Law will become the pleasure-ground of man. Such earth is solid; the feet do not slip upon it.

The Law of God is also described as the Holy City, the New Jerusalem. It is evident that the New Jerusalem which descends from heaven is not a city of stone, mortar, bricks, earth and wood. It is the Law of God which descends from heaven and is called new, for it is clear that the Jerusalem which is of stone and earth does not descend from heaven, and that it is not renewed; but that which is renewed is the Law of God.

The Law of God is also compared to an adorned bride who appears with most beautiful ornaments, as it has been said in chapter 21 of the Revelation of St. John: "And I John saw the holy city, new Jerusalem, coming down from God out of heaven, prepared as a bride adorned for her husband."[1] And in chapter 12, verse 1, it is said: "And there appeared a great wonder in heaven; a woman clothed with the sun, and the moon under her feet, and upon her head a crown of twelve stars." This woman is that bride, the Law of God that descended upon Muḥammad. The sun with which she was clothed, and the moon which was under her feet, are the two nations which are under the shadow of that Law, the Persian and Ottoman kingdoms; for the emblem of Persia is the sun, and that of the Ottoman Empire is the crescent moon. Thus the sun and moon are the emblems of two kingdoms which are under the power of the Law of God. Afterward it is said: "upon her head is a crown of twelve stars." These twelve stars are the twelve Imáms, who were the promoters of the Law of Muḥammad and the educators of the people, shining like stars in the heaven of guidance.

Then it is said in the second verse: "and she being with child cried," meaning that this Law fell into the greatest difficulties and endured great troubles and afflictions until

1. Rev. 21:2.

a perfect offspring was produced—that is, the coming Manifestation, the Promised One, Who is the perfect offspring, and Who was reared in the bosom of this Law, which is as its mother. The child Who is referred to is the Báb, the Primal Point, Who was in truth born from the Law of Muḥammad—that is to say, the Holy Reality, Who is the child and outcome of the Law of God, His mother, and Who is promised by that religion, finds a reality in the kingdom of that Law; but because of the despotism of the dragon the child was carried up to God. After twelve hundred and sixty days the dragon was destroyed, and the child of the Law of God, the Promised One, became manifest.

Verses 3 and 4. "And there appeared a great wonder in heaven; and behold a great red dragon, having seven heads and ten horns, and seven crowns upon his heads. And his tail drew the third part of the stars of heaven, and did cast them to the earth."[1] These signs are an allusion to the dynasty of the Umayyads who dominated the Muḥammadan religion. Seven heads and seven crowns mean seven countries and dominions over which the Umayyads had power: they were the Roman dominion around Damascus; and the Persian, Arabian and Egyptian dominions, together with the dominion of Africa—that is to say, Tunis, Morocco and Algeria; the dominion of Andalusia, which is now Spain; and the dominion of the Turks of Transoxania. The Umayyads had power over these countries. The ten horns mean the names of the Umayyad rulers—that is, without repetition, there were ten names of rulers, meaning ten names of commanders and chiefs—the first is Abú Sufyán and the last Marván—but several of them bear the same name. So there are two Mu'ávíya, three Yazíd, two Valíd, and two Marván; but if the names were counted without repetition

1. Cf. Rev. 12:3–4.

there would be ten. The Umayyads, of whom the first was Abú Sufyán, Amír of Mecca and chief of the dynasty of the Umayyads, and the last was Marván, destroyed the third part of the holy and saintly people of the lineage of Muḥammad who were like the stars of heaven.

Verse 4. "And the dragon stood before the woman which was ready to be delivered, for to devour the child as soon as it was born."[1] As we have before explained, this woman is the Law of God. The dragon was standing near the woman to devour her child, and this child was the promised Manifestation, the offspring of the Law of Muḥammad. The Umayyads were always waiting to get possession of the Promised One, Who was to come from the line of Muḥammad, to destroy and annihilate Him; for they much feared the appearance of the promised Manifestation, and they sought to kill any of Muḥammad's descendants who might be highly esteemed.

Verse 5. "And she brought forth a man child, Who was to rule all nations with a rod of iron." This great son is the promised Manifestation Who was born of the Law of God and reared in the bosom of the divine teachings. The iron rod is a symbol of power and might—it is not a sword—and means that with divine power and might He will shepherd all the nations of the earth. This son is the Báb.

Verse 5. "And her child was caught up unto God, and to His throne." This is a prophecy of the Báb, Who ascended to the heavenly realm, to the Throne of God, and to the center of His Kingdom. Consider how all this corresponds to what happened.

Verse 6. "And the woman fled into the wilderness"—that is to say, the Law of God fled to the wilderness, meaning the vast desert of Ḥijáz, and the Arabian Peninsula.

Verse 6. "Where she had a place prepared of God."[2]

1. Cf. Rev. 12:4.
2. Cf. Rev. 12:6.

The Arabian Peninsula became the abode and dwelling place, and the center of the Law of God.

Verse 6. "That they should feed her there a thousand two hundred and threescore days." In the terminology of the Holy Book these twelve hundred and sixty days mean the twelve hundred and sixty years that the Law of God was set up in the wilderness of Arabia, the great desert: from it the Promised One has come. After twelve hundred and sixty years that Law will have no more influence, for the fruit of that tree will have appeared, and the result will have been produced.

Consider how the prophecies correspond to one another. In the Apocalypse, the appearance of the Promised One is appointed after forty-two months, and Daniel expresses it as three times and a half, which is also forty-two months, which are twelve hundred and sixty days. In another passage of John's Revelation it is clearly spoken of as twelve hundred and sixty days, and in the Holy Book it is said that each day signifies one year. Nothing could be clearer than this agreement of the prophecies with one another. The Báb appeared in the year 1260 of the Hejira of Muḥammad, which is the beginning of the universal era-reckoning of all Islám. There are no clearer proofs than this in the Holy Books for any Manifestation. For him who is just, the agreement of the times indicated by the tongues of the Great Ones is the most conclusive proof. There is no other possible explanation of these prophecies. Blessed are the just souls who seek the truth. But failing justice, the people attack, dispute and openly deny the evidence, like the Pharisees who, at the manifestation of Christ, denied with the greatest obstinacy the explanations of Christ and of His disciples. They obscured Christ's Cause before the ignorant people, saying, "These prophecies are not of Jesus, but of the Promised One Who shall come later, according to the conditions mentioned in the Bible." Some of these conditions were that He must have a kingdom, be seated on the throne of David, enforce the Law of the Bible, and manifest such justice that the wolf and the lamb shall gather at the same spring.

And thus they prevented the people from knowing Christ.

Note. —In these last conversations 'Abdu'l-Bahá wishes to reconcile in a new interpretation the apocalyptic prophecies of the Jews, the Christians and the Muslims, rather than to show their supernatural character. On the powers of the Prophets, cf. "The Knowledge of the Divine Manifestations," p. 157; and "Visions and Communication with Spirits," p. 251.

14

SPIRITUAL PROOFS

In this material world time has cycles; places change through alternating seasons, and for souls there are progress, retrogression and education.

At one time it is the season of spring; at another it is the season of autumn; and again it is the season of summer or the season of winter.

In the spring there are the clouds which send down the precious rain, the musk-scented breezes and life-giving zephyrs; the air is perfectly temperate, the rain falls, the sun shines, the fecundating wind wafts the clouds, the world is renewed, and the breath of life appears in plants, in animals and in men. Earthly beings pass from one condition to another. All things are clothed in new garments, and the black earth is covered with herbage; mountains and plains are adorned with verdure; trees bear leaves and blossoms; gardens bring forth flowers and fragrant herbs. The world becomes another world, and it attains to a life-giving spirit. The earth was a lifeless body; it finds a new spirit, and produces endless beauty, grace and freshness. Thus the spring is the cause of new life and infuses a new spirit.

Afterward comes the summer, when the heat increases, and growth and development attain their greatest power. The energy of life in the vegetable kingdom reaches to the degree of perfection, the fruit appears, and the time of harvest ripens; a seed has become a sheaf, and the food is stored for winter. Afterward comes tumultuous autumn when unwholesome and sterile winds blow; it is the season of sickness, when all things are withered, and the balmy air is vitiated. The breezes of spring are changed to autumn winds; the fertile green trees have become withered and bare; flowers and fragrant herbs fade away; the beautiful garden becomes a dustheap. Following this comes the season of winter, with cold and tempests. It snows, rains, hails, storms, thunders and lightens, freezes and congeals; all plants die, and animals languish and are wretched.

When this state is reached, again a new life-giving spring returns, and the cycle is renewed. The season of spring with its hosts of freshness and beauty spreads its tent on the plains and mountains with great pomp and magnificence. A second time the form of the creatures is renewed, and the creation of beings begins afresh; bodies grow and develop, the plains and wildernesses become green and fertile, trees bring forth blossoms, and the spring of last year returns in the utmost fullness and glory. Such is, and such ought to be, the cycle and succession of existence. Such is the cycle and revolution of the material world.

It is the same with the spiritual cycles of the Prophets—that is to say, the day of the appearance of the Holy Manifestations is the spiritual springtime; it is the divine splendor; it is the heavenly bounty, the breeze of life, the rising of the Sun of Reality. Spirits are quickened; hearts are refreshed and invigorated; souls become good; existence is set in motion; human realities are gladdened, and grow and develop in good qualities and perfections. General progress is achieved and revival takes place, for it is the day of resurrection, the time of excitement and ferment, and the season of bliss, of joy and of intense rapture.

Afterward the life-giving spring ends in fruitful summer. The word of God is exalted, the Law of God is promulgated; all things reach perfection. The heavenly table is spread, the holy breezes perfume the East and the

West, the teachings of God conquer the world, men become educated, praiseworthy results are produced, universal progress appears in the world of humanity, and the divine bounties surround all things. The Sun of Reality rises from the horizon of the Kingdom with the greatest power and heat. When it reaches the meridian, it will begin to decline and descend, and the spiritual summer will be followed by autumn, when growth and development are arrested. Breezes change into blighting winds, and the unwholesome season dissipates the beauty and freshness of the gardens, plains and bowers—that is to say, attraction and goodwill do not remain, divine qualities are changed, the radiance of hearts is dimmed, the spirituality of souls is altered, virtues are replaced by vices, and holiness and purity disappear. Only the name of the Religion of God remains, and the exoteric forms of the divine teachings. The foundations of the Religion of God are destroyed and annihilated, and nothing but forms and customs exist. Divisions appear, firmness is changed into instability, and spirits become dead; hearts languish, souls become inert, and winter arrives—that is to say, the coldness of ignorance envelops the world, and the darkness of human error prevails. After this come indifference, disobedience, inconsiderateness, indolence, baseness, animal instincts and the coldness and insensibility of stones. It is like the season of winter when the terrestrial globe, deprived of the effect of the heat of the sun, becomes desolate and dreary. When the world of intelligence and thought has reached to this state, there remain only continual death and perpetual nonexistence.

When the season of winter has had its effect, again the spiritual springtime returns, and a new cycle appears. Spiritual breezes blow, the luminous dawn gleams, the divine clouds give rain, the rays of the Sun of Reality shine forth, the contingent world attains unto a new life and is clad in a wonderful garment. All the signs and the gifts of the past springtime reappear, with perhaps even greater splendor in this new season.

The spiritual cycles of the Sun of Reality are like the cycles of the material sun: they are always revolving and being renewed. The Sun of Reality, like the material sun, has numerous rising and dawning places: one day it rises from the zodiacal sign of Cancer, another day from the sign of Libra or Aquarius; another time it is from the sign of Aries that it diffuses its rays. But the sun is one sun and one reality; the people of knowledge are lovers of the sun, and are not fascinated by the places of its rising and dawning. The people of perception are the seekers of the truth, and not of the places of its appearance, nor of its dawning points; therefore, they will adore the Sun from whatever point in the zodiac it may appear, and they will seek the Reality in every Sanctified Soul Who manifests it. Such people always attain to the truth and are not veiled from the Sun of the Divine World. So the lover of the sun and the seeker of the light will always turn toward the sun, whether it shines from the sign of Aries or gives its bounty from the sign of Cancer, or radiates from Gemini; but the ignorant and uninstructed are lovers of the signs of the zodiac, and enamored and fascinated by the rising-places, and not by the sun. When it was in the sign of Cancer, they turned toward it, though afterward the sun changed to the sign of Libra; as they were lovers of the sign, they turned toward it and attached themselves to it, and were deprived of the influences of the sun merely because it had changed its place. For example, once the Sun of Reality poured forth its rays from the sign of Abraham, and then it dawned from the sign of Moses and illuminated the horizon. Afterward it rose with the greatest power and brilliancy from the sign of Christ. Those who were the seekers of Reality worshiped that Reality wherever they saw it, but those who were attached to Abraham were deprived of its influences when it shone upon Sinai and illuminated the reality of Moses. Those who held fast to Moses, when the Sun of Reality shone from Christ with the utmost radiance and lordly splendor, were also veiled; and so forth.

Therefore, man must be the seeker after the Reality, and he will find that Reality in each of the Sanctified Souls. He must be fascinated and enraptured, and attracted to the divine bounty; he must be like the butterfly who is the lover of the light from whatever lamp it may shine, and like the nightingale who is the lover of the rose in whatever garden it may grow.

If the sun were to rise in the West, it would still be the sun; one must not withdraw from it on account of its rising-place, nor consider the West to be always the place of sunset. In the same way, one must look for the heavenly bounties and seek for the Divine Aurora. In every place where it appears, one must become its distracted lover. Consider that if the Jews had not kept turning to the horizon of Moses, and had only regarded the Sun of Reality, without any doubt they would have recognized the Sun in the dawning-place of the reality of Christ, in the greatest divine splendor. But, alas! a thousand times alas! attaching themselves to the outward words of Moses, they were deprived of the divine bounties and the lordly splendors!

15

TRUE WEALTH

THE honor and exaltation of every existing being depends upon causes and circumstances.

The excellency, the adornment and the perfection of the earth is to be verdant and fertile through the bounty of the clouds of springtime. Plants grow; flowers and fragrant herbs spring up; fruit-bearing trees become full of blossoms and bring forth fresh and new fruit. Gardens become beautiful, and meadows adorned; mountains and plains are clad in a green robe, and gardens, fields, villages and cities are decorated. This is the prosperity of the mineral world.

The height of exaltation and the perfection of the vegetable world is that a tree should grow on the bank of a stream of fresh water, that a gentle breeze should blow on it, that the warmth of the sun should shine on it, that a gardener should attend to its cultivation, and that day by day it should develop and yield fruit. But its real prosperity is to progress into the animal and human world, and replace that which has been exhausted in the bodies of animals and men.

The exaltation of the animal world is to possess perfect members, organs and powers, and to have all its needs supplied. This is its chief glory, its honor and exaltation. So the supreme happiness of an animal is to have possession of a green and fertile meadow, perfectly pure flowing water, and a lovely, verdant forest. If these things are provided for it, no greater prosperity can be imagined. For example, if a bird builds its nest in a green and fruitful forest, in a beautiful high place, upon a strong tree, and at the top of a lofty branch, and if it finds all it needs of seeds and water, this is its perfect prosperity.

But real prosperity for the animal consists in passing from the animal world to the human world, like the microscopic beings that, through the water and air, enter into man and are assimilated, and replace that which has been consumed in his body. This is the great honor and prosperity for the animal world; no greater honor can be conceived for it.

Therefore, it is evident and clear that this wealth, this comfort and this material abundance form the complete prosperity of minerals, vegetables and animals. No riches, wealth, comfort or ease of the material world is equal to the wealth of a bird; all the areas of these plains and mountains are its dwelling, and all the seeds and harvests are its food and wealth, and all the lands, villages, meadows, pastures, forests and wildernesses are its possessions. Now, which is the richer, this bird, or the most wealthy man? for no matter how many seeds it may take or bestow, its wealth does not decrease.

Then it is clear that the honor and exaltation of man must be something more than material riches. Material comforts are only a branch, but the root of the exaltation of man is the good attributes and virtues which are the adornments of his reality. These are the divine appearances, the heavenly bounties, the sublime emotions, the love and knowledge of God; universal wisdom, intellectual perception, scientific discoveries, justice, equity, truthfulness, benevolence, natural courage and innate fortitude; the respect for rights and the keeping of agreements and covenants; rectitude in all circumstances; serving the truth under all conditions; the sacrifice of one's life for the good of all people; kindness and esteem for all nations; obedience to the teachings of God; service in the Divine Kingdom; the guidance of the people, and the education of the nations and races. This is the prosperity of the human world! This is the exaltation of man in the world! This is eternal life and heavenly honor!

These virtues do not appear from the reality of man except through the power of God and the divine teachings, for they need supernatural power for their manifestation. It may be that in the world of nature a trace of these perfections may appear, but they are unstable and ephemeral; they are like the rays of the sun upon the wall.

As the compassionate God has placed such a wonderful crown upon the head of man, man should strive that its brilliant jewels may become visible in the world.

Part Two

SOME CHRISTIAN SUBJECTS

16

OUTWARD FORMS AND SYMBOLS
MUST BE USED TO CONVEY
INTELLECTUAL CONCEPTIONS

A SUBJECT that is essential[1] for the comprehension of the
questions that we have mentioned, and of others of which
we are about to speak, so that the essence of the problems
may be understood, is this: that human knowledge is of
two kinds. One is the knowledge of things perceptible to
the senses—that is to say, things which the eye, or ear, or
smell, or taste, or touch can perceive, which are called objective or sensible. So the sun, because it can be seen, is
said to be objective; and in the same way sounds are sensible because the ear hears them; perfumes are sensible because they can be inhaled and the sense of smell perceives
them; foods are sensible because the palate perceives their
sweetness, sourness or saltness; heat and cold are sensible
because the feelings perceive them. These are said to be
sensible realities.

The other kind of human knowledge is intellectual—
that is to say, it is a reality of the intellect; it has no outward form and no place and is not perceptible to the
senses. For example, the power of intellect is not sensible;
none of the inner qualities of man is a sensible thing; on the
contrary, they are intellectual realities. So love is a mental
reality and not sensible; for this reality the ear does not
hear, the eye does not see, the smell does not perceive, the
taste does not discern, the touch does not feel. Even

1. Lit., the pivot.

ethereal matter, the forces of which are said in physics to be heat, light, electricity and magnetism, is an intellectual reality, and is not sensible. In the same way, nature, also, in its essence is an intellectual reality and is not sensible; the human spirit is an intellectual, not sensible reality. In explaining these intellectual realities, one is obliged to express them by sensible figures because in exterior existence there is nothing that is not material. Therefore, to explain the reality of the spirit—its condition, its station—one is obliged to give explanations under the forms of sensible things because in the external world all that exists is sensible. For example, grief and happiness are intellectual things; when you wish to express those spiritual qualities you say: "My heart is oppressed; my heart is dilated," though the heart of man is neither oppressed nor dilated. This is an intellectual or spiritual state, to explain which you are obliged to have recourse to sensible figures. Another example: you say, "such an individual made great progress," though he is remaining in the same place; or again, "such a one's position was exalted," although, like everyone else, he walks upon the earth. This exaltation and this progress are spiritual states and intellectual realities, but to explain them you are obliged to have recourse to sensible figures because in the exterior world there is nothing that is not sensible.

So the symbol of knowledge is light, and of ignorance, darkness; but reflect, is knowledge sensible light, or ignorance sensible darkness? No, they are merely symbols. These are only intellectual states, but when you desire to express them outwardly, you call knowledge light, and ignorance darkness. You say: "My heart was gloomy, and it became enlightened." Now, that light of knowledge, and that darkness of ignorance, are intellectual realities, not sensible ones; but when we seek for explanations in the external world, we are obliged to give them a sensible form.

Then it is evident that the dove which descended upon Christ was not a material dove, but it was a spiritual state, which, that it might be comprehensible, was expressed by a sensible figure. Thus in the Old Testament it is said that God appeared as a pillar of fire: this does not signify the material form; it is an intellectual reality which is expressed by a sensible image.

Christ says, "The Father is in the Son, and the Son is in the Father." Was Christ within God, or God within Christ? No, in the name of God! On the contrary, this is an intellectual state which is expressed in a sensible figure.

We come to the explanation of the words of Bahá'u'lláh when He says: "O king! I was but a man like others, asleep upon My couch, when lo, the breezes of the All-Glorious were wafted over Me, and taught Me the knowledge of all that hath been. This thing is not from Me, but from One Who is Almighty and All-Knowing."[1] This is the state of manifestation: it is not sensible; it is an intellectual reality, exempt and freed from time, from past, present and future; it is an explanation, a simile, a metaphor and is not to be accepted literally; it is not a state that can be comprehended by man. Sleeping and waking is passing from one state to another. Sleeping is the condition of repose, and wakefulness is the condition of movement. Sleeping is the state of silence; wakefulness is the state of speech. Sleeping is the state of mystery; wakefulness is the state of manifestation.

For example, it is a Persian and Arabic expression to say that the earth was asleep, and the spring came, and it awoke; or the earth was dead, and the spring came, and it revived. These expressions are metaphors, allegories, mystic explanations in the world of signification.

Briefly, the Holy Manifestations have ever been, and ever will be, Luminous Realities; no change or variation

1. Extract from the letter to Náṣiri'd-Dín Sháh.

takes place in Their essence. Before declaring Their manifestation, They are silent and quiet like a sleeper, and after Their manifestation, They speak and are illuminated, like one who is awake.

17

THE BIRTH OF CHRIST

Question. —How was Christ born of the Holy Spirit?

Answer. —In regard to this question, theologians and materialists disagree. The theologians believe that Christ was born of the Holy Spirit, but the materialists think this is impossible and inadmissible, and that without doubt He had a human father.

In the Qur'án it is said: "And We sent Our Spirit unto her, and He appeared unto her in the shape of a perfect man,"[1] meaning that the Holy Spirit took the likeness of the human form, as an image is produced in a mirror, and he addressed Mary.

The materialists believe that there must be marriage, and say that a living body cannot be created from a lifeless body, and without male and female there cannot be fecundation. And they think that not only with man, but also with animals and plants, it is impossible. For this union of the male and female exists in all living beings and plants. This pairing of things is even shown forth in the Qur'án: "Glory be to Him Who has created all the pairs: of such things as the earth produceth, and of themselves; and of things which they know not"[2]—that is to say, men, animals and plants are all in pairs—"and of everything have We created two kinds"—that is to say, We have created all the beings through pairing.

Briefly, they say a man without a human father cannot be imagined. In answer, the theologians say: "This thing

1. Cf. Qur'án 19:17.
2. Qur'án 36:35.

is not impossible and unachievable, but it has not been seen; and there is a great difference between a thing which is impossible and one which is unknown. For example, in former times the telegraph, which causes the East and the West to communicate, was unknown but not impossible; photography and phonography were unknown but not impossible."

The materialists insist upon this belief, and the theologians reply: "Is this globe eternal or phenomenal?" The materialists answer that, according to science and important discoveries, it is established that it is phenomenal; in the beginning it was a flaming globe, and gradually it became temperate; a crust was formed around it, and upon this crust plants came into existence, then animals, and finally man.

The theologians say: "Then from your statement it has become evident and clear that mankind is phenomenal upon the globe, and not eternal. Then surely the first man had neither father nor mother, for the existence of man is phenomenal. Is not the creation of man without father and mother, even though gradually, more difficult than if he had simply come into existence without a father? As you admit that the first man came into existence without father or mother—whether it be gradually or at once—there can remain no doubt that a man without a human father is also possible and admissible; you cannot consider this impossible; otherwise, you are illogical. For example, if you say that this lamp has once been lighted without wick and oil, and then say that it is impossible to light it without the wick, this is illogical." Christ had a mother; the first man, as the materialists believe, had neither father nor mother.[1]

---

1. This conversation shows the uselessness of discussions upon such questions; the teachings of 'Abdu'l-Bahá upon the birth of Christ will be found in the following chapter.

18

THE GREATNESS OF CHRIST IS DUE
TO HIS PERFECTIONS

A GREAT man is a great man, whether born of a human father or not. If being without a father is a virtue, Adam is greater and more excellent than all the Prophets and Messengers, for He had neither father nor mother. That which causes honor and greatness is the splendor and bounty of the divine perfections. The sun is born from substance and form, which can be compared to father and mother, and it is absolute perfection; but the darkness has neither substance nor form, neither father nor mother, and it is absolute imperfection. The substance of Adam's physical life was earth, but the substance of Abraham was pure sperm; it is certain that the pure and chaste sperm is superior to earth.

Furthermore, in the first chapter of the Gospel of John, verses 12 and 13, it is said: "But as many as received Him, to them gave He power to become the sons of God, even to them that believed on His name:

"Which were born, not of blood, nor of the will of the flesh, nor of the will of man, but of God."[1]

From these verses it is obvious that the being of a disciple also is not created by physical power, but by the spiritual reality. The honor and greatness of Christ is not due to the fact that He did not have a human father, but to His perfections, bounties and divine glory. If the greatness of Christ is His being fatherless, then Adam is greater than Christ, for He had neither father nor mother. It is

1. Cf. John 1:12–13.

89

said in the Old Testament, "And the Lord God formed man of the dust of the ground, and breathed into his nostrils the breath of life; and man became a living soul."[1] Observe that it is said that Adam came into existence from the Spirit of life. Moreover, the expression which John uses in regard to the disciples proves that they also are from the Heavenly Father. Hence it is evident that the holy reality, meaning the real existence of every great man, comes from God and owes its being to the breath of the Holy Spirit.

The purport is that, if to be without a father is the greatest human glory, then Adam is greater than all, for He had neither father nor mother. Is it better for a man to be created from a living substance or from earth? Certainly it is better if he be created from a living substance. But Christ was born and came into existence from the Holy Spirit.

To conclude: the splendor and honor of the holy souls and the Divine Manifestations come from Their heavenly perfections, bounties and glory, and from nothing else.

1. Gen. 2:7.

19

THE BAPTISM OF CHRIST

Question.—It is said in the Gospel of St. Matthew, chapter 3, verses 13, 14, 15: "Then cometh Jesus from Galilee to Jordan unto John, to be baptized of him. But John forbade Him, saying, I have need to be baptized of Thee, and comest Thou to me? And Jesus answering said unto him, Suffer it to be so now: for thus it becometh us to fulfil all righteousness. Then he suffered Him."

What is the wisdom of this: since Christ possessed all essential perfection, why did He need baptism?

Answer.—The principle of baptism is purification by repentance. John admonished and exhorted the people, and caused them to repent; then he baptized them. Therefore, it is apparent that this baptism is a symbol of repentance from all sin: its meaning is expressed in these words: "O God! as my body has become purified and cleansed from physical impurities, in the same way purify and sanctify my spirit from the impurities of the world of nature, which are not worthy of the Threshold of Thy Unity!" Repentance is the return from disobedience to obedience. Man, after remoteness and deprivation from God, repents and undergoes purification: and this is a symbol signifying "O God! make my heart good and pure, freed and sanctified from all save Thy love."

As Christ desired that this institution of John should be used at that time by all, He Himself conformed to it in order to awaken the people and to complete the law of the former religion. Although the ablution of repentance was the institution of John, it was in reality formerly practiced in the religion of God.

Christ was not in need of baptism; but as at that time it was an acceptable and praiseworthy action, and a sign of the glad tidings of the Kingdom, therefore, He confirmed it. However, afterward He said the true baptism is not with material water, but it must be with spirit and with water. In this case water does not signify material water, for elsewhere it is explicitly said baptism is with spirit and with fire, from which it is clear that the reference is not to material fire and material water, for baptism with fire is impossible.

Therefore, the spirit is the bounty of God, the water is knowledge and life, and the fire is the love of God. For material water does not purify the heart of man; no, it cleanses his body. But the heavenly water and spirit, which are knowledge and life, make the human heart good and pure; the heart which receives a portion of the bounty of the Spirit becomes sanctified, good and pure—that is to say, the reality of man becomes purified and sanctified from the impurities of the world of nature. These natural impurities are evil qualities: anger, lust, worldliness, pride, lying, hypocrisy, fraud, self-love, etc.

Man cannot free himself from the rage of the carnal passions except by the help of the Holy Spirit. That is why He says baptism with the spirit, with water and with fire is necessary, and that it is essential—that is to say, the spirit of divine bounty, the water of knowledge and life, and the fire of the love of God. Man must be baptized with this spirit, this water and this fire so as to become filled with the eternal bounty. Otherwise, what is the use of baptizing with material water? No, this baptism with water was a symbol of repentance, and of seeking forgiveness of sins.

But in the cycle of Bahá'u'lláh there is no longer need of this symbol; for its reality, which is to be baptized with the spirit and love of God, is understood and established.

20

THE NECESSITY OF BAPTISM

Question.—Is the ablution of baptism useful and necessary, or is it useless and unnecessary? In the first case, if it is useful, why was it abrogated? And in the second case, if it is useless, why did John practice it?

Answer.—The change in conditions, alterations and transformations are necessities of the essence of beings, and essential necessities cannot be separated from the reality of things. So it is absolutely impossible to separate heat from fire, humidity from water, or light from the sun, for they are essential necessities. As the change and alteration of conditions are necessities for beings, so laws also are changed and altered in accordance with the changes and alterations of the times. For example, in the time of Moses, His Law was conformed and adapted to the conditions of the time; but in the days of Christ these conditions had changed and altered to such an extent that the Mosaic Law was no longer suited and adapted to the needs of mankind; and it was, therefore, abrogated. Thus it was that Christ broke the Sabbath and forbade divorce. After Christ four disciples, among whom were Peter and Paul, permitted the use of animal food forbidden by the Bible, except the eating of those animals which had been strangled, or which were sacrificed to idols, and of blood.[1] They also forbade fornication. They maintained these four commandments. Afterward, Paul permitted even the eating of strangled animals, those sacrificed to idols, and blood, and only maintained the prohibition of fornication.

1. Acts 15:20.

So in chapter 14, verse 14 of his Epistle to the Romans, Paul writes: "I know, and am persuaded by the Lord Jesus, that there is nothing unclean of itself: but to him that esteemeth any thing to be unclean, to him it is unclean."

Also in the Epistle of Paul to Titus, chapter 1, verse 15: "Unto the pure all things are pure: but unto them that are defiled and unbelieving is nothing pure; but even their mind and conscience is defiled."

Now this change, these alterations and this abrogation are due to the impossibility of comparing the time of Christ with that of Moses. The conditions and requirements in the later period were entirely changed and altered. The former laws were, therefore, abrogated.

The existence of the world may be compared to that of a man, and the Prophets and Messengers of God to skillful doctors. The human being cannot remain in one condition: different maladies occur which have each a special remedy. The skillful physician does not give the same medicine to cure each disease and each malady, but he changes remedies and medicines according to the different necessities of the diseases and constitutions. One person may have a severe illness caused by fever, and the skilled doctor will give him cooling remedies; and when at some other time the condition of this person has changed, and fever is replaced by chills, without doubt the skilled doctor will discard cooling medicine and permit the use of heating drugs. This change and alteration is required by the condition of the patient and is an evident proof of the skill of the physician.

Consider, could the Law of the Old Testament be enforced at this epoch and time? No, in the name of God! it would be impossible and impracticable; therefore, most certainly God abrogated the laws of the Old Testament at the time of Christ. Reflect, also, that baptism in the days of John the Baptist was used to awaken and admonish the people to repent from all sin, and to watch for the appearance of the Kingdom of Christ. But at present in Asia, the Catholics and the Orthodox Church plunge newly born children into water mixed with olive oil, and many of them become ill from the shock; at the time of baptism they struggle and become agitated. In other places, the clergy sprinkle the water of baptism on the forehead. But neither from the first form nor from the second do the children derive any spiritual benefit. Then what result is obtained from this form? Other peoples are amazed and wonder why the infant is plunged into the water, since this is neither the cause of the spiritual awakening of the child, nor of its faith or conversion, but it is only a custom which is followed. In the time of John the Baptist it was not so; no, at first John used to exhort the people, and to guide them to repentance from sin, and to fill them with the desire to await the manifestation of Christ. Whoever received the ablution of baptism, and repented of sins in absolute humility and meekness, would also purify and cleanse his body from outward impurities. With perfect yearning, night and day, he would constantly wait for the manifestation of Christ, and the entrance to the Kingdom of the Spirit of God.[1]

To recapitulate: our meaning is that the change and modification of conditions, and the altered requirements of different centuries and times, are the cause of the abrogation of laws. For a time comes when these laws are no longer suitably adapted to conditions. Consider how very different are the requirements of the first centuries, of the Middle Ages, and of modern times. Is it possible that the laws of the first centuries could be enforced at present? It is evident that it would be impossible and impracticable. In the same manner, after the lapse of a few centuries, the requirements of the present time will not be the same as

1. i.e., of Christ, Whom the Muslims frequently designate by the title of *Rúḥu'lláh*, the Spirit of God.

those of the future, and certainly there will be change and alteration. In Europe the laws are unceasingly altered and modified; in bygone years, how many laws existed in the organizations and systems of Europe, which are now abrogated! These changes and alterations are due to the variation and mutation of thought, conditions and customs. If it were not so, the prosperity of the world of humanity would be wrecked.

For example, there is in the Pentateuch a law that if anyone break the Sabbath, he shall be put to death. Moreover, there are ten sentences of death in the Pentateuch. Would it be possible to keep these laws in our time? It is clear that it would be absolutely impossible. Consequently, there are changes and modifications in the laws, and these are a sufficient proof of the supreme wisdom of God.

This subject needs deep thought. Then the cause of these changes will be evident and apparent.

Blessed are those who reflect!

21

THE SYMBOLISM OF THE BREAD
AND THE WINE

Question. —The Christ said: "I am the living bread which came down from heaven, that a man may eat thereof and not die."[1] What is the meaning of this utterance?

Answer. —This bread signifies the heavenly food and divine perfections. So, "If any man eateth of this bread" means if any man acquires heavenly bounty, receives the divine light, or partakes of Christ's perfections, he thereby gains everlasting life. The blood also signifies the spirit of life and the divine perfections, the lordly splendor and eternal bounty. For all the members of the body gain vital substance from the circulation of the blood.

In the Gospel of St. John, chapter 6, verse 26, it is written: "Ye seek Me, not because ye saw the miracles, but because ye did eat of the loaves, and were filled."

It is evident that the bread of which the disciples ate and were filled was the heavenly bounty; for in verse 33 of the same chapter it is said: "For the bread of God is He which cometh down from heaven, and giveth life unto the world." It is clear that the body of Christ did not descend from heaven, but it came from the womb of Mary; and that which descended from the heaven of God was the spirit of Christ. As the Jews thought that Christ spoke of His body, they made objections, for it is said in the 42nd verse of the same chapter: "And they said, Is not this Jesus, the son of Joseph, whose father and mother we

1. Cf. John 6:51, 50.

know? how is it then that he saith, I came down from heaven?"

Reflect how clear it is that what Christ meant by the heavenly bread was His spirit, His bounties, His perfections and His teachings; for it is said in the 63rd verse: "It is the spirit that quickeneth; the flesh profiteth nothing."

Therefore, it is evident that the spirit of Christ is a heavenly grace which descends from heaven; whosoever receives light from that spirit in abundance—that is to say, the heavenly teachings—finds everlasting life. That is why it is said in the 35th verse: "And Jesus said unto them, I am the bread of life: he that cometh to Me shall never hunger; and he that believeth on Me shall never thirst."

Notice that "coming to Him" He expresses as eating, and "belief in Him" as drinking. Then it is evident and established that the celestial food is the divine bounties, the spiritual splendors, the heavenly teachings, the universal meaning of Christ. To eat is to draw near to Him, and to drink is to believe in Him. For Christ had an elemental body and a celestial form. The elemental body was crucified, but the heavenly form is living and eternal, and the cause of everlasting life; the first was the human nature, and the second is the divine nature. It is thought by some that the Eucharist is the reality of Christ, and that the Divinity and the Holy Spirit descend into and exist in it. Now when once the Eucharist is taken, after a few moments it is simply disintegrated and entirely transformed. Therefore, how can such a thought be conceived? God forbid! certainly it is an absolute fantasy.

To conclude: through the manifestation of Christ, the divine teachings, which are an eternal bounty, were spread abroad, the light of guidance shone forth, and the spirit of life was conferred on man. Whoever found guidance became living; whoever remained lost was seized by enduring death. This bread which came down from heaven was the divine body of Christ, His spiritual elements, which the disciples ate, and through which they gained eternal life.

The disciples had taken many meals from the hand of Christ; why was the last supper distinguished from the others? It is evident that the heavenly bread did not signify this material bread, but rather the divine nourishment of the spiritual body of Christ, the divine graces and heavenly perfections of which His disciples partook, and with which they became filled.

In the same way, reflect that when Christ blessed the bread and gave it to His disciples, saying, "This is My body,"[1] and gave grace to them, He was with them in person, in presence, and form. He was not transformed into bread and wine; if He had been turned into bread and wine, He could not have remained with the disciples in body, in person and in presence.

Then it is clear that the bread and wine were symbols which signified: I have given you My bounties and perfections, and when you have received this bounty, you have gained eternal life and have partaken of your share and your portion of the heavenly nourishment.

1. Matt. 26:26.

22

MIRACLES

Question.—It is recorded that miracles were performed by Christ. Are the reports of these miracles really to be accepted literally, or have they another meaning? It has been proved by exact science that the essence of things does not change, and that all beings are under one universal law and organization from which they cannot deviate; and, therefore, that which is contrary to universal law is impossible.

Answer.—The Holy Manifestations are the sources of miracles and the originators of wonderful signs. For Them, any difficult and impracticable thing is possible and easy. For through a supernatural power wonders appear from Them; and by this power, which is beyond nature, They influence the world of nature. From all the Manifestations marvelous things have appeared.

But in the Holy Books an especial terminology is employed, and for the Manifestations these miracles and wonderful signs have no importance. They do not even wish to mention them. For if we consider miracles a great proof, they are still only proofs and arguments for those who are present when they are performed, and not for those who are absent.

For example, if we relate to a seeker, a stranger to Moses and Christ, marvelous signs, he will deny them and will say: "Wonderful signs are also continually related of false gods by the testimony of many people, and they are affirmed in the Books. The Brahmans have written a book about wonderful prodigies from Brahma." He will also say: "How can we know that the Jews and the Christians speak the truth, and that the Brahmans tell a lie? For both are generally admitted traditions, which are collected in books, and may be supposed to be true or false." The same may be said of other religions: if one is true, all are true; if one is accepted, all must be accepted. Therefore, miracles are not a proof. For if they are proofs for those who are present, they fail as proofs to those who are absent.

But in the day of the Manifestation the people with insight see that all the conditions of the Manifestation are miracles, for They are superior to all others, and this alone is an absolute miracle. Recollect that Christ, solitary and alone, without a helper or protector, without armies and legions, and under the greatest oppression, uplifted the standard of God before all the people of the world, and withstood them, and finally conquered all, although outwardly He was crucified. Now this is a veritable miracle which can never be denied. There is no need of any other proof of the truth of Christ.

The outward miracles have no importance for the people of Reality. If a blind man receive sight, for example, he will finally again become sightless, for he will die and be deprived of all his senses and powers. Therefore, causing the blind man to see is comparatively of little importance, for this faculty of sight will at last disappear. If the body of a dead person be resuscitated, of what use is it since the body will die again? But it is important to give perception and eternal life—that is, the spiritual and divine life. For this physical life is not immortal, and its existence is equivalent to nonexistence. So it is that Christ said to one of His disciples: "Let the dead bury their dead;" for "That which is born of the flesh is flesh; and that which is born of the Spirit is spirit."[1]

Observe: those who in appearance were physically alive, Christ considered dead; for life is the eternal life, and existence is the real existence. Wherever in the Holy

1. Matt. 8:22; John 3:6.

Books they speak of raising the dead, the meaning is that the dead were blessed by eternal life; where it is said that the blind received sight, the signification is that he obtained the true perception; where it is said a deaf man received hearing, the meaning is that he acquired spiritual and heavenly hearing. This is ascertained from the text of the Gospel where Christ said: "These are like those of whom Isaiah said, They have eyes and see not, they have ears and hear not; and I healed them."[1]

The meaning is not that the Manifestations are unable to perform miracles, for They have all power. But for Them inner sight, spiritual healing and eternal life are the valuable and important things. Consequently, whenever it is recorded in the Holy Books that such a one was blind and recovered his sight, the meaning is that he was inwardly blind, and that he obtained spiritual vision, or that he was ignorant and became wise, or that he was negligent and became heedful, or that he was worldly and became heavenly.

As this inner sight, hearing, life and healing are eternal, they are of importance. What, comparatively, is the importance, the value and the worth of this animal life with its powers? In a few days it will cease like fleeting thoughts. For example, if one relights an extinguished lamp, it will again become extinguished; but the light of the sun is always luminous. This is of importance.

1. Cf. Matt. 13:14 and John 12:40–41.

23

THE RESURRECTION OF CHRIST

Question.—What is the meaning of Christ's resurrection after three days?

Answer.—The resurrections of the Divine Manifestations are not of the body. All Their states, Their conditions, Their acts, the things They have established, Their teachings, Their expressions, Their parables and Their instructions have a spiritual and divine signification, and have no connection with material things. For example, there is the subject of Christ's coming from heaven: it is clearly stated in many places in the Gospel that the Son of man came from heaven, He is in heaven, and He will go to heaven. So in chapter 6, verse 38, of the Gospel of John it is written: "For I came down from heaven"; and also in verse 42 we find: "And they said, Is not this Jesus, the son of Joseph, whose father and mother we know? how is it then that he saith, I came down from heaven?" Also in John, chapter 3, verse 13: "And no man hath ascended up to heaven, but He that came down from heaven, even the Son of man which is in heaven."

Observe that it is said, "The Son of man is in heaven," while at that time Christ was on earth. Notice also that it is said that Christ came from heaven, though He came from the womb of Mary, and His body was born of Mary. It is clear, then, that when it is said that the Son of man is come from heaven, this has not an outward but an inward signification; it is a spiritual, not a material, fact. The meaning is that though, apparently, Christ was born from the womb of Mary, in reality He came from heaven, from the center of the Sun of Reality, from the Divine World, and the Spiritual Kingdom. And as it has become evident that Christ came from the spiritual heaven of the Divine Kingdom, therefore, His disappearance under the earth for three days has an inner signification and is not an outward fact. In the same way, His resurrection from the interior of the earth is also symbolical; it is a spiritual and divine fact, and not material; and likewise His ascension to heaven is a spiritual and not material ascension.

Beside these explanations, it has been established and proved by science that the visible heaven is a limitless area, void and empty, where innumerable stars and planets revolve.

Therefore, we say that the meaning of Christ's resurrection is as follows: the disciples were troubled and agitated after the martyrdom of Christ. The Reality of Christ, which signifies His teachings, His bounties, His perfections and His spiritual power, was hidden and concealed for two or three days after His martyrdom, and was not resplendent and manifest. No, rather it was lost, for the believers were few in number and were troubled and agitated. The Cause of Christ was like a lifeless body; and when after three days the disciples became assured and steadfast, and began to serve the Cause of Christ, and resolved to spread the divine teachings, putting His counsels into practice, and arising to serve Him, the Reality of Christ became resplendent and His bounty appeared; His religion found life; His teachings and His admonitions became evident and visible. In other words, the Cause of Christ was like a lifeless body until the life and the bounty of the Holy Spirit surrounded it.

Such is the meaning of the resurrection of Christ, and this was a true resurrection. But as the clergy have neither understood the meaning of the Gospels nor comprehended the symbols, therefore, it has been said that religion is in contradiction to science, and science in opposition to religion, as, for example, this subject of the ascension of Christ with an elemental body to the visible heaven is contrary to the science of mathematics. But when the truth of this subject becomes clear, and the symbol is explained, science in no way contradicts it; but, on the contrary, science and the intelligence affirm it.

24

THE DESCENT OF THE HOLY SPIRIT
UPON THE APOSTLES

Question.—What is the manner, and what is the meaning, of the descent of the Holy Spirit upon the Apostles, as described in the Gospel?

Answer.—The descent of the Holy Spirit is not like the entrance of air into man; it is an expression and a simile, rather than an exact or a literal image. No, rather it is like the entrance of the image of the sun into the mirror—that is to say, its splendor becomes apparent in it.

After the death of Christ the disciples were troubled, and their ideas and thoughts were discordant and contradictory; later they became firm and united, and at the feast of Pentecost they gathered together and detached themselves from the things of this world. Disregarding themselves, they renounced their comfort and worldly happiness, sacrificing their body and soul to the Beloved, abandoning their houses, and becoming wanderers and homeless, even forgetting their own existence. Then they received the help of God, and the power of the Holy Spirit became manifested; the spirituality of Christ triumphed, and the love of God reigned. They were given help at that time and dispersed in different directions, teaching the Cause of God, and giving forth proofs and evidences.

So the descent of the Holy Spirit upon the Apostles means their attraction by the Christ Spirit, whereby they acquired stability and firmness. Through the spirit of the love of God they gained a new life, and they saw Christ living, helping and protecting them. They were like drops, and they became seas; they were like feeble insects, and they became majestic eagles; they were weak and became powerful. They were like mirrors facing the sun; verily, some of the light became manifest in them.

25

THE HOLY SPIRIT

Question. —What is the Holy Spirit?

Answer. —The Holy Spirit is the Bounty of God and the luminous rays which emanate from the Manifestations; for the focus of the rays of the Sun of Reality was Christ, and from this glorious focus, which is the Reality of Christ, the Bounty of God reflected upon the other mirrors which were the reality of the Apostles. The descent of the Holy Spirit upon the Apostles signifies that the glorious divine bounties reflected and appeared in their reality. Moreover, entrance and exit, descent and ascent, are characteristics of bodies and not of spirits—that is to say, sensible realities enter and come forth, but intellectual subtleties and mental realities, such as intelligence, love, knowledge, imagination and thought, do not enter, nor come forth, nor descend, but rather they have direct connection.

For example, knowledge, which is a state attained to by the intelligence, is an intellectual condition; and entering and coming out of the mind are imaginary conditions; but the mind is connected with the acquisition of knowledge, like images reflected in a mirror.

Therefore, as it is evident and clear that the intellectual realities do not enter and descend, and it is absolutely impossible that the Holy Spirit should ascend and descend, enter, come out or penetrate, it can only be that the Holy Spirit appears in splendor, as the sun appears in the mirror.

In some passages in the Holy Books the Spirit is spoken

of, signifying a certain person, as it is currently said in speech and conversation that such a person is an embodied spirit, or he is a personification of mercy and generosity. In this case, it is the light we look at, and not the glass.

In the Gospel of John, in speaking of the Promised One Who was to come after Christ, it is said in chapter 16, verses 12, 13: "I have yet many things to say unto you, but ye cannot bear them now. Howbeit when He, the Spirit of truth, is come, He will guide you into all truth: for He shall not speak of Himself; but whatsoever He shall hear, that shall He speak."

Now consider carefully that from these words, "for He shall not speak of Himself; but whatsoever He shall hear, that shall He speak," it is clear that the Spirit of truth is embodied in a Man Who has individuality, Who has ears to hear and a tongue to speak. In the same way the name "Spirit of God" is used in relation to Christ, as you speak of a light, meaning both the light and the lamp.

26

THE SECOND COMING OF CHRIST AND
THE DAY OF JUDGMENT

IT is said in the Holy Books that Christ will come again, and that His coming depends upon the fulfillment of certain signs: when He comes, it will be with these signs. For example, "The sun will be darkened, and the moon shall not give her light, and the stars shall fall from heaven. . . . And then shall appear the sign of the Son of man in heaven: and then shall all the tribes of the earth mourn, and they shall see the Son of man coming in the clouds of heaven with power and great glory."[1] Bahá'u'lláh has explained these verses in the Kitáb-i-Íqán.[2] There is no need of repetition; refer to it, and you will understand these sayings.

But I have something further to say upon this subject. At His first coming Christ also came from heaven, as it is explicity stated in the Gospel. Christ Himself says: "And no man hath ascended up to heaven, but He that came down from heaven, even the Son of man which is in heaven."[3]

It is clear to all that Christ came from heaven, although apparently He came from the womb of Mary. At the first coming He came from heaven, though apparently from the womb; in the same way, also, at His second coming He will come from heaven, though apparently from the

1. Cf. Matt. 24:29–30.
2. Kitáb-i-Íqán, one of the first works of Bahá'u'lláh, written at Baghdád, before the declaration of His manifestation.
3. John 3:13.

womb. The conditions that are indicated in the Gospel for the second coming of Christ are the same as those that were mentioned for the first coming, as we said before.

The Book of Isaiah announces that the Messiah will conquer the East and the West, and all nations of the world will come under His shadow, that His Kingdom will be established, that He will come from an unknown place, that the sinners will be judged, and that justice will prevail to such a degree that the wolf and the lamb, the leopard and the kid, the sucking child and the asp, shall all gather at one spring, and in one meadow, and one dwelling.[1] The first coming was also under these conditions, though outwardly none of them came to pass. Therefore, the Jews rejected Christ, and, God forbid! called the Messiah *masíkh*,[2] considered Him to be the destroyer of the edifice of God, regarded Him as the breaker of the Sabbath and the Law, and sentenced Him to death. Nevertheless, each one of these conditions had a signification that the Jews did not understand; therefore, they were debarred from perceiving the truth of Christ.

The second coming of Christ also will be in like manner: the signs and conditions which have been spoken of all have meanings, and are not to be taken literally. Among other things it is said that the stars will fall upon the earth. The stars are endless and innumerable, and modern mathematicians have established and proved scientifically that the globe of the sun is estimated to be about one million and a half times greater than the earth, and each of the fixed stars to be a thousand times larger than the sun. If these stars were to fall upon the surface of the earth, how could they find place there? It would be as though a

1. In these conversations, as the reader will have already observed, 'Abdu'l-Bahá desires rather to indicate the meaning of certain passages of the Scriptures than to quote the exact text.

2. *Masíkh*—i.e., the monster. In Arabic there is a play upon the words *Masíh*, the Messiah, and *masíkh*, the monster.

thousand million of Himalaya mountains were to fall upon a grain of mustard seed. According to reason and science this thing is quite impossible. What is even more strange is that Christ said: "Perhaps I shall come when you are yet asleep, for the coming of the Son of man is like the coming of a thief."[1] Perhaps the thief will be in the house, and the owner will not know it.

It is clear and evident that these signs have symbolic signification, and that they are not literal. They are fully explained in the Kitáb-i-Íqán. Refer to it.

---

1. Cf. 1 Thess. 5:2; 2 Pet. 3:10.

27

THE TRINITY

Question.—What is the meaning of the Trinity, of the Three Persons in One?

Answer.—The Divine Reality, which is purified and sanctified from the understanding of human beings and which can never be imagined by the people of wisdom and of intelligence, is exempt from all conception. That Lordly Reality admits of no division; for division and multiplicity are properties of creatures which are contingent existences, and not accidents which happen to the self-existent.

The Divine Reality is sanctified from singleness, then how much more from plurality. The descent of that Lordly Reality into conditions and degrees would be equivalent to imperfection and contrary to perfection, and is, therefore, absolutely impossible. It perpetually has been, and is, in the exaltation of holiness and sanctity. All that is mentioned of the Manifestations and Dawning-places of God signifies the divine reflection, and not a descent into the conditions of existence.[1]

God is pure perfection, and creatures are but imperfections. For God to descend into the conditions of existence would be the greatest of imperfections; on the contrary, His manifestation, His appearance, His rising are like the reflection of the sun in a clear, pure, polished mirror. All the creatures are evident signs of God, like the earthly beings upon all of which the rays of the sun shine. But upon the plains, the mountains, the trees and fruits, only a por-

1. Cf. "Pantheism," p. 290.

tion of the light shines, through which they become visible, and are reared, and attain to the object of their existence, while the Perfect Man[1] is in the condition of a clear mirror in which the Sun of Reality becomes visible and manifest with all its qualities and perfections. So the Reality of Christ was a clear and polished mirror of the greatest purity and fineness. The Sun of Reality, the Essence of Divinity, reflected itself in this mirror and manifested its light and heat in it; but from the exaltation of its holiness, and the heaven of its sanctity, the Sun did not descend to dwell and abide in the mirror. No, it continues to subsist in its exaltation and sublimity, while appearing and becoming manifest in the mirror in beauty and perfection.

Now if we say that we have seen the Sun in two mirrors—one the Christ and one the Holy Spirit—that is to say, that we have seen three Suns, one in heaven and the two others on the earth, we speak truly. And if we say that there is one Sun, and it is pure singleness, and has no partner and equal, we again speak truly.

The epitome of the discourse is that the Reality of Christ was a clear mirror, and the Sun of Reality—that is to say, the Essence of Oneness, with its infinite perfections and attributes—became visible in the mirror. The meaning is not that the Sun, which is the Essence of the Divinity, became divided and multiplied—for the Sun is one—but it appeared in the mirror. This is why Christ said, "The Father is in the Son," meaning that the Sun is visible and manifest in this mirror.

The Holy Spirit is the Bounty of God which becomes visible and evident in the Reality of Christ. The Sonship station is the heart of Christ, and the Holy Spirit is the station of the spirit of Christ. Hence it has become certain and proved that the Essence of Divinity is absolutely unique and has no equal, no likeness, no equivalent.

1. The Divine Manifestation.

This is the signification of the Three Persons of the Trinity. If it were otherwise, the foundations of the Religion of God would rest upon an illogical proposition which the mind could never conceive, and how can the mind be forced to believe a thing which it cannot conceive? A thing cannot be grasped by the intelligence except when it is clothed in an intelligible form; otherwise, it is but an effort of the imagination.

It has now become clear, from this explanation, what is the meaning of the Three Persons of the Trinity. The Oneness of God is also proved.

28

EXPLANATION OF VERSE FIVE, CHAPTER SEVENTEEN, OF THE GOSPEL OF ST. JOHN

"AND now, O Father, glorify Thou Me with Thine own self, with the glory which I had with Thee before the world was."[1]

There are two kinds of priorities: one is essential and is not preceded by a cause, but its existence is in itself, as, for example, the sun has light in itself, for its shining is not dependent on the light of other stars. This is called an essential light. But the light of the moon is received from the sun, for the moon is dependent on the sun for its light; therefore, the sun, with regard to light, is the cause, and the moon becomes the effect. The former is the ancient, the precedent, the antecedent, while the latter is the preceded and the last.

The second sort of preexistence is the preexistence of time, and that has no beginning. The Word of God is sanctified from time.[2] The past, the present, the future, all, in relation to God, are equal. Yesterday, today, tomorrow do not exist in the sun.

In the same way there is a priority with regard to glory—that is to say, the most glorious precedes the glorious. Therefore, the Reality of Christ, Who is the Word of God, with regard to essence, attributes and glory, certainly precedes the creatures. Before appearing in the human form, the Word of God was in the utmost sanctity

1. John 17:5.
2. i.e., the Reality of Christ.

and glory, existing in perfect beauty and splendor in the height of its magnificence. When through the wisdom of God the Most High it shone from the heights of glory in the world of the body, the Word of God, through this body, became oppressed, so that it fell into the hands of the Jews, and became the captive of the tyrannical and ignorant, and at last was crucified. That is why He addressed God, saying: "Free Me from the bonds of the world of the body, and liberate Me from this cage, so that I may ascend to the heights of honor and glory, and attain unto the former grandeur and might which existed before the bodily world, that I may rejoice in the eternal world and may ascend to the original abode, the placeless world, the invisible kingdom."

It is thus that you see even in the kingdom of this world—that is to say, in the realm of souls and countries—that the glory and the grandeur of Christ appeared in this earth after His ascension. When in the world of the body He was subject to the contempt and jeers of the weakest nation of the world, the Jews, who thought it fitting to set a crown of thorns upon His sacred head. But after His ascension the bejeweled crowns of all the kings were humbled and bowed before the crown of thorns.

Behold the glory that the Word of God attained even in this world!

29

EXPLANATION OF VERSE TWENTY-TWO, CHAPTER FIFTEEN, OF THE FIRST EPISTLE OF ST. PAUL TO THE CORINTHIANS

Question.—In verse 22 of chapter 15 of 1 Corinthians it is written: "For as in Adam all die, even so in Christ shall all be made alive." What is the meaning of these words?

Answer.—Know that there are two natures in man: the physical nature and the spiritual nature. The physical nature is inherited from Adam, and the spiritual nature is inherited from the Reality of the Word of God, which is the spirituality of Christ. The physical nature is born of Adam, but the spiritual nature is born from the bounty of the Holy Spirit. The first is the source of all imperfection; the second is the source of all perfection.

The Christ sacrificed Himself so that men might be freed from the imperfections of the physical nature and might become possessed of the virtues of the spiritual nature. This spiritual nature, which came into existence through the bounty of the Divine Reality, is the union of all perfections and appears through the breath of the Holy Spirit. It is the divine perfections; it is light, spirituality, guidance, exaltation, high aspiration, justice, love, grace, kindness to all, philanthropy, the essence of life. It is the reflection of the splendor of the Sun of Reality.

The Christ is the central point of the Holy Spirit: He is born of the Holy Spirit; He is raised up by the Holy Spirit; He is the descendant of the Holy Spirit—that is to say, that the Reality of Christ does not descend from

Adam; no, it is born of the Holy Spirit. Therefore, this verse in Corinthians, "As in Adam all die, even so in Christ shall all be made alive," means, according to this terminology, that Adam[1] is the father of man—that is to say, He is the cause of the physical life of mankind; His was the physical fatherhood. He is a living soul, but He is not the giver of spiritual life, whereas Christ is the cause of the spiritual life of man, and with regard to the spirit, His was the spiritual fatherhood. Adam is a living soul; Christ is a quickening spirit.

This physical world of man is subject to the power of the lusts, and sin is the consequence of this power of the lusts, for it is not subject to the laws of justice and holiness. The body of man is a captive of nature; it will act in accordance with whatever nature orders. It is, therefore, certain that sins such as anger, jealousy, dispute, covetousness, avarice, ignorance, prejudice, hatred, pride and tyranny exist in the physical world. All these brutal qualities exist in the nature of man. A man who has not had a spiritual education is a brute. Like the savages of Africa, whose actions, habits and morals are purely sensual, they act according to the demands of nature to such a degree that they rend and eat one another. Thus it is evident that the physical world of man is a world of sin. In this physical world man is not distinguished from the animal.

All sin comes from the demands of nature, and these demands, which arise from the physical qualities, are not sins with respect to the animals, while for man they are sin. The animal is the source of imperfections, such as anger, sensuality, jealousy, avarice, cruelty, pride: all these defects are found in animals but do not constitute sins. But in man they are sins.

Adam is the cause of man's physical life; but the Reality of Christ—that is to say, the Word of God—is the cause of

1. *Abu'l-bashar*, i.e., the father of man, is one of the titles given by the Muslims to Adam.

spiritual life. It is "a quickening spirit," meaning that all
the imperfections which come from the requirements of
the physical life of man are transformed into human perfections by the teachings and education of that spirit.
Therefore, Christ was a quickening spirit, and the cause of
life in all mankind.

Adam was the cause of physical life, and as the physical
world of man is the world of imperfections, and imperfections are the equivalent of death, Paul compared the
physical imperfections to death.

But the mass of the Christians believe that, as Adam ate
of the forbidden tree, He sinned in that He disobeyed, and
that the disastrous consequences of this disobedience have
been transmitted as a heritage and have remained among
His descendants. Hence Adam became the cause of the
death of humanity. This explanation is unreasonable and
evidently wrong, for it means that all men, even the
Prophets and the Messengers of God, without committing
any sin or fault, but simply because they are the posterity
of Adam, have become without reason guilty sinners, and
until the day of the sacrifice of Christ were held captive in
hell in painful torment. This is far from the justice of God.
If Adam was a sinner, what is the sin of Abraham? What is
the fault of Isaac, or of Joseph? Of what is Moses guilty?

But Christ, Who is the Word of God, sacrificed Himself. This has two meanings, an apparent and an esoteric
meaning. The outward meaning is this: Christ's intention
was to represent and promote a Cause which was to educate the human world, to quicken the children of Adam,
and to enlighten all mankind; and since to represent such a
great Cause—a Cause which was antagonistic to all the
people of the world and all the nations and kingdoms—
meant that He would be killed and crucified, so Christ in
proclaiming His mission sacrificed His life. He regarded
the cross as a throne, the wound as a balm, the poison as
honey and sugar. He arose to teach and educate men, and

so He sacrificed Himself to give the spirit of life. He perished in body so as to quicken others by the spirit.

The second meaning of sacrifice is this: Christ was like a seed, and this seed sacrificed its own form so that the tree might grow and develop. Although the form of the seed was destroyed, its reality became apparent in perfect majesty and beauty in the form of a tree.

The position of Christ was that of absolute perfection; He made His divine perfections shine like the sun upon all believing souls, and the bounties of the light shone and radiated in the reality of men. This is why He says: "I am the bread which descended from heaven; whosoever shall eat of this bread will not die"[1]—that is to say, that whosoever shall partake of this divine food will attain unto eternal life: that is, every one who partakes of this bounty and receives these perfections will find eternal life, will obtain preexistent favors, will be freed from the darkness of error, and will be illuminated by the light of His guidance.

The form of the seed was sacrificed for the tree, but its perfections, because of this sacrifice, became evident and apparent—the tree, the branches, the leaves and the blossoms being concealed in the seed. When the form of the seed was sacrificed, its perfections appeared in the perfect form of leaves, blossoms and fruits.

1. Cf. John 6:41, 50, 58.

30

ADAM AND EVE

Question.—What is the truth of the story of Adam, and His eating of the fruit of the tree?

Answer.—In the Bible it is written that God put Adam in the garden of Eden, to cultivate and take care of it, and said to Him: "Eat of every tree of the garden except the tree of good and evil, for if You eat of that, You will die."[1] Then it is said that God caused Adam to sleep, and He took one of His ribs and created woman in order that she might be His companion. After that it is said the serpent induced the woman to eat of the tree, saying: "God has forbidden you to eat of the tree in order that your eyes may not be opened, and that you may not know good from evil."[2] Then Eve ate from the tree and gave unto Adam, Who also ate; their eyes were opened, they found themselves naked, and they hid their bodies with leaves. In consequence of this act they received the reproaches of God. God said to Adam: "Hast Thou eaten of the forbidden tree?" Adam answered: "Eve tempted Me, and I did eat." God then reproved Eve; Eve said: "The serpent tempted me, and I did eat." For this the serpent was cursed, and enmity was put between the serpent and Eve, and between their descendants. And God said: "The man is become like unto Us, knowing good and evil, and perhaps He will eat of the tree of life and live forever." So God guarded the tree of life.[3]

1. Cf. Gen. 2:16–17.
2. Cf. Gen. 3:5.
3. Cf. Gen. 3:11–15, 22.

If we take this story in its apparent meaning, according to the interpretation of the masses, it is indeed extraordinary. The intelligence cannot accept it, affirm it, or imagine it; for such arrangements, such details, such speeches and reproaches are far from being those of an intelligent man, how much less of the Divinity—that Divinity Who has organized this infinite universe in the most perfect form, and its innumerable inhabitants with absolute system, strength and perfection.

We must reflect a little: if the literal meaning of this story were attributed to a wise man, certainly all would logically deny that this arrangement, this invention, could have emanated from an intelligent being. Therefore, this story of Adam and Eve who ate from the tree, and their expulsion from Paradise, must be thought of simply as a symbol. It contains divine mysteries and universal meanings, and it is capable of marvelous explanations. Only those who are initiated into mysteries, and those who are near the Court of the All-Powerful, are aware of these secrets. Hence these verses of the Bible have numerous meanings.

We will explain one of them, and we will say: Adam signifies the heavenly spirit of Adam, and Eve His human soul. For in some passages in the Holy Books where women are mentioned, they represent the soul of man. The tree of good and evil signifies the human world; for the spiritual and divine world is purely good and absolutely luminous, but in the human world light and darkness, good and evil, exist as opposite conditions.

The meaning of the serpent is attachment to the human world. This attachment of the spirit to the human world led the soul and spirit of Adam from the world of freedom to the world of bondage and caused Him to turn from the Kingdom of Unity to the human world. When the soul and spirit of Adam entered the human world, He came out from the paradise of freedom and fell into the world of

bondage. From the height of purity and absolute goodness, He entered into the world of good and evil.

The tree of life is the highest degree of the world of
existence: the position of the Word of God, and the supreme Manifestation. Therefore, that position has been
preserved; and, at the appearance of the most noble supreme Manifestation, it became apparent and clear. For
the position of Adam, with regard to the appearance and
manifestation of the divine perfections, was in the embryonic condition; the position of Christ was the condition
of maturity and the age of reason; and the rising of the
Greatest Luminary[1] was the condition of the perfection of
the essence and of the qualities. This is why in the supreme Paradise the tree of life is the expression for the
center of absolutely pure sanctity—that is to say, of the
divine supreme Manifestation. From the days of Adam
until the days of Christ, They spoke little of eternal life
and the heavenly universal perfections. This tree of life
was the position of the Reality of Christ; through His
manifestation it was planted and adorned with everlasting
fruits.

Now consider how far this meaning conforms to the
reality. For the spirit and the soul of Adam, when they
were attached to the human world, passed from the world
of freedom into the world of bondage, and His descendants continued in bondage. This attachment of the soul
and spirit to the human world, which is sin, was inherited
by the descendants of Adam, and is the serpent which is
always in the midst of, and at enmity with, the spirits and
the descendants of Adam. That enmity continues and
endures. For attachment to the world has become the
cause of the bondage of spirits, and this bondage is identical with sin, which has been transmitted from Adam to
His posterity. It is because of this attachment that men

1. Bahá'u'lláh.

have been deprived of essential spirituality and exalted position.

When the sanctified breezes of Christ and the holy light of the Greatest Luminary[1] were spread abroad, the human realities—that is to say, those who turned toward the Word of God and received the profusion of His bounties—were saved from this attachment and sin, obtained everlasting life, were delivered from the chains of bondage, and attained to the world of liberty. They were freed from the vices of the human world, and were blessed by the virtues of the Kingdom. This is the meaning of the words of Christ, "I gave My blood for the life of the world"[2]—that is to say, I have chosen all these troubles, these sufferings, calamities, and even the greatest martyrdom, to attain this object, the remission of sins (that is, the detachment of spirits from the human world, and their attraction to the divine world) in order that souls may arise who will be the very essence of the guidance of mankind, and the manifestations of the perfections of the Supreme Kingdom.

Observe that if, according to the suppositions of the People of the Book,[3] the meaning were taken in its exoteric sense, it would be absolute injustice and complete predestination. If Adam sinned by going near the forbidden tree, what was the sin of the glorious Abraham, and what was the error of Moses the Interlocutor? What was the crime of Noah the Prophet? What was the transgression of Joseph the Truthful? What was the iniquity of the Prophets of God, and what was the trespass of John the Chaste? Would the justice of God have allowed these enlightened Manifestations, on account of the sin of Adam, to find torment in hell until Christ came and by the sacrifice of Himself saved them from excruciating tortures? Such an

1. Bahá'u'lláh.
2. Cf. John 6:51.
3. Jews and Christians.

idea is beyond every law and rule and cannot be accepted by any intelligent person.

No; it means what has already been said: Adam is the spirit of Adam, and Eve is His soul; the tree is the human world, and the serpent is that attachment to this world which constitutes sin, and which has infected the descendants of Adam. Christ by His holy breezes saved men from this attachment and freed them from this sin. The sin in Adam is relative to His position. Although from this attachment there proceed results, nevertheless, attachment to the earthly world, in relation to attachment to the spiritual world, is considered as a sin. The good deeds of the righteous are the sins of the Near Ones. This is established. So bodily power is not only defective in relation to spiritual power; it is weakness in comparison. In the same way, physical life, in comparison with eternal life in the Kingdom, is considered as death. So Christ called the physical life death, and said: "Let the dead bury their dead."[1] Though those souls possessed physical life, yet in His eyes that life was death.

This is one of the meanings of the biblical story of Adam. Reflect until you discover the others.

Salutations be upon you.

1. Matt. 8:22.

31

EXPLANATION OF BLASPHEMY
AGAINST THE HOLY SPIRIT

Question.—"Wherefore I say unto you, All manner of sin and blasphemy shall be forgiven unto men: but the blasphemy against the Holy Ghost shall not be forgiven unto men. And whosoever speaketh a word against the Son of man, it shall be forgiven him: but whosoever speaketh against the Holy Ghost, it shall not be forgiven him, neither in this world, neither in the world to come."— (Matt. 12:31–32)

Answer.—The holy realities of the Manifestations of God have two spiritual positions. One is the place of manifestation, which can be compared to the position of the globe of the sun, and the other is the resplendency of the manifestation, which is like its light and radiance; these are the perfections of God—in other words, the Holy Spirit. For the Holy Spirit is the divine bounties and lordly perfections, and these divine perfections are as the rays and heat of the sun. The brilliant rays of the sun constitute its being, and without them it would not be the sun. If the manifestation and the reflection of the divine perfections were not in Christ, Jesus would not be the Messiah. He is a Manifestation because He reflects in Himself the divine perfections. The Prophets of God are manifestations for the lordly perfections—that is, the Holy Spirit is apparent in Them.

If a soul remains far from the manifestation, he may yet be awakened; for he did not recognize the manifestation of the divine perfections. But if he loathe the divine perfec-

127

tions themselves—in other words, the Holy Spirit—it is evident that he is like a bat which hates the light.

This detestation of the light has no remedy and cannot be forgiven—that is to say, it is impossible for him to come near unto God. This lamp is a lamp because of its light; without the light it would not be a lamp. Now if a soul has an aversion for the light of the lamp, he is, as it were, blind, and cannot comprehend the light; and blindness is the cause of everlasting banishment from God.

It is evident that the souls receive grace from the bounty of the Holy Spirit which appears in the Manifestations of God, and not from the personality of the Manifestation. Therefore, if a soul does not receive grace from the bounties of the Holy Spirit, he remains deprived of the divine gift, and the banishment itself puts the soul beyond the reach of pardon.

This is why many people who were the enemies of the Manifestations, and who did not recognize Them, when once they had known Them became Their friends. So enmity toward the Manifestation did not become the cause of perpetual banishment, for they who indulged in it were the enemies of the light-holders, not knowing that They were the shining lights of God. They were not the enemies of the light, and when once they understood that the light-holder was the place of manifestation of the light, they became sincere friends of it.

The meaning is this: to remain far from the light-holder does not entail everlasting banishment, for one may become awakened and vigilant; but enmity toward the light is the cause of everlasting banishment, and for this there is no remedy.

32

EXPLANATION OF THE VERSE "FOR MANY ARE CALLED BUT FEW ARE CHOSEN"

Question.—In the Gospel Christ said: "Many are called, but few are chosen,"[1] and in the Qur'án it is written: "He will confer particular mercy on whom He pleaseth." What is the wisdom of this?

Answer.—Know that the order and the perfection of the whole universe require that existence should appear in numberless forms. For existing beings could not be embodied in only one degree, one station, one kind, one species and one class; undoubtedly, the difference of degrees and distinction of forms, and the variety of genus and species, are necessary—that is to say, the degree of mineral, vegetable, animal substances, and of man, are inevitable; for the world could not be arranged, adorned, organized and perfected with man alone. In the same way, with only animals, only plants or only minerals, this world could not show forth beautiful scenery, exact organization and exquisite adornment. Without doubt it is because of the varieties of degrees, stations, species and classes that existence becomes resplendent with utmost perfection.

For example, if this tree were entirely fruit, the vegetable perfections could not be attained; for leaves, blossoms and fruits are all necessary so that the tree may be adorned with utmost beauty and perfection.

In the same way consider the body of man. It must be composed of different organs, parts and members. Hu-

1. Matt. 22:14.

man beauty and perfection require the existence of the ear, the eye, the brain and even that of the nails and hair; if man were all brain, eyes or ears, it would be equivalent to imperfection. So the absence of hair, eyelashes, teeth and nails would be an absolute defect, though in comparison with the eye they are without feeling, and in this resemble the mineral and plant; but their absence in the body of man is necessarily faulty and displeasing.

As the degrees of existence are different and various, some beings are higher in the scale than others. Therefore, it is by the will and wish of God that some creatures are chosen for the highest degree, as man, and some others are placed in the middle degree, as the vegetable, and some are left in the lowest degree, like the mineral.

It is from the bounty of God that man is selected for the highest degree; and the differences which exist between men in regard to spiritual progress and heavenly perfections are also due to the choice of the Compassionate One. For faith, which is life eternal, is the sign of bounty, and not the result of justice. The flame of the fire of love, in this world of earth and water, comes through the power of attraction and not by effort and striving. Nevertheless, by effort and perseverance, knowledge, science and other perfections can be acquired; but only the light of the Divine Beauty can transport and move the spirits through the force of attraction. Therefore, it is said: "Many are called, but few are chosen."[1]

But the material beings are not despised, judged and held responsible for their own degree and station. For example, mineral, vegetable and animal in their various degrees are acceptable; but if in their own degree they remain imperfect, they are blamable, the degree itself being purely perfect.

The differences among mankind are of two sorts: one is a difference of station, and this difference is not

1. Matt. 22:14.

blameworthy. The other is a difference of faith and assurance; the loss of these is blameworthy, for then the soul is overwhelmed by his desires and passions, which deprive him of these blessings and prevent him from feeling the power of attraction of the love of God. Though that man is praiseworthy and acceptable in his station, yet as he is deprived of the perfections of that degree, he will become a source of imperfections, for which he is held responsible.[1]

1. Cf. "The Causes of Differences in the Characters of Men," p. 212.

33

THE "RETURN" SPOKEN OF BY
THE PROPHETS

Question. —Will you explain the subject of Return?

Answer. —Bahá'u'lláh has explained this question fully
and clearly in the *Íqán*.[1] Read it, and the truth of this subject will become apparent. But since you have asked about
it, I will explain it briefly. We will begin to elucidate it
from the Gospel, for there it is plainly said that when
John, the son of Zacharias, appeared and gave to men the
glad tidings of the Kingdom of God, they asked him,
"Who art thou? Art thou the promised Messiah?" He replied, "I am not the Messiah." Then they asked him, "Art
thou Elijah?" He said, "I am not."[2] These words prove
and show that John, the son of Zacharias, was not the
promised Elias. But on the day of the transfiguration on
Mount Tabor Christ said plainly that John, the son of
Zacharias, was the promised Elias.

In chapter 9, verses 11–13, of the Gospel of Mark, it is
said: "And they asked Him, saying, Why say the scribes
that Elias must first come? And He answered and told
them, Elias verily cometh first, and restoreth all things;
and how it is written of the Son of man, that He must suffer many things, and be set at nought. But I say unto you,
That Elias is indeed come, and they have done unto him
whatsoever they listed, as it is written of him."

In chapter 17, verse 13, of Matthew, it is said: "Then

1. Cf. p. 110, n. 2.
2. Cf. John 1:19–21.

the disciples understood that He spake unto them of John the Baptist."

They asked John the Baptist, "Are you Elias?" He answered, "No, I am not," although it is said in the Gospel that John was the promised Elias, and Christ also said so clearly.[1] Then if John was Elias, why did he say, "I am not"? And if he was not Elias, why did Christ say that he was?

The explanation is this: not the personality, but the reality of the perfections, is meant—that is to say, the same perfections that were in Elias existed in John the Baptist and were exactly realized in him. Therefore, John the Baptist was the promised Elias. In this case not the essence,[2] but the qualities, are regarded. For example, there was a flower last year, and this year there is also a flower; I say the flower of last year has returned. Now, I do not mean that same flower in its exact individuality has come back; but as this flower has the same qualities as that of last year—as it has the same perfume, delicacy, color and form—I say the flower of last year has returned, and this flower is the former flower. When spring comes, we say last year's spring has come back because all that was found in last year's spring exists in this spring. That is why Christ said, "You will see all that happened in the days of the former Prophets."

We will give another illustration. The seed of last year is sown, branches and leaves grow forth, blossoms and fruits appear, and all has again returned to seed. When this second seed is planted, a tree will grow from it, and once more those branches, leaves, blossoms and fruits will return, and that tree will appear in perfection. As the beginning was a seed and the end is a seed, we say that the seed has returned. When we look at the substance of the tree, it

1. Cf. John 1:21.
2. i.e., the individuality.

is another substance, but when we look at the blossoms, leaves and fruits, the same fragrance, delicacy and taste are produced. Therefore, the perfection of the tree has returned a second time.

In the same way, if we regard the return of the individual, it is another individual; but if we regard the qualities and perfections, the same have returned. Therefore, when Christ said, "This is Elias," He meant: this person is a manifestation of the bounty, the perfections, the character, the qualities and the virtues of Elias. John the Baptist said, "I am not Elias." Christ considered the qualities, the perfections, the character and the virtues of both, and John regarded his substance and individuality. It is like this lamp: it was here last night, and tonight it is also lighted, and tomorrow night it will also shine. We say that the lamp of this night is the same light as that of last night, and that it has returned. It refers to the light, and not to the oil, the wick or the holder.

This subject is fully and clearly explained in the Kitáb-i-Íqán.

34

PETER'S CONFESSION OF FAITH

Question.—In the Gospel of St. Matthew it is said: "Thou art Peter, and upon this rock I will build My church."[1] What is the meaning of this verse?

Answer.—This utterance of Christ is a confirmation of the statement of Peter, when Christ asked: Whom do you believe Me to be? and Peter answered: I believe that "Thou art the Son of the living God." Then Christ said to him: "Thou art Peter"[2]—for Cephas in Aramaic means rock—"and upon this rock I will build My church." For the others in answer to Christ said that He was Elias, and some said John the Baptist, and some others Jeremias or one of the Prophets.[3]

Christ wished by suggestion, or an allusion, to confirm the words of Peter; so on account of the suitability of his name, Peter, He said: "and upon this rock I will build My church," meaning, thy belief that Christ is the Son of the living God will be the foundation of the Religion of God, and upon this belief the foundation of the church of God—which is the Law of God—shall be established.

The existence of the tomb of Peter in Rome is doubtful; it is not authenticated. Some say it is in Antioch.

Moreover, let us compare the lives of some of the Popes with the religion of Christ. Christ, hungry and without shelter, ate herbs in the wilderness, and was unwilling to

1. Matt. 16:18.
2. It is well known that Peter's real name was Simon, but Christ called him Cephas, which corresponds to the Greek word *petras*, which means rock.
3. Cf. Matt. 16:14–18.

hurt the feelings of anyone. The Pope sits in a carriage covered with gold and passes his time in the utmost splendor, amidst such pleasures and luxuries, such riches and adoration, as kings have never had.

Christ hurt no one, but some of the Popes killed innocent people: refer to history. How much blood the Popes have shed merely to retain temporal power! For mere differences of opinion they arrested, imprisoned and slew thousands of the servants of the world of humanity and learned men who had discovered the secrets of nature. To what a degree they opposed the truth!

Reflect upon the instructions of Christ, and investigate the habits and customs of the Popes. Consider: is there any resemblance between the instructions of Christ and the manner of government of the Popes? We do not like to criticize, but the history of the Vatican is very extraordinary. The purport of our argument is this, that the instructions of Christ are one thing, and the manner of the Papal government is quite another; they do not agree. See how many Protestants have been killed by the order of the Popes, how many tyrannies and oppressions have been countenanced, and how many punishments and tortures have been inflicted! Can any of the sweet fragrances of Christ be detected in these actions? No! in the name of God! These people did not obey Christ, while Saint Barbara, whose picture is before us, did obey Christ, and followed in His footsteps, and put His commands into practice. Among the Popes there are also some blessed souls who followed in the footsteps of Christ, particularly in the first centuries of the Christian era when temporal things were lacking and the tests of God were severe. But when they came into possession of governmental power, and worldly honor and prosperity were gained, the Papal government entirely forgot Christ and was occupied with temporal power, grandeur, comfort and luxuries. It killed people, opposed the diffusion of learning, tormented the men of science, obstructed the light of knowledge, and gave the order to slay and to pillage. Thousands of souls, men of science and learning, and sinless ones, perished in the prisons of Rome. With all these proceedings and actions, how can the Vicarship of Christ be believed in?

The Papal See has constantly opposed knowledge; even in Europe it is admitted that religion is the opponent of science, and that science is the destroyer of the foundations of religion. While the religion of God is the promoter of truth, the founder of science and knowledge, it is full of goodwill for learned men; it is the civilizer of mankind, the discoverer of the secrets of nature, and the enlightener of the horizons of the world. Consequently, how can it be said to oppose knowledge? God forbid! Nay, for God, knowledge is the most glorious gift of man and the most noble of human perfections. To oppose knowledge is ignorant, and he who detests knowledge and science is not a man, but rather an animal without intelligence. For knowledge is light, life, felicity, perfection, beauty and the means of approaching the Threshold of Unity. It is the honor and glory of the world of humanity, and the greatest bounty of God. Knowledge is identical with guidance, and ignorance is real error.

Happy are those who spend their days in gaining knowledge, in discovering the secrets of nature, and in penetrating the subtleties of pure truth! Woe to those who are contented with ignorance, whose hearts are gladdened by thoughtless imitation, who have fallen into the lowest depths of ignorance and foolishness, and who have wasted their lives!

35

PREDESTINATION

Question. —If God has knowledge of an action which will be performed by someone, and it has been written on the Tablet of Fate, is it possible to resist it?

Answer. —The foreknowledge of a thing is not the cause of its realization; for the essential knowledge of God surrounds, in the same way, the realities of things, before as well as after their existence, and it does not become the cause of their existence. It is a perfection of God. But that which was prophesied by the inspiration of God through the tongues of the Prophets, concerning the appearance of the Promised One of the Bible, was not the cause of the manifestation of Christ.

The hidden secrets of the future were revealed to the Prophets, and They thus became acquainted with the future events which They announced. This knowledge and these prophecies were not the cause of the occurrences. For example, tonight everyone knows that after seven hours the sun will rise, but this general foreknowledge does not cause the rising and appearance of the sun.

Therefore, the knowledge of God in the realm of contingency does not produce the forms of the things. On the contrary, it is purified from the past, present and future. It is identical with the reality of the things; it is not the cause of their occurrence.

In the same way, the record and the mention of a thing in the Book does not become the cause of its existence. The Prophets, through the divine inspiration, knew what would come to pass. For instance, through the divine inspiration They knew that Christ would be martyred, and They announced it. Now, was Their knowledge and information the cause of the martyrdom of Christ? No; this knowledge is a perfection of the Prophets and did not cause the martyrdom.

The mathematicians by astronomical calculations know that at a certain time an eclipse of the moon or the sun will occur. Surely this discovery does not cause the eclipse to take place. This is, of course, only an analogy and not an exact image.

Part Three

ON THE POWERS AND CONDITIONS
OF THE MANIFESTATIONS
OF GOD

36

THE FIVE ASPECTS OF SPIRIT

KNOW that, speaking generally, there are five divisions of the spirit. First the vegetable spirit: this is a power which results from the combination of elements and the mingling of substances by the decree of the Supreme God, and from the influence, the effect and connection of other existences. When these substances and elements are separated from each other, the power of growth also ceases to exist. So, to use another figure, electricity results from the combination of elements, and when these elements are separated, the electric force is dispersed and lost. Such is the vegetable spirit.

After this is the animal spirit, which also results from the mingling and combination of elements. But this combination is more complete, and through the decree of the Almighty Lord a perfect mingling is obtained, and the animal spirit—in other words, the power of the senses —is produced. It will perceive the reality of things from that which is seen and visible, audible, edible, tangible, and that which can be smelled. After the dissociation and decomposition of the combined elements this spirit also will naturally disappear. It is like this lamp which you see: when the oil and wick and fire are brought together, light is the result; but when the oil is finished and the wick consumed, the light will also vanish and be lost.

The human spirit may be likened to the bounty of the sun shining on a mirror. The body of man, which is composed from the elements, is combined and mingled in the most perfect form; it is the most solid construction, the noblest combination, the most perfect existence. It grows and develops through the animal spirit. This perfected body can be compared to a mirror, and the human spirit to the sun. Nevertheless, if the mirror breaks, the bounty of the sun continues; and if the mirror is destroyed or ceases to exist, no harm will happen to the bounty of the sun, which is everlasting. This spirit has the power of discovery; it encompasses all things. All these wonderful signs, these scientific discoveries, great enterprises and important historical events which you know are due to it. From the realm of the invisible and hidden, through spiritual power, it brought them to the plane of the visible. So man is upon the earth, yet he makes discoveries in the heavens. From known realities—that is to say, from the things which are known and visible—he discovers unknown things. For example, man is in this hemisphere; but, like Columbus, through the power of his reason he discovers another hemisphere—that is, America—which was until then unknown. His body is heavy, but through the help of vehicles which he invents, he is able to fly. He is slow of movement, but by vehicles which he invents he travels to the East and West with extreme rapidity. Briefly, this power embraces all things.

But the spirit of man has two aspects: one divine, one satanic—that is to say, it is capable of the utmost perfection, or it is capable of the utmost imperfection. If it acquires virtues, it is the most noble of the existing beings; and if it acquires vices, it becomes the most degraded existence.

The fourth degree of spirit is the heavenly spirit; it is the spirit of faith and the bounty of God; it comes from the breath of the Holy Spirit, and by the divine power it becomes the cause of eternal life. It is the power which makes the earthly man heavenly, and the imperfect man perfect.

It makes the impure to be pure, the silent eloquent; it purifies and sanctifies those made captive by carnal desires; it makes the ignorant wise.

The fifth spirit is the Holy Spirit. This Holy Spirit is the mediator between God and His creatures. It is like a mirror facing the sun. As the pure mirror receives light from the sun and transmits this bounty to others, so the Holy Spirit is the mediator of the Holy Light from the Sun of Reality, which it gives to the sanctified realities. It is adorned with all the divine perfections. Every time it appears, the world is renewed, and a new cycle is founded. The body of the world of humanity puts on a new garment. It can be compared to the spring; whenever it comes, the world passes from one condition to another. Through the advent of the season of spring the black earth and the fields and wildernesses will become verdant and blooming, and all sorts of flowers and sweet-scented herbs will grow; the trees will have new life, and new fruits will appear, and a new cycle is founded. The appearance of the Holy Spirit is like this. Whenever it appears, it renews the world of humanity and gives a new spirit to the human realities: it arrays the world of existence in a praiseworthy garment, dispels the darkness of ignorance, and causes the radiation of the light of perfections. Christ with this power has renewed this cycle; the heavenly spring with the utmost freshness and sweetness spread its tent in the world of humanity, and the life-giving breeze perfumed the nostrils of the enlightened ones.

In the same way, the appearance of Bahá'u'lláh was like a new springtime which appeared with holy breezes, with the hosts of everlasting life, and with heavenly power. It established the Throne of the Divine Kingdom in the center of the world and, by the power of the Holy Spirit, revived souls and established a new cycle.

37

THE DIVINITY CAN ONLY BE
COMPREHENDED THROUGH THE
DIVINE MANIFESTATIONS

Question.—What connection has the Reality of Divinity with the Lordly Rising-places and the Divine Dawning-points?

Answer.—Know that the Reality of Divinity or the substance of the Essence of Oneness is pure sanctity and absolute holiness—that is to say, it is sanctified and exempt from all praise. The whole of the supreme attributes of the degrees of existence, in reference to this plane, are only imaginations. It is invisible, incomprehensible, inaccessible, a pure essence which cannot be described, for the Divine Essence surrounds all things. Verily, that which surrounds is greater than the surrounded, and the surrounded cannot contain that by which it is surrounded, nor comprehend its reality. However far mind may progress, though it may reach to the final degree of comprehension, the limit of understanding, it beholds the divine signs and attributes in the world of creation and not in the world of God. For the essence and the attributes of the Lord of Unity are in the heights of sanctity, and for the minds and understandings there is no way to approach that position. "The way is closed, and seeking is forbidden."

It is evident that the human understanding is a quality of the existence of man, and that man is a sign of God: how can the quality of the sign surround the creator of the sign?—that is to say, how can the understanding, which is a quality of the existence of man, comprehend God? Therefore, the Reality of the Divinity is hidden from all comprehension, and concealed from the minds of all men. It is absolutely impossible to ascend to that plane. We see that everything which is lower is powerless to comprehend the reality of that which is higher. So the stone, the earth, the tree, however much they may evolve, cannot comprehend the reality of man and cannot imagine the powers of sight, of hearing, and of the other senses, although they are all alike created. Therefore, how can man, the created, understand the reality of the pure Essence of the Creator? This plane is unapproachable by the understanding; no explanation is sufficient for its comprehension, and there is no power to indicate it. What has an atom of dust to do with the pure world, and what relation is there between the limited mind and the infinite world? Minds are powerless to comprehend God, and the souls become bewildered in explaining Him. "The eyes see Him not, but He seeth the eyes. He is the Omniscient, the Knower."[1]

Consequently, with reference to this plane of existence, every statement and elucidation is defective, all praise and all description are unworthy, every conception is vain, and every meditation is futile. But for this Essence of the essences, this Truth of truths, this Mystery of mysteries, there are reflections, auroras, appearances and resplendencies in the world of existence. The dawning-place of these splendors, the place of these reflections, and the appearance of these manifestations are the Holy Dawning-places, the Universal Realities and the Divine Beings, Who are the true mirrors of the sanctified Essence of God. All the perfections, the bounties, the splendors which come from God are visible and evident in the Reality of the Holy Manifestations, like the sun which is resplendent in a clear polished mirror with all its perfections and boun-

1. Cf. Qur'án 6:104.

ties. If it be said that the mirrors are the manifestations of the sun and the dawning-places of the rising star, this does not mean that the sun has descended from the height of its sanctity and become incorporated in the mirror, nor that the Unlimited Reality is limited to this place of appearance. God forbid! This is the belief of the adherents of anthropomorphism. No; all the praises, the descriptions and exaltations refer to the Holy Manifestations—that is to say, all the descriptions, the qualities, the names and the attributes which we mention return to the Divine Manifestations; but as no one has attained to the reality of the Essence of Divinity, so no one is able to describe, explain, praise or glorify it. Therefore, all that the human reality knows, discovers and understands of the names, the attributes and the perfections of God refer to these Holy Manifestations. There is no access to anything else: "the way is closed, and seeking is forbidden."

Nevertheless, we speak of the names and attributes of the Divine Reality, and we praise Him by attributing to Him sight, hearing, power, life and knowledge. We affirm these names and attributes, not to prove the perfections of God, but to deny that He is capable of imperfections. When we look at the existing world, we see that ignorance is imperfection and knowledge is perfection; therefore, we say that the sanctified Essence of God is wisdom. Weakness is imperfection, and power is perfection; consequently, we say that the sanctified Essence of God is the acme of power. It is not that we can comprehend His knowledge, His sight, His power and life, for it is beyond our comprehension; for the essential names and attributes of God are identical with His Essence, and His Essence is above all comprehension. If the attributes are not identical with the Essence, there must also be a multiplicity of preexistences, and differences between the attributes and the Essence must also exist; and as Preexistence is necessary, therefore, the sequence of preexistences would become infinite. This is an evident error.

Accordingly all these attributes, names, praises and eulogies apply to the Places of Manifestation; and all that we imagine and suppose beside them is mere imagination, for we have no means of comprehending that which is invisible and inaccessible. This is why it is said: "All that you have distinguished through the illusion of your imagination in your subtle mental images is but a creation like unto yourself, and returns to you."[1] It is clear that if we wish to imagine the Reality of Divinity, this imagination is the surrounded, and we are the surrounding one; and it is sure that the one who surrounds is greater than the surrounded. From this it is certain and evident that if we imagine a Divine Reality outside of the Holy Manifestations, it is pure imagination, for there is no way to approach the Reality of Divinity which is not cut off to us, and all that we imagine is mere supposition.

Therefore, reflect that different peoples of the world are revolving around imaginations and are worshipers of the idols of thoughts and conjectures. They are not aware of this; they consider their imaginations to be the Reality which is withdrawn from all comprehension and purified from all descriptions. They regard themselves as the people of Unity, and the others as worshipers of idols; but idols at least have a mineral existence, while the idols of thoughts and the imaginations of man are but fancies; they have not even mineral existence. "Take heed ye who are endued with discernment."[2]

Know that the attributes of perfection, the splendor of the divine bounties, and the lights of inspiration are visible and evident in all the Holy Manifestations; but the glorious Word of God, Christ, and the Greatest Name,

1. From a ḥadíth.
2. Qur'án 59:2.

Bahá'u'lláh, are manifestations and evidences which are beyond imagination, for They possess all the perfections of the former Manifestations; and more than that, They possess some perfections which make the other Manifestations dependent upon Them. So all the Prophets of Israel were centers of inspiration; Christ also was a receiver of inspiration, but what a difference between the inspiration of the Word of God and the revelations of Isaiah, Jeremiah and Elijah!

Reflect that light is the expression of the vibrations of the etheric matter: the nerves of the eye are affected by these vibrations, and sight is produced. The light of the lamp exists through the vibration of the etheric matter; so also does that of the sun, but what a difference between the light of the sun and that of the stars or the lamp!

The spirit of man appears and is manifest in the embryonic condition, and also in that of childhood and of maturity, and it is resplendent and evident in the condition of perfection. The spirit is one, but in the embryonic condition the power of sight and of hearing is lacking. In the state of maturity and perfection it appears in the utmost splendor and brilliance. In the same way the seed in the beginning becomes leaves and is the place where the vegetable spirit appears; in the condition of fruit it manifests the same spirit—that is to say, the power of growth appears in the utmost perfection; but what a difference between the condition of the leaves and that of the fruit! For from the fruit a hundred thousand leaves appear, though they all grow and develop through the same vegetable spirit. Notice the difference between the virtues and perfections of Christ, the splendors and brilliance of Bahá'u'lláh, and the virtues of the Prophets of Israel, such as Ezekiel or Samuel. All were the manifestations of inspiration, but between them there is an infinite difference. Salutations!

38

THE THREE STATIONS OF THE DIVINE MANIFESTATIONS

Know that the Holy Manifestations, though They have the degrees of endless perfections, yet, speaking generally, have only three stations. The first station is the physical; the second station is the human, which is that of the rational soul; the third is that of the divine appearance and the heavenly splendor.

The physical station is phenomenal; it is composed of elements, and necessarily everything that is composed is subject to decomposition. It is not possible that a composition should not be disintegrated.

The second is the station of the rational soul, which is the human reality. This also is phenomenal, and the Holy Manifestations share it with all mankind.

Know that, although the human soul has existed on the earth for prolonged times and ages, yet it is phenomenal.[1] As it is a divine sign, when once it has come into existence, it is eternal. The spirit of man has a beginning, but it has no end; it continues eternally. In the same way the species existing on this earth are phenomenal, for it is established that there was a time when these species did not exist on the surface of the earth. Moreover, the earth has not always existed, but the world of existence has always been, for the universe is not limited to this terrestrial globe. The meaning of this is that, although human souls are phenomenal, they are nevertheless immortal, everlasting and

1. i.e., at its birth.

151

perpetual; for the world of things is the world of imperfection in comparison with that of man, and the world of
man is the world of perfection in comparison with that of
things. When imperfections reach the station of perfection, they become eternal.[1] This is an example of which
you must comprehend the meaning.

The third station is that of the divine appearance and
heavenly splendor: it is the Word of God, the Eternal
Bounty, the Holy Spirit. It has neither beginning nor end,
for these things are related to the world of contingencies
and not to the divine world. For God the end is the same
thing as the beginning. So the reckoning of days, weeks,
months and years, of yesterday and today, is connected
with the terrestrial globe; but in the sun there is no such
thing—there is neither yesterday, today nor tomorrow,
neither months nor years: all are equal. In the same way
the Word of God is purified from all these conditions and
is exempt from the boundaries, the laws and the limits of
the world of contingency. Therefore, the reality of
prophethood, which is the Word of God and the perfect
state of manifestation, did not have any beginning and will
not have any end; its rising is different from all others and
is like that of the sun. For example, its dawning in the sign
of Christ was with the utmost splendor and radiance, and
this is eternal and everlasting. See how many conquering
kings there have been, how many statesmen and princes,
powerful organizers, all of whom have disappeared,
whereas the breezes of Christ are still blowing; His light is
still shining; His melody is still resounding; His standard
is still waving; His armies are still fighting; His heavenly
voice is still sweetly melodious; His clouds are still show-
ering gems; His lightning is still flashing; His reflection is

1. i.e., in the kingdom of man, where alone the Spirit manifests
immortality. Cf. "Five Aspects of Spirit," p. 143; "The State of Man
and His Progress after Death," p. 235, etc.

still clear and brilliant; His splendor is still radiating and luminous; and it is the same with those souls who are under His protection and are shining with His light.

Then it is evident that the Manifestations possess three conditions: the physical condition, the condition of the rational soul, and the condition of the divine appearance and heavenly splendor. The physical condition will certainly become decomposed, but the condition of the rational soul, though it has a beginning, has no end: nay, it is endowed with everlasting life. But the Holy Reality, of which Christ says, "The Father is in the Son,"[1] has neither beginning nor end. When beginning is spoken of, it signifies the state of manifesting; and, symbolically, the condition of silence is compared to sleep. For example, a man is sleeping—when he begins to speak, he is awake— but it is always the same individual, whether he be asleep or awake; no difference has occurred in his station, his elevation, his glory, his reality or his nature. The state of silence is compared to sleep, and that of manifestation to wakefulness. A man sleeping or waking is the same man; sleep is one state, and wakefulness is another. The time of silence is compared to sleep, and manifestation and guidance are compared to wakefulness.

In the Gospel it is said, "In the beginning was the Word, and the Word was with God."[2] Then it is evident and clear that Christ did not reach to the station of Messiahship and its perfections at the time of baptism, when the Holy Spirit descended upon Him in the likeness of a dove. Nay, the Word of God from all eternity has always been, and will be, in the exaltation of sanctification.

1. Cf. John 14:11; 17:21.
2. John 1:1.

39

THE HUMAN CONDITION
AND THE SPIRITUAL CONDITION OF
THE DIVINE MANIFESTATIONS

WE said that the Manifestations have three planes. First, the physical reality, which depends upon the body; second, the individual reality, that is to say, the rational soul; third, the divine appearance, which is the divine perfections, the cause of the life of existence, of the education of souls, of the guidance of people, and of the enlightenment of the contingent world.

The physical state is the human state which perishes because it is composed of elements, and all that is composed of elements will necessarily be decomposed and dispersed.

But the individual reality of the Manifestations of God is a holy reality, and for that reason it is sanctified and, in that which concerns its nature and quality, is distinguished from all other things. It is like the sun, which by its essential nature produces light and cannot be compared to the moon, just as the particles that compose the globe of the sun cannot be compared with those which compose the moon. The particles and organization of the former produce rays, but the particles of which the moon is composed do not produce rays but need to borrow light. So other human realities are those souls who, like the moon, take light from the sun; but that Holy Reality is luminous in Himself.

The third plane of that Being[1] is the Divine Bounty, the

1. The Manifestation.

splendor of the Preexistent Beauty, and the radiance of the light of the Almighty. The individual realities of the Divine Manifestations have no separation from the Bounty of God and the Lordly Splendor. In the same way, the orb of the sun has no separation from the light. Therefore, it may be said that the ascension of the Holy Manifestation is simply the leaving of this elemental form. For example, if a lamp illumines this niche, and if its light ceases to illuminate it because the niche is destroyed, the bounty of the lamp is not cut off. Briefly, in the Holy Manifestations the Preexistent Bounty is like the light, the individuality is represented by the glass globe, and the human body is like the niche: if the niche is destroyed, the lamp continues to burn. The Divine Manifestations are so many different mirrors because They have a special individuality, but that which is reflected in the mirrors is one sun. It is clear that the reality of Christ is different from that of Moses.

Verily, from the beginning that Holy Reality[1] is conscious of the secret of existence, and from the age of childhood signs of greatness appear and are visible in Him. Therefore, how can it be that with all these bounties and perfections He should have no consciousness?

We have mentioned that the Holy Manifestations have three planes. The physical condition, the individual reality, and the center of the appearance of perfection: it is like the sun, its heat and its light. Other individuals have the physical plane, the plane of the rational soul—the spirit and mind.[2] So the saying, "I was asleep, and the divine breezes passed over Me, and I awoke," is like Christ's saying, "The body is sad, and the spirit is happy," or again, "I am afflicted," or "I am at ease," or "I am troubled"—these refer to the physical condition and have no reference to the individual reality nor to the manifestation of the Divine Reality. Thus consider what thousands

1. The Manifestation.
2. Cf. "Soul, Spirit and Mind," p. 208.

of vicissitudes can happen to the body of man, but the spirit is not affected by them; it may even be that some members of the body are entirely crippled, but the essence of the mind remains and is everlasting. A thousand accidents may happen to a garment, but for the wearer of it there is no danger. These words which Bahá'u'lláh said, "I was asleep, and the breeze passed over Me, and awakened Me," refer to the body.

In the world of God there is no past, no future and no present; all are one. So when Christ said, "In the beginning was the Word"[1]—that means it was, is and shall be; for in the world of God there is no time. Time has sway over creatures but not over God. For example, in the prayer He says, "Hallowed be Thy name"; the meaning is that Thy name was, is and shall be hallowed.[2] Morning, noon and evening are related to this earth, but in the sun there is neither morning, noon nor evening.

1. Cf. John 1:1.
2. Matt. 6:9; Luke 11:2.

40

THE KNOWLEDGE OF THE DIVINE MANIFESTATIONS

Question.—One of the powers possessed by the Divine Manifestations is knowledge. To what extent is it limited?

Answer.—Knowledge is of two kinds. One is subjective and the other objective knowledge—that is to say, an intuitive knowledge and a knowledge derived from perception.

The knowledge of things which men universally have is gained by reflection or by evidence—that is to say, either by the power of the mind the conception of an object is formed, or from beholding an object the form is produced in the mirror of the heart. The circle of this knowledge is very limited because it depends upon effort and attainment.

But the second sort of knowledge, which is the knowledge of being, is intuitive; it is like the cognizance and consciousness that man has of himself.

For example, the mind and the spirit of man are cognizant of the conditions and states of the members and component parts of the body, and are aware of all the physical sensations; in the same way, they are aware of their power, of their feelings, and of their spiritual conditions. This is the knowledge of being which man realizes and perceives, for the spirit surrounds the body and is aware of its sensations and powers. This knowledge is not the outcome of effort and study. It is an existing thing; it is an absolute gift.

Since the Sanctified Realities, the supreme Manifestations of God, surround the essence and qualities of the creatures, transcend and contain existing realities and understand all things, therefore, Their knowledge is divine knowledge, and not acquired—that is to say, it is a holy bounty; it is a divine revelation.

We will mention an example expressly for the purpose of comprehending this subject. The most noble being on the earth is man. He embraces the animal, vegetable and mineral kingdoms—that is to say, these conditions are contained in him to such an extent that he is the possessor of these conditions and states; he is aware of their mysteries and of the secrets of their existence. This is simply an example and not an analogy. Briefly, the supreme Manifestations of God are aware of the reality of the mysteries of beings. Therefore, They establish laws which are suitable and adapted to the state of the world of man, for religion is the essential connection which proceeds from the realities of things. The Manifestation—that is, the Holy Lawgiver—unless He is aware of the realities of beings, will not comprehend the essential connection which proceeds from the realities of things, and He will certainly not be able to establish a religion conformable to the facts and suited to the conditions. The Prophets of God, the supreme Manifestations, are like skilled physicians, and the contingent world is like the body of man: the divine laws are the remedy and treatment. Consequently, the doctor must be aware of, and know, all the members and parts, as well as the constitution and state of the patient, so that he can prescribe a medicine which will be beneficial against the violent poison of the disease. In reality the doctor deduces from the disease itself the treatment which is suited to the patient, for he diagnoses the malady, and afterward prescribes the remedy for the illness. Until the malady be discovered, how can the remedy and treatment be prescribed? The doctor then must have a thorough knowledge of the constitution, members, organs and state of the patient, and be acquainted with all diseases and all remedies, in order to prescribe a fitting medicine.

Religion, then, is the necessary connection which emanates from the reality of things; and as the supreme Manifestations of God are aware of the mysteries of beings, therefore, They understand this essential connection, and by this knowledge establish the Law of God.

41

THE UNIVERSAL CYCLES

Question.—What is the real explanation of the cycles which occur in the world of existence?

Answer.—Each one of the luminous bodies in this limitless firmament has a cycle of revolution which is of a different duration, and every one revolves in its own orbit, and again begins a new cycle. So the earth, every three hundred and sixty-five days, five hours, forty-eight minutes and a fraction, completes a revolution; and then it begins a new cycle—that is to say, the first cycle is again renewed. In the same way, for the whole universe, whether for the heavens or for men, there are cycles of great events, of important facts and occurrences. When a cycle is ended, a new cycle begins; and the old one, on account of the great events which take place, is completely forgotten, and not a trace or record of it will remain. As you see, we have no records of twenty thousand years ago, although we have before proved by argument that life on this earth is very ancient. It is not one hundred thousand, or two hundred thousand, or one million or two million years old; it is very ancient, and the ancient records and traces are entirely obliterated.

Each of the Divine Manifestations has likewise a cycle, and during the cycle His laws and commandments prevail and are performed. When His cycle is completed by the appearance of a new Manifestation, a new cycle begins. In this way cycles begin, end and are renewed, until a universal cycle is completed in the world, when important events and great occurrences will take place which entirely efface every trace and every record of the past; then a new universal cycle begins in the world, for this universe has no beginning. We have before stated proofs and evidences concerning this subject; there is no need of repetition.

Briefly, we say a universal cycle in the world of existence signifies a long duration of time, and innumerable and incalculable periods and epochs. In such a cycle the Manifestations appear with splendor in the realm of the visible until a great and supreme Manifestation makes the world the center of His radiance. His appearance causes the world to attain to maturity, and the extension of His cycle is very great. Afterward, other Manifestations will arise under His shadow, Who according to the needs of the time will renew certain commandments relating to material questions and affairs, while remaining under His shadow.

We are in the cycle which began with Adam, and its supreme Manifestation is Bahá'u'lláh.

42

THE POWER AND INFLUENCE OF THE DIVINE MANIFESTATIONS

Question.—What is the degree of the power and the perfections of the Thrones of Reality, the Manifestations of God, and what is the limit of Their influence?

Answer.—Consider the world of existence—that is to say, the world of material things. The solar system is dark and obscure, and in it the sun is the center of light, and all the planets of the system revolve around its might and are partakers of its bounty. The sun is the cause of life and illumination, and the means of the growth and development of all the beings of the solar system; for without the bounty of the sun no living being could exist: all would be dark and destroyed. Therefore, it is evident and clear that the sun is the center of light and the cause of the life of the beings of the solar system.

In like manner, the Holy Manifestations of God are the centers of the light of reality, of the source of mysteries, and of the bounties of love. They are resplendent in the world of hearts and thoughts, and shower eternal graces upon the world of spirits; They give spiritual life and are shining with the light of realities and meanings. The enlightenment of the world of thought comes from these centers of light and sources of mysteries. Without the bounty of the splendor and the instructions of these Holy Beings the world of souls and thoughts would be opaque darkness. Without the irrefutable teachings of those sources of mysteries the human world would become the pasture of animal appetites and qualities, the existence of everything would be unreal, and there would be no true life. That is why it is said in the Gospel: "In the beginning was the Word," meaning that it became the cause of all life.[1]

Now consider the influence of the sun upon the earthly beings, what signs and results become evident and clear from its nearness and remoteness, from its rising or its setting. At one time it is autumn, at another time spring; or again it is summer or winter. When the sun passes the line of the equator, the life-giving spring will become manifest in splendor, and when it is in the summer solstice, the fruits will attain to the acme of perfection, grains and plants will yield their produce, and earthly beings will attain their most complete development and growth.

In like manner, when the Holy Manifestation of God, Who is the sun of the world of His creation, shines upon the worlds of spirits, of thoughts and of hearts, then the spiritual spring and new life appear, the power of the wonderful springtime becomes visible, and marvelous benefits are apparent. As you have observed, at the time of the appearance of each Manifestation of God extraordinary progress has occurred in the world of minds, thoughts and spirits. For example, in this divine age see what development has been attained in the world of minds and thoughts, and it is now only the beginning of its dawn. Before long you will see that new bounties and divine teachings will illuminate this dark world and will transform these sad regions into the paradise of Eden.

If we were to explain the signs and bounties of each of the Holy Manifestations, it would take too long. Think and reflect upon it yourself, and then you will attain to the truth of this subject.

1. John 1:1.

43

THE TWO CLASSES OF PROPHETS

Question. —How many kinds of Prophets are there?

Answer. —Universally, the Prophets are of two kinds. One are the independent Prophets Who are followed; the other kind are not independent and are themselves followers.

The independent Prophets are the lawgivers and the founders of a new cycle. Through Their appearance the world puts on a new garment, the foundations of religion are established, and a new book is revealed. Without an intermediary They receive bounty from the Reality of the Divinity, and Their illumination is an essential illumination. They are like the sun which is luminous in itself: the light is its essential necessity; it does not receive light from any other star. These Dawning-places of the morn of Unity are the sources of bounty and the mirrors of the Essence of Reality.

The other Prophets are followers and promoters, for they are branches and not independent; they receive the bounty of the independent Prophets, and they profit by the light of the Guidance of the universal Prophets. They are like the moon, which is not luminous and radiant in itself, but receives its light from the sun.

The Manifestations of universal Prophethood Who appeared independently are, for example, Abraham, Moses, Christ, Muḥammad, the Báb and Bahá'u'lláh. But the others who are followers and promoters are like Solomon, David, Isaiah, Jeremiah and Ezekiel. For the independent

Prophets are founders; They establish a new religion and make new creatures of men; They change the general morals, promote new customs and rules, renew the cycle and the Law. Their appearance is like the season of spring, which arrays all earthly beings in a new garment, and gives them a new life.

With regard to the second sort of Prophets who are followers, these also promote the Law of God, make known the Religion of God, and proclaim His word. Of themselves they have no power and might, except what they receive from the independent Prophets.

Question.—To which category do Buddha and Confucius belong?

Answer.—Buddha also established a new religion, and Confucius renewed morals and ancient virtues, but their institutions have been entirely destroyed. The beliefs and rites of the Buddhists and Confucianists have not continued in accordance with their fundamental teachings. The founder of Buddhism was a wonderful soul. He established the Oneness of God, but later the original principles of His doctrines gradually disappeared, and ignorant customs and ceremonials arose and increased until they finally ended in the worship of statues and images.

Now, consider: Christ frequently repeated that the Ten Commandments in the Pentateuch were to be followed, and He insisted that they should be maintained. Among the Ten Commandments is one which says: "Do not worship any picture or image."[1] At present in some of the Christian churches many pictures and images exist. It is, therefore, clear and evident that the Religion of God does not maintain its original principles among the people, but that it has gradually changed and altered until it has been entirely destroyed and annihilated. Because of this the manifestation is renewed, and a new religion estab-

1. Cf. Exod. 20:4–5; Deut. 5:8–9.

lished. But if religions did not change and alter, there would be no need of renewal.

In the beginning the tree was in all its beauty, and full of blossoms and fruits, but at last it became old and entirely fruitless, and it withered and decayed. This is why the True Gardener plants again an incomparable young tree of the same kind and species, which grows and develops day by day, and spreads a wide shadow in the divine garden, and yields admirable fruit. So it is with religions; through the passing of time they change from their original foundation, the truth of the Religion of God entirely departs, and the spirit of it does not stay; heresies appear, and it becomes a body without a soul. That is why it is renewed.

The meaning is that the Buddhists and Confucianists now worship images and statues. They are entirely heedless of the Oneness of God and believe in imaginary gods like the ancient Greeks. But in the beginning it was not so; there were different principles and other ordinances.

Again, consider how much the principles of the religion of Christ have been forgotten, and how many heresies have appeared. For example, Christ forbade revenge and transgression; furthermore, He commanded benevolence and mercy in return for injury and evil. Now reflect: among the Christian nations themselves how many sanguinary wars have taken place, and how much oppression, cruelty, rapacity and bloodthirstiness have occurred! Many of these wars were carried on by command of the Popes. It is then clear and evident that in the passage of time religions become entirely changed and altered. Therefore, they are renewed.

44

EXPLANATION OF THE REBUKES ADDRESSED BY GOD TO THE PROPHETS

Question. —In the Holy Books there are some addresses of reproach and rebuke directed to the Prophets. Who is addressed, and for whom is the rebuke?

Answer. —All the divine discourses containing reproof, though apparently addressed to the Prophets, in reality are directed to the people, through a wisdom which is absolute mercy, in order that the people may not be discouraged and disheartened. They, therefore, appear to be addressed to the Prophets; but though outwardly for the Prophets, they are in truth for the people and not for the Prophets.

Moreover, the powerful and independent king represents his country: that which he says is the word of all, and every agreement that he makes is the agreement of all, for the wishes and desires of all his subjects are included in his wishes and desires. In the same way, every Prophet is the expression of the whole of the people. So the promise and speech of God addressed to Him is addressed to all. Generally the speech of reproach and rebuke is rather too severe for the people and would be heartbreaking to them. So the Perfect Wisdom makes use of this form of address, as is clearly shown in the Bible itself, as, for example, when the children of Israel rebelled and said to Moses: "We cannot fight with the Amalekites, for they are powerful, mighty and courageous." God then rebuked Moses and Aaron, though Moses was in complete obedience and not in rebellion. Surely such a great Man, Who is the mediator of the Divine Bounty and the deliverer of the Law, must necessarily obey the commands of God. These Holy Souls are like the leaves of a tree which are put in motion by the blowing of the wind, and not by Their own desire; for They are attracted by the breeze of the love of God, and Their will is absolutely submissive. Their word is the word of God; Their commandment is the commandment of God; Their prohibition is the prohibition of God. They are like the glass globe which receives light from the lamp. Although the light appears to emanate from the glass, in reality it is shining from the lamp. In the same way for the Prophets of God, the centers of manifestation, Their movement and repose come from divine inspiration, not from human passions. If it were not so, how could the Prophet be worthy of trust, and how could He be the Messenger of God, delivering the commands and the prohibitions of God? All the defects that are mentioned in the Holy Books with reference to the Manifestations refer to questions of this kind.

Praise be to God that you have come here and have met the servants of God! Have you perceived in them anything except the fragrance of the pleasure of God? Indeed, no. You have seen with your own eyes that day and night they endeavor and strive, and that they have no aim except the exaltation of the word of God, the education of men, the improvement of the masses, spiritual progress, the promulgation of universal peace, goodwill to all mankind, and kindness toward all nations. Sacrificing themselves for the good of humanity, they are detached from material advantages, and labor to give virtues to mankind.

But let us return to our subject. For example, in the Old Testament it is said in the Book of Isaiah, chapter 48, verse 12: "Hearken unto Me, O Jacob and Israel, My called; I

am He; I am the first, I also am the last." It is evident that it
does not mean Jacob who was Israel, but the people of Israel. Also in the Book of Isaiah, chapter 43, verse 1, it is
said: "But now thus saith the Lord that created thee, O
Jacob, and He that formed thee, O Israel, Fear not: for I
have redeemed thee, I have called thee by thy name; thou
art Mine."

Furthermore, in Numbers, chapter 20, verse 23: "And
the Lord spake unto Moses and Aaron in mount Hor, by
the coast of the land of Edom, saying, Aaron shall be
gathered unto his people: for he shall not enter into the
land which I have given unto the children of Israel, because ye rebelled against My word at the water of
Meribah";[1] and in verse 13: "This is the water of Meribah;
because the children of Israel strove with the Lord, and
He was sanctified in them."

Observe: the people of Israel rebelled, but apparently
the reproach was for Moses and Aaron. As it is said in the
Book of Deuteronomy, chapter 3, verse 26: "But the Lord
was wroth with Me for your sakes, and would not hear
Me: and the Lord said unto Me, Let it suffice Thee; speak
no more unto Me of this matter."

Now this discourse and reproach really refer to the
children of Israel, who, for having rebelled against the
command of God, were held captive a long time in the arid
desert, on the other side of Jordan, until the time of
Joshua—upon him be salutations. This address and reproach appeared to be for Moses and Aaron, but in reality
they were for the people of Israel.

In the same way in the Qur'án it is said to Muḥammad:
"We have granted Thee a manifest victory, so that God
may forgive Thee Thy preceding and subsequent sin."[2]
This address, although apparently directed to Muḥam-

1. Num. 20:23–24.
2. Cf. Qur'án 48:1–2.

mad, was in reality for all the people. This mode of address, as before said, was used by the perfect wisdom of God, so that the hearts of the people might not be troubled, anxious and tormented.

How often the Prophets of God and His supreme Manifestations in Their prayers confess Their sins and faults! This is only to teach other men, to encourage and incite them to humility and meekness, and to induce them to confess their sins and faults. For these Holy Souls are pure from every sin and sanctified from faults. In the Gospel it is said that a man came to Christ and called Him "Good Master." Christ answered, "Why callest thou Me good? there is none good but One, that is, God."[1] This did not mean—God forbid!—that Christ was a sinner; but the intention was to teach submission, humility, meekness and modesty to the man to whom He spoke. These Holy Beings are lights, and light does not unite itself with darkness. They are life, and life and death are not confounded. They are for guidance, and guidance and error cannot be together. They are the essence of obedience, and obedience cannot exist with rebellion.

To conclude, the addresses in the form of reproach which are in the Holy Books, though apparently directed to the Prophets—that is to say, to the Manifestations of God—in reality are intended for the people. This will become evident and clear to you when you have diligently examined the Holy Books.

Salutations be upon you.

---

1. Matt. 19:16, 17.

45

EXPLANATION OF THE VERSE OF THE KITÁB-I-AQDAS, "THERE IS NO PARTNER FOR HIM WHO IS THE DAYSPRING OF REVELATION IN HIS MOST GREAT INFALLIBILITY"

It is said in the holy verse: "There is no partner for Him Who is the Dayspring of Revelation[1] in His Most Great Infallibility. He is, in truth, the exponent of 'God doeth whatsoever He willeth' in the kingdom of creation. Indeed the Almighty hath exclusively reserved this station for Himself and to none is given a share in this sublime and highly exalted distinction."[2]

Know that infallibility is of two kinds: essential infallibility and acquired infallibility. In like manner there is essential knowledge and acquired knowledge; and so it is with other names and attributes. Essential infallibility is peculiar to the supreme Manifestation, for it is His essential requirement, and an essential requirement cannot be separated from the thing itself. The rays are the essential necessity of the sun and are inseparable from it. Knowledge is an essential necessity of God and is inseparable from Him. Power is an essential necessity of God and is inseparable from Him. If it could be separated from Him, He would not be God. If the rays could be separated from the sun, it would not be the sun. Therefore, if one imag-

---

1. The Manifestation of God.
2. Kitáb-i-Aqdas: i.e., The Most Holy Book. The principal work of Bahá'u'lláh, which contains the greater part of the commandments. It is the basis of the principles of the Bahá'í Faith.

ines separation of the Most Great Infallibility from the supreme Manifestation, He would not be the supreme Manifestation, and He would lack the essential perfections.

But acquired infallibility is not a natural necessity; on the contrary, it is a ray of the bounty of infallibility which shines from the Sun of Reality upon hearts, and grants a share and portion of itself to souls. Although these souls have not essential infallibility, still they are under the protection of God—that is to say, God preserves them from error. Thus many of the holy beings who were not dawning-points of the Most Great Infallibility, were yet kept and preserved from error under the shadow of the protection and guardianship of God, for they were the mediators of grace between God and men. If God did not protect them from error, their error would cause believing souls to fall into error, and thus the foundation of the Religion of God would be overturned, which would not be fitting nor worthy of God.

To epitomize: essential infallibility belongs especially to the supreme Manifestations, and acquired infallibility is granted to every holy soul. For instance, the Universal House of Justice,[1] if it be established under the necessary conditions—with members elected from all the people—that House of Justice will be under the protection and the unerring guidance of God. If that House of Justice shall decide unanimously, or by a majority, upon any question not mentioned in the Book, that decision and command will be guarded from mistake. Now the mem-

1. The House of Justice (*Baytu'l-Adl*) is an institution created by Bahá'u'lláh. He refers to two levels of this institution: the Local Houses of Justice, responsible for each town or village, and the Universal House of Justice. 'Abdu'l-Bahá, in His Will and Testament, added an intermediate level, the Secondary Houses of Justice. It is only on the Universal House of Justice that infallibility has been conferred. At the present time, to stress their purely spiritual functions, the Local and Secondary Houses of Justice are designated Local and National Spiritual Assemblies.

bers of the House of Justice have not, individually, essential infallibility; but the body of the House of Justice is under the protection and unerring guidance of God: this is called conferred infallibility.

Briefly, it is said that the "Dayspring of Revelation" is the manifestation of these words, "He doeth whatsoever He willeth"; this condition is peculiar to that Holy Being, and others have no share of this essential perfection. That is to say, that as the supreme Manifestations certainly possess essential infallibility, therefore whatever emanates from Them is identical with the truth, and conformable to reality. They are not under the shadow of the former laws. Whatever They say is the word of God, and whatever They perform is an upright action. No believer has any right to criticize; his condition must be one of absolute submission, for the Manifestation arises with perfect wisdom—so that whatever the supreme Manifestation says and does is absolute wisdom, and is in accordance with reality.

If some people do not understand the hidden secret of one of His commands and actions, they ought not to oppose it, for the supreme Manifestation does what He wishes. How often it has occurred, when an act has been performed by a wise, perfect, intelligent man, that others incapable of comprehending its wisdom have objected to it and been amazed that this wise man could say or do such a thing. This opposition comes from their ignorance, and the wisdom of the sage is pure and exempt from error. In the same way, the skilled doctor in treating the patient does what he wishes, and the patient has no right to object; whatever the doctor says and does is right; all ought to consider him the manifestation of these words, "He doeth whatsoever He willeth, and commandeth whatever He desireth." It is certain that the doctor will use some medicine contrary to the ideas of other people; now opposition is not permitted to those who have not the advantage of science and the medical art. No, in the name of God! on the contrary, all ought to be submissive and to perform whatever the skilled doctor says. Therefore, the skilled doctor does what he wishes, and the patients have no share in this right. The skill of the doctor must be first ascertained; but when the skill of the doctor is once established, he does what he wishes.

So also, when the head of the army is unrivaled in the art of war, in what he says and commands he does what he wishes. When the captain of a ship is proficient in the art of navigation, in whatever he says and commands he does what he wishes. And as the real educator is the Perfect Man, in whatever He says and commands He does what He wishes.

In short, the meaning of "He doeth whatsoever He willeth" is that if the Manifestation says something, or gives a command, or performs an action, and believers do not understand its wisdom, they still ought not to oppose it by a single thought, seeking to know why He spoke so, or why He did such a thing. The other souls who are under the shadow of the supreme Manifestations are submissive to the commandments of the Law of God, and are not to deviate as much as a hairsbreadth from it; they must conform their acts and words to the Law of God. If they do deviate from it, they will be held responsible and reproved in the presence of God. It is certain that they have no share in the permission "He doeth whatsoever He willeth," for this condition is peculiar to the supreme Manifestations.

So Christ—may my spirit be sacrificed to Him!—was the manifestation of these words, "He doeth whatsoever He willeth," but the disciples were not partakers of this condition; for as they were under the shadow of Christ, they could not deviate from His command and will.

Part Four

ON THE ORIGIN, POWERS AND
CONDITIONS OF MAN

46

MODIFICATION OF SPECIES

WE have now come to the question of the modification of species and of organic development—that is to say, to the point of inquiring whether man's descent is from the animal.

This theory has found credence in the minds of some European philosophers, and it is now very difficult to make its falseness understood, but in the future it will become evident and clear, and the European philosophers will themselves realize its untruth. For, verily, it is an evident error. When man looks at the beings with a penetrating regard, and attentively examines the condition of existences, and when he sees the state, the organization and the perfection of the world, he will be convinced that in the possible world there is nothing more wonderful than that which already exists. For all existing beings, terrestrial and celestial, as well as this limitless space and all that is in it, have been created and organized, composed, arranged and perfected as they ought to be; the universe has no imperfection, so that if all beings became pure intelligence and reflected for ever and ever, it is impossible that they could imagine anything better than that which exists.

If, however, the creation in the past had not been adorned with utmost perfection, then existence would have been imperfect and meaningless, and in this case creation would have been incomplete. This question needs to be considered with the greatest attention and thought. For example, imagine that the contingent world resembles in a general way the body of man. If this composition, organization, perfection, beauty and completeness which now exist in the human body were different, it would be absolute imperfection. Now, if we imagine a time when man belonged to the animal world, or when he was merely an animal, we shall find that existence would have been imperfect—that is to say, there would have been no man, and this chief member, which in the body of the world is like the brain and mind in man, would have been missing. The world would then have been quite imperfect. It is thus proved that if there had been a time when man was in the animal kingdom, the perfection of existence would have been destroyed; for man is the greatest member of this world, and if the body was without this chief member, surely it would be imperfect. We consider man as the greatest member because, among the creatures, he is the sum of all existing perfections. When we speak of man, we mean the perfect one, the foremost individual in the world, who is the sum of spiritual and apparent perfections, and who is like the sun among the beings. Then imagine that at one time the sun did not exist, but that it was a planet; surely at such a time the relations of existence would be disordered. How can such a thing be imagined? To a man who examines the world of existence what we have said is sufficient.

There is another more subtle proof: all these endless beings which inhabit the world, whether man, animal, vegetable, mineral—whatever they may be—are surely, each one of them, composed of elements. There is no doubt that this perfection which is in all beings is caused by the creation of God from the composing elements, by their appropriate mingling and proportionate quantities, the mode of their composition, and the influence of other beings. For all beings are connected together like a chain; and reciprocal help, assistance and interaction belonging to the properties of things are the causes of the existence, development and growth of created beings. It is confirmed through evidences and proofs that every being universally acts upon other beings, either absolutely or through association. Finally, the perfection of each individual being—that is to say, the perfection which you now see in man or apart from him, with regard to their atoms, members or powers—is due to the composition of the elements, to their measure, to their balance, to the mode of their combination, and to mutual influence. When all these are gathered together, then man exists.

As the perfection of man is entirely due to the composition of the atoms of the elements, to their measure, to the method of their combination, and to the mutual influence and action of the different beings—then, since man was produced ten or a hundred thousand years ago from these earthly elements with the same measure and balance, the same method of combination and mingling, and the same influence of the other beings, exactly the same man existed then as now. This is evident and not worth debating. A thousand million years hence, if these elements of man are gathered together and arranged in this special proportion, and if the elements are combined according to the same method, and if they are affected by the same influence of other beings, exactly the same man will exist. For example, if after a hundred thousand years there is oil, fire, a wick, a lamp and the lighter of the lamp—briefly, if there are all the necessaries which now exist, exactly the same lamp will be obtained.

These are conclusive and evident facts. But the arguments which these European philosophers have used raise doubtful proofs and are not conclusive.

47

THE UNIVERSE IS WITHOUT BEGINNING

THE ORIGIN OF MAN

KNOW that it is one of the most abstruse spiritual truths that the world of existence—that is to say, this endless universe—has no beginning.

We have already explained that the names and attributes of the Divinity themselves require the existence of beings. Although this subject has been explained in detail, we will speak of it again briefly. Know that an educator without pupils cannot be imagined; a monarch without subjects could not exist; a master without scholars cannot be appointed; a creator without a creature is impossible; a provider without those provided for cannot be conceived; for all the divine names and attributes demand the existence of beings. If we could imagine a time when no beings existed, this imagination would be the denial of the Divinity of God. Moreover, absolute nonexistence cannot become existence. If the beings were absolutely nonexistent, existence would not have come into being. Therefore, as the Essence of Unity (that is, the existence of God) is everlasting and eternal—that is to say, it has neither beginning nor end—it is certain that this world of existence, this endless universe, has neither beginning nor end. Yes, it may be that one of the parts of the universe, one of the globes, for example, may come into existence, or may be disintegrated, but the other endless globes are still existing; the universe would not be disordered nor destroyed.

On the contrary, existence is eternal and perpetual. As each globe has a beginning, necessarily it has an end because every composition, collective or particular, must of necessity be decomposed. The only difference is that some are quickly decomposed, and others more slowly, but it is impossible that a composed thing should not eventually be decomposed.

It is necessary, therefore, that we should know what each of the important existences was in the beginning— for there is no doubt that in the beginning the origin was one: the origin of all numbers is one and not two. Then it is evident that in the beginning matter was one, and that one matter appeared in different aspects in each element. Thus various forms were produced, and these various aspects as they were produced became permanent, and each element was specialized. But this permanence was not definite, and did not attain realization and perfect existence until after a very long time. Then these elements became composed, and organized and combined in infinite forms; or rather from the composition and combination of these elements innumerable beings appeared.

This composition and arrangement, through the wisdom of God and His preexistent might, were produced from one natural organization, which was composed and combined with the greatest strength, conformable to wisdom, and according to a universal law. From this it is evident that it is the creation of God, and is not a fortuitous composition and arrangement. This is why from every natural composition a being can come into existence, but from an accidental composition no being can come into existence. For example, if a man of his own mind and intelligence collects some elements and combines them, a living being will not be brought into existence since the system is unnatural. This is the answer to the implied question that, since beings are made by the composition and the combination of elements, why is it not possible for us to gather elements and mingle them together, and so create a living being. This is a false supposition, for the origin of this composition is from God; it is God Who makes the combination, and as it is done according to the natural system, from each composition one being is produced, and an existence is realized. A composition made by man produces nothing because man cannot create.

Briefly, we have said that from the composition and combination of elements, from their decomposition, from their measure, and from the effect of other beings upon them, resulted forms, endless realities and innumerable beings. But it is clear that this terrestrial globe in its present form did not come into existence all at once, but that this universal existence gradually passed through different phases until it became adorned with its present perfection. Universal beings resemble and can be compared to particular beings, for both are subjected to one natural system, one universal law and divine organization. So you will find the smallest atoms in the universal system are similar to the greatest beings of the universe. It is clear that they come into existence from one laboratory of might under one natural system and one universal law; therefore, they may be compared to one another. Thus the embryo of man in the womb of the mother gradually grows and develops, and appears in different forms and conditions, until in the degree of perfect beauty it reaches maturity and appears in a perfect form with the utmost grace. And in the same way, the seed of this flower which you see was in the beginning an insignificant thing, and very small; and it grew and developed in the womb of the earth and, after appearing in various forms, came forth in this condition with perfect freshness and grace. In the same manner, it is evident that this terrestrial globe, having once found existence, grew and developed in the matrix of the universe, and came forth in different forms and conditions, until gradually it attained this present perfection, and became adorned with innumerable beings, and appeared as a finished organization.

Then it is clear that original matter, which is in the embryonic state, and the mingled and composed elements which were its earliest forms, gradually grew and developed during many ages and cycles, passing from one shape and form to another, until they appeared in this perfection, this system, this organization and this establishment, through the supreme wisdom of God.

Let us return to our subject that man, in the beginning of his existence and in the womb of the earth, like the embryo in the womb of the mother, gradually grew and developed, and passed from one form to another, from one shape to another, until he appeared with this beauty and perfection, this force and this power. It is certain that in the beginning he had not this loveliness and grace and elegance, and that he only by degrees attained this shape, this form, this beauty and this grace. There is no doubt that the human embryo did not at once appear in this form; neither did it then become the manifestation of the words "Blessed, therefore, be God, the most excellent of Makers."[1] Gradually it passed through various conditions and different shapes, until it attained this form and beauty, this perfection, grace and loveliness. Thus it is evident and confirmed that the development and growth of man on this earth, until he reached his present perfection, resembled the growth and development of the embryo in the womb of the mother: by degrees it passed from condition to condition, from form to form, from one shape to another, for this is according to the requirement of the universal system and Divine Law.

That is to say, the embryo passes through different states and traverses numerous degrees, until it reaches the form in which it manifests the words "Praise be to God,

1. Qur'án 23:14.

the best of Creators," and until the signs of reason and
maturity appear. And in the same way, man's existence on
this earth, from the beginning until it reaches this state,
form and condition, necessarily lasts a long time, and goes
through many degrees until it reaches this condition. But
from the beginning of man's existence he is a distinct species. In the same way, the embryo of man in the womb of
the mother was at first in a strange form; then this body
passes from shape to shape, from state to state, from form
to form, until it appears in utmost beauty and perfection.
But even when in the womb of the mother and in this
strange form, entirely different from his present form and
figure, he is the embryo of the superior species, and not of
the animal; his species and essence undergo no change.
Now, admitting that the traces of organs which have disappeared actually exist, this is not a proof of the imperma-
nence and the nonoriginality of the species. At the most it
proves that the form, and fashion, and the organs of man
have progressed. Man was always a distinct species, a
man, not an animal. So, if the embryo of man in the womb
of the mother passes from one form to another so that the
second form in no way resembles the first, is this a proof
that the species has changed? that it was at first an animal,
and that its organs progressed and developed until it became a man? No, indeed! How puerile and unfounded is
this idea and this thought! For the proof of the originality
of the human species, and of the permanency of the nature
of man, is clear and evident.

48

THE DIFFERENCE EXISTING BETWEEN MAN AND ANIMAL

ALREADY we have talked once or twice on the subject of the spirit, but our words have not been written down.

Know that people belong to two categories—that is to say, they constitute two parties. One party deny the spirit and say that man also is a species of animal; for they say: Do we not see that animals and men share the same powers and senses? These simple, single elements which fill space are endlessly combined, and from each of these combinations one of the beings is produced. Among these beings is the possessor of spirit,[1] of the powers and of the senses. The more perfect the combination, the nobler is the being. The combination of the elements in the body of man is more perfect than the composition of any other being; it is mingled in absolute equilibrium; therefore, it is more noble and more perfect. "It is not," they say, "that he has a special power and spirit which the other animals lack: animals possess sensitive bodies, but man in some powers has more sensation, although, in what concerns the outer senses, such as hearing, sight, taste, smell, touch and even in some interior powers like memory, the animal is more richly endowed than man." "The animal, too," they say, "has intelligence and perception." All that they concede is that man's intelligence is greater.

This is what the philosophers of the present state; this is their saying, this is their supposition, and thus their

1. Man.

imagination decrees. So with powerful arguments and proofs they make the descent of man go back to the animal, and say that there was once a time when man was an animal, that then the species changed and progressed little by little until it reached the present status of man.

But the theologians say: No, this is not so. Though man has powers and outer senses in common with the animal, yet an extraordinary power exists in him of which the animal is bereft. The sciences, arts, inventions, trades and discoveries of realities are the results of this spiritual power. This is a power which encompasses all things, comprehends their realities, discovers all the hidden mysteries of beings, and through this knowledge controls them. It even perceives things which do not exist outwardly—that is to say, intellectual realities which are not sensible, and which have no outward existence because they are invisible; so it comprehends the mind, the spirit, the qualities, the characters, the love and sorrow of man, which are intellectual realities. Moreover, these existing sciences, arts, laws and endless inventions of man at one time were invisible, mysterious and hidden secrets; it is only the all-encompassing human power which has discovered and brought them out from the plane of the invisible to the plane of the visible. So telegraphy, photography, phonography and all such inventions and wonderful arts were at one time hidden mysteries. The human reality discovered and brought them out from the plane of the invisible to the plane of the visible. There was even a time when the qualities of this iron which you see— indeed of all the minerals—were hidden mysteries; men discovered this mineral, and wrought it in this industrial form. It is the same with all the other discoveries and inventions of man, which are innumerable.

This we cannot deny. If we say that these are effects of powers which animals also have, and of the powers of the bodily senses, we see clearly and evidently that the animals are, in regard to these powers, superior to man. For example, the sight of animals is much more keen than the sight of man; so also is their power of smell and taste. Briefly, in the powers which animals and men have in common, the animal is often the more powerful. For example, let us take the power of memory. If you carry a pigeon from here to a distant country, and there set it free, it will return, for it remembers the way. Take a dog from here to the center of Asia, set him free, and he will come back here and never once lose the road. So it is with the other powers such as hearing, sight, smell, taste and touch.

Thus it is clear that if there were not in man a power different from any of those of the animals, the latter would be superior to man in inventions and the comprehension of realities. Therefore, it is evident that man has a gift which the animal does not possess. Now, the animal perceives sensible things but does not perceive intellectual realities. For example, that which is within the range of its vision the animal sees, but that which is beyond the range of sight it is not possible for it to perceive, and it cannot imagine it. So it is not possible for the animal to understand that the earth has the form of a globe. But man from known things proves unknown things and discovers unknown truths. For example, man sees the curve of the horizon, and from this he infers the roundness of the earth. The Pole Star at 'Akká, for instance, is at 33°—that is to say, it is 33° above the horizon. When a man goes toward the North Pole, the Pole Star rises one degree above the horizon for each degree of distance that he travels—that is to say, the altitude of the Pole Star will be 34°, then 40°, then 50°, then 60°, then 70°. If he reaches the North Pole the altitude of the Pole Star will be 90° or have attained the zenith—that is to say, will be directly overhead. This Pole Star and its ascension are sensible things. The further one goes toward the Pole, the higher the Pole

Star rises; from these two known truths an unknown thing
has been discovered—that is, that the horizon is curved,
meaning that the horizon of each degree of the earth is a
different horizon from that of another degree. Man perceives this and proves from it an invisible thing which is
the roundness of the earth. This it is impossible for the
animal to perceive. In the same way, it cannot understand
that the sun is the center and that the earth revolves
around it. The animal is the captive of the senses and
bound by them; all that is beyond the senses, the things
that they do not control, the animal can never understand,
although in the outer senses it is greater than man. Hence
it is proved and verified that in man there is a power of discovery by which he is distinguished from the animals, and
this is the spirit of man.

Praise be to God! man is always turned toward the
heights, and his aspiration is lofty; he always desires to
reach a greater world than the world in which he is, and to
mount to a higher sphere than that in which he is. The love
of exaltation is one of the characteristics of man. I am as-
tonished that certain philosophers of America and Europe
are content to gradually approach the animal world and so
to go backward; for the tendency of existence must be
toward exaltation. Nevertheless, if you said to one of
them, "You are an animal," he would be extremely hurt
and angry.

What a difference between the human world and the
world of the animal, between the elevation of man and the
abasement of the animal, between the perfections of man
and the ignorance of the animal, between the light of man
and the darkness of the animal, between the glory of man
and the degradation of the animal! An Arab child of ten
years can manage two or three hundred camels in the desert, and with his voice can lead them forward or turn them
back. A weak Hindu can so control a huge elephant that
the elephant becomes the most obedient of servants. All

things are subdued by the hand of man; he can resist nature while all other creatures are captives of nature: none
can depart from her requirements. Man alone can resist
nature. Nature attracts bodies to the center of the earth;
man through mechanical means goes far from it and soars
in the air. Nature prevents man from crossing the seas;
man builds a ship, and he travels and voyages across the
great ocean, and so on; the subject is endless. For example,
man drives engines over the mountains and through the
wildernesses, and gathers in one spot the news of the
events of the East and West. All this is contrary to nature.
The sea with its grandeur cannot deviate by an atom from
the laws of nature; the sun in all its magnificence cannot
deviate as much as a needle's point from the laws of nature,
and can never comprehend the conditions, the state, the
qualities, the movements and the nature of man.

What, then, is the power in this small body of man
which encompasses all this? What is this ruling power by
which he subdues all things?

One more point remains. Modern philosophers say:
"We have never seen the spirit in man, and in spite of our
researches into the secrets of the human body, we do not
perceive a spiritual power. How can we imagine a power
which is not sensible?" The theologians reply: "The spirit
of the animal also is not sensible, and through its bodily
powers it cannot be perceived. By what do you prove the
existence of the spirit of the animal? There is no doubt that
from its effects you prove that in the animal there is a
power which is not in the plant, and this is the power of
the senses—that is to say, sight, hearing and also other
powers; from these you infer that there is an animal spirit.
In the same way, from the proofs and signs we have mentioned, we argue that there is a human spirit. Since in the
animal there are signs which are not in the plant, you say
this power of sensation is a property of the animal spirit;
you also see in man signs, powers and perfections which

do not exist in the animal; therefore, you infer that there is a power in him which the animal is without."

If we wish to deny everything that is not sensible, then we must deny the realities which unquestionably exist. For example, ethereal matter is not sensible, though it has an undoubted existence. The power of attraction is not sensible, though it certainly exists. From what do we affirm these existences? From their signs. Thus this light is the vibration of that ethereal matter, and from this vibration we infer the existence of ether.

49

THE GROWTH AND DEVELOPMENT OF THE HUMAN RACE

Question.—What do you say with regard to the theories held by some European philosophers on the growth and development of beings?

Answer.—This subject was spoken of the other day, but we will speak of it again. Briefly, this question will be decided by determining whether species are original or not—that is to say, has the species of man been established from its origin, or was it afterward derived from the animals?

Certain European philosophers agree that the species grows and develops, and that even change and alteration are also possible. One of the proofs that they give for this theory is that through the attentive study and verification of the science of geology it has become clear that the existence of the vegetable preceded that of the animal, and that of the animal preceded that of man. They admit that both the vegetable and the animal species have changed, for in some of the strata of the earth they have discovered plants which existed in the past and are now extinct; they have progressed, grown in strength, their form and appearance have changed, and so the species have altered. In the same way, in the strata of the earth there are some species of animals which have changed and are transformed. One of these animals is the serpent. There are indications that the serpent once had feet, but through the lapse of time those members have disappeared. In the same way, in the vertebral column of man there is an indication which amounts to a proof that, like other animals, he once had a tail. At one time that member was useful, but when man developed, it was no longer of use; and, therefore, it gradually disappeared. As the serpent took refuge under the ground and became a creeping animal, it was no longer in need of feet, so they disappeared; but their traces survive. The principal argument is this: that the existence of traces of members proves that they once existed, and as now they are no longer of service, they have gradually disappeared. Therefore, while the perfect and necessary members have remained, those which are unnecessary have gradually disappeared by the modification of the species, but the traces of them continue.

The first answer to this argument is the fact that the animal having preceded man is not a proof of the evolution, change and alteration of the species, nor that man was raised from the animal world to the human world. For while the individual appearance of these different beings is certain, it is possible that man came into existence after the animal. So when we examine the vegetable kingdom, we see that the fruits of the different trees do not arrive at maturity at one time; on the contrary, some come first and others afterward. This priority does not prove that the later fruit of one tree was produced from the earlier fruit of another tree.

Second, these slight signs and traces of members have perhaps a great reason of which the mind is not yet cognizant. How many things exist of which we do not yet know the reason! So the science of physiology—that is to say, the knowledge of the composition of the members— records that the reason and cause of the difference in the colors of animals, and of the hair of men, of the redness of the lips, and of the variety of the colors of birds, is still unknown; it is secret and hidden. But it is known that the pupil of the eye is black so as to attract the rays of the sun, for if it were another color—that is, uniformly white—it would not attract the rays of the sun. Therefore, as the reason of the things we have mentioned is unknown, it is possible that the reason and the wisdom of these traces of members, whether they be in the animal or man, are equally unknown. Certainly there is a reason, even though it is not known.

Third, let us suppose that there was a time when some animals, or even man, possessed some members which have now disappeared; this is not a sufficient proof of the change and evolution of the species. For man, from the beginning of the embryonic period till he reaches the degree of maturity, goes through different forms and appearances. His aspect, his form, his appearance and color change; he passes from one form to another, and from one appearance to another. Nevertheless, from the beginning of the embryonic period he is of the species of man—that is to say, an embryo of a man and not of an animal; but this is not at first apparent, but later it becomes visible and evident. For example, let us suppose that man once resembled the animal, and that now he has progressed and changed. Supposing this to be true, it is still not a proof of the change of species. No, as before mentioned, it is merely like the change and alteration of the embryo of man until it reaches the degree of reason and perfection. We will state it more clearly. Let us suppose that there was a time when man walked on his hands and feet, or had a tail; this change and alteration is like that of the fetus in the womb of the mother. Although it changes in all ways, and grows and develops until it reaches the perfect form, from the beginning it is a special species. We also see in the vegetable kingdom that the original species of the genus do not change and alter, but the form, color and bulk will change and alter, or even progress.

To recapitulate: as man in the womb of the mother passes from form to form, from shape to shape, changes and develops, and is still the human species from the beginning of the embryonic period—in the same way man, from the beginning of his existence in the matrix of the world, is also a distinct species—that is, man—and has gradually evolved from one form to another. Therefore, this change of appearance, this evolution of members, this development and growth, even though we admit the reality of growth and progress,[1] does not prevent the species from being original. Man from the beginning was in this perfect form and composition, and possessed capacity and aptitude for acquiring material and spiritual perfections, and was the manifestation of these words, "We will make man in Our image and likeness."[2] He has only become more pleasing, more beautiful and more graceful. Civilization has brought him out of his wild state, just as the wild fruits which are cultivated by a gardener become finer, sweeter and acquire more freshness and delicacy.

The gardeners of the world of humanity are the Prophets of God.

1. i.e., if we admit, for example, that man had formerly been a quadruped, or had had a tail.
2. Cf. Gen. 1:26.

50

SPIRITUAL PROOFS OF THE
ORIGIN OF MAN

THE proofs which we have adduced relative to the origin
of the human species were logical proofs. Now we will
give the spiritual proofs, which are essential. For, as we
have proved Divinity by logical arguments, and have also
proved logically that man exists from his origin and foundation as man, and that his species has existed from all
eternity, now we will establish spiritual proofs that
human existence—that is, the species of man—is a necessary existence, and that without man the perfections of
Divinity would not appear. But these are spiritual proofs,
not logical proofs.

We have many times demonstrated and established that
man is the noblest of beings, the sum of all perfections,
and that all beings and all existences are the centers from
which the glory of God is reflected—that is to say, the
signs of the Divinity of God are apparent in the realities of
things and of creatures. Just as the terrestrial globe is the
place where the rays of the sun are reflected—as its light,
its heat and its influence are apparent and visible in all the
atoms of the earth—so, in the same way, the atoms of beings, in this infinite space, proclaim and prove one of the
divine perfections. Nothing is deprived of this benefit;
either it is a sign of the mercy of God, or it is a sign of His
power, His greatness, His justice, His nurturing providence; or it is a sign of the generosity of God, His vision,
His hearing, His knowledge, His grace and so on.

Without doubt each being is the center of the shining

forth of the glory of God—that is to say, the perfections of God appear from it and are resplendent in it. It is like the sun, which is resplendent in the desert, upon the sea, in the trees, in the fruits and blossoms, and in all earthly things. The world, indeed each existing being, proclaims to us one of the names of God, but the reality of man is the collective reality, the general reality, and is the center where the glory of all the perfections of God shine forth—that is to say, for each name, each attribute, each perfection which we affirm of God there exists a sign in man. If it were otherwise, man could not imagine these perfections and could not understand them. So we say that God is the seer, and the eye is the sign of His vision; if this sight were not in man, how could we imagine the vision of God? for the blind (that is, one born blind) cannot imagine sight; and the deaf (that is, one deaf from birth) cannot imagine hearing; and the dead cannot realize life. Consequently, the Divinity of God, which is the sum of all perfections, reflects itself in the reality of man—that is to say, the Essence of Oneness is the gathering of all perfections, and from this unity He casts a reflection upon the human reality. Man, then, is the perfect mirror facing the Sun of Truth and is the center of radiation: the Sun of Truth shines in this mirror. The reflection of the divine perfections appears in the reality of man, so he is the representative of God, the messenger of God. If man did not exist, the universe would be without result, for the object of existence is the appearance of the perfections of God.

Therefore, it cannot be said there was a time when man was not. All that we can say is that this terrestrial globe at one time did not exist, and at its beginning man did not appear upon it. But from the beginning which has no beginning, to the end which has no end, a Perfect Manifestation always exists. This Man of Whom we speak is not every man; we mean the Perfect Man. For the noblest part of the tree is the fruit, which is the reason of its existence. If the tree had no fruit, it would have no meaning. Therefore, it cannot be imagined that the worlds of existence, whether the stars or this earth, were once inhabited by the donkey, cow, mouse and cat, and that they were without man! This supposition is false and meaningless. The word of God is clear as the sun. This is a spiritual proof, but one which we cannot at the beginning put forth for the benefit of the materialists. First we must speak of the logical proofs, afterward the spiritual proofs.

51

THE SPIRIT AND MIND OF MAN
HAVE EXISTED FROM
THE BEGINNING

Question. —Does man in the beginning possess mind and spirit, or are they an outcome of his evolution?

Answer. —The beginning of the existence of man on the terrestrial globe resembles his formation in the womb of the mother. The embryo in the womb of the mother gradually grows and develops until birth, after which it continues to grow and develop until it reaches the age of discretion and maturity. Though in infancy the signs of the mind and spirit appear in man, they do not reach the degree of perfection; they are imperfect. Only when man attains maturity do the mind and the spirit appear and become evident in utmost perfection.

So also the formation of man in the matrix of the world was in the beginning like the embryo; then gradually he made progress in perfectness, and grew and developed until he reached the state of maturity, when the mind and spirit became visible in the greatest power. In the beginning of his formation the mind and spirit also existed, but they were hidden; later they were manifested. In the womb of the world mind and spirit also existed in the embryo, but they were concealed; afterward they appeared. So it is that in the seed the tree exists, but it is hidden and concealed; when it develops and grows, the complete tree appears. In the same way the growth and development of all beings is gradual; this is the universal divine organiza-

tion and the natural system. The seed does not at once become a tree; the embryo does not at once become a man;
the mineral does not suddenly become a stone. No, they
grow and develop gradually and attain the limit of perfection.

All beings, whether large or small, were created perfect
and complete from the first, but their perfections appear in
them by degrees. The organization of God is one; the
evolution of existence is one; the divine system is one.
Whether they be small or great beings, all are subject to
one law and system. Each seed has in it from the first all
the vegetable perfections. For example, in the seed all the
vegetable perfections exist from the beginning, but not
visibly; afterward little by little they appear. So it is first
the shoot which appears from the seed, then the branches,
leaves, blossoms and fruits; but from the beginning of its
existence all these things are in the seed, potentially,
though not apparently.

In the same way, the embryo possesses from the first all
perfections, such as the spirit, the mind, the sight, the
smell, the taste—in one word, all the powers—but they
are not visible and become so only by degrees.

Similarly, the terrestrial globe from the beginning was
created with all its elements, substances, minerals, atoms
and organisms; but these only appeared by degrees: first
the mineral, then the plant, afterward the animal, and
finally man. But from the first these kinds and species
existed, but were undeveloped in the terrestrial globe, and
then appeared only gradually. For the supreme organization of God, and the universal natural system, surround
all beings, and all are subject to this rule. When you consider this universal system, you see that there is not one of
the beings which at its coming into existence has reached
the limit of perfection. No, they gradually grow and develop, and then attain the degree of perfection.

52

THE APPEARING OF THE SPIRIT
IN THE BODY

Question. —What is the wisdom of the spirit's appearing in the body?

Answer. —The wisdom of the appearance of the spirit in the body is this: the human spirit is a Divine Trust, and it must traverse all conditions, for its passage and movement through the conditions of existence will be the means of its acquiring perfections. So when a man travels and passes through different regions and numerous countries with system and method, it is certainly a means of his acquiring perfection, for he will see places, scenes and countries, from which he will discover the conditions and states of other nations. He will thus become acquainted with the geography of countries and their wonders and arts; he will familiarize himself with the habits, customs and usages of peoples; he will see the civilization and progress of the epoch; he will become aware of the policy of governments and the power and capacity of each country. It is the same when the human spirit passes through the conditions of existence: it will become the possessor of each degree and station. Even in the condition of the body it will surely acquire perfections.

Besides this, it is necessary that the signs of the perfection of the spirit should be apparent in this world, so that the world of creation may bring forth endless results, and this body may receive life and manifest the divine bounties. So, for example, the rays of the sun must shine upon the earth, and the solar heat develop the earthly beings; if the rays and heat of the sun did not shine upon the earth, the earth would be uninhabited, without meaning; and its development would be retarded. In the same way, if the perfections of the spirit did not appear in this world, this world would be unenlightened and absolutely brutal. By the appearance of the spirit in the physical form, this world is enlightened. As the spirit of man is the cause of the life of the body, so the world is in the condition of the body, and man is in the condition of the spirit. If there were no man, the perfections of the spirit would not appear, and the light of the mind would not be resplendent in this world. This world would be like a body without a soul.

This world is also in the condition of a fruit tree, and man is like the fruit; without fruit the tree would be useless.

Moreover, these members, these elements, this composition, which are found in the organism of man, are an attraction and magnet for the spirit; it is certain that the spirit will appear in it. So a mirror which is clear will certainly attract the rays of the sun. It will become luminous, and wonderful images will appear in it—that is to say, when these existing elements are gathered together according to the natural order, and with perfect strength, they become a magnet for the spirit, and the spirit will become manifest in them with all its perfections.

Under these conditions it cannot be said, "What is the necessity for the rays of the sun to descend upon the mirror?"—for the connection which exists between the reality of things, whether they be spiritual or material, requires that when the mirror is clear and faces the sun, the light of the sun must become apparent in it. In the same way, when the elements are arranged and combined in the most glorious system, organization and manner, the human spirit will appear and be manifest in them. This is the decree of the Powerful, the Wise.

53

THE RELATION BETWEEN GOD
AND THE CREATURE

Question.—What is the nature of the connection between
God and the creature—that is to say, between the Independent, the Most High, and the other beings?

Answer.—The connection between God and the creatures is that of the creator to the creation; it is like the connection between the sun and the dark bodies of contingent
beings, and is the connection between the maker and the
things that he has made. The sun in its own essence is independent of the bodies which it lights, for its light is in
itself and is free and independent of the terrestrial globe;
so the earth is under the influence of the sun and receives
its light, whereas the sun and its rays are entirely independent of the earth. But if there were no sun, the earth and all
earthly beings could not exist.

The dependence of the creatures upon God is a dependence of emanation—that is to say, creatures emanate
from God; they do not manifest Him.[1] The relation is that
of emanation and not that of manifestation. The light of
the sun emanates from the sun; it does not manifest it. The
appearance through emanation is like the appearance of
the rays from the luminary of the horizons of the
world—that is to say, the holy essence of the Sun of Truth
is not divided and does not descend to the condition of the
creatures. In the same way, the globe of the sun does not
become divided and does not descend to the earth. No, the

1. This subject, of emanation and manifestation, is more fully explained in the following chapter.

rays of the sun, which are its bounty, emanate from it and illumine the dark bodies.

But the appearance through manifestation is the manifestation of the branches, leaves, blossoms and fruit from the seed; for the seed in its own essence becomes branches and fruits, and its reality enters into the branches, the leaves and fruits. This appearance through manifestation would be for God, the Most High, simple imperfection; and this is quite impossible, for the implication would be that the Absolute Preexistent is qualified with phenomenal attributes. But if this were so, pure independence would become mere poverty, and true existence would become nonexistence, and this is impossible.

Therefore, all creatures emanate from God—that is to say, it is by God that all things are realized, and by Him that all beings have attained to existence. The first thing which emanated from God is that universal reality, which the ancient philosophers termed the "First Mind," and which the people of Bahá call the "First Will." This emanation, in that which concerns its action in the world of God, is not limited by time or place; it is without beginning or end—beginning and end in relation to God are one. The preexistence of God is the preexistence of essence, and also preexistence of time, and the phenomenality of contingency is essential and not temporal, as we have already explained one day at table.[1]

Though the "First Mind" is without beginning, it does not become a sharer in the preexistence of God, for the existence of the universal reality in relation to the existence of God is nothingness, and it has not the power to become an associate of God and like unto Him in preexistence. This subject has been before explained.

The existence of living things signifies composition, and their death, decomposition. But universal matter and the elements do not become absolutely annihilated and de-

1. Cf. "Real Preexistence," p. 280.

stroyed. No, their nonexistence is simply transformation. For instance, when man is annihilated, he becomes dust; but he does not become absolutely nonexistent. He still exists in the shape of dust, but transformation has taken place, and this composition is accidentally decomposed. The annihilation of the other beings is the same, for existence does not become absolute nonexistence, and absolute nonexistence does not become existence.

54

ON THE PROCEEDING OF THE
HUMAN SPIRIT FROM GOD

Question. —In the Bible it is said that God breathed the spirit into the body of man. What is the meaning of this verse?

Answer. —Know that proceeding is of two kinds: the proceeding and appearance through emanation, and the proceeding and appearance through manifestation. The proceeding through emanation is like the coming forth of the action from the actor, of the writing from the writer. Now the writing emanates from the writer, and the discourse emanates from the speaker, and in the same way the human spirit emanates from God. It is not that it manifests God—that is to say, no part has been detached from the Divine Reality to enter the body of man. No, as the discourse emanates from the speaker, the spirit appears in the body of man.

But the proceeding through manifestation is the manifestation of the reality of a thing in other forms, like the coming forth of this tree from the seed of the tree, or the coming forth of the flower from the seed of the flower, for it is the seed itself which appears in the form of the branches, leaves and flowers. This is called the proceeding through manifestation. The spirits of men, with reference to God, have dependence through emanation, just as the discourse proceeds from the speaker and the writing from the writer—that is to say, the speaker himself does not become the discourse, nor does the writer himself become the writing; no, rather they have the proceeding of emanation. The speaker has perfect ability and power, and the discourse emanates from him, as the action does from the actor. The Real Speaker, the Essence of Unity, has always been in one condition, which neither changes nor alters, has neither transformation nor vicissitude. He is the Eternal, the Immortal. Therefore, the proceeding of the human spirits from God is through emanation. When it is said in the Bible that God breathed His spirit into man, this spirit is that which, like the discourse, emanates from the Real Speaker, taking effect in the reality of man.

But the proceeding through manifestation (if by this is meant the divine appearance, and not division into parts), we have said, is the proceeding and the appearance of the Holy Spirit and the Word, which is from God. As it is said in the Gospel of John, "In the beginning was the Word, and the Word was with God";[1] then the Holy Spirit and the Word are the appearance of God. The Spirit and the Word mean the divine perfections that appeared in the Reality of Christ, and these perfections were with God; so the sun manifests all its glory in the mirror. For the Word does not signify the body of Christ, no, but the divine perfections manifested in Him. For Christ was like a clear mirror which was facing the Sun of Reality; and the perfections of the Sun of Reality—that is to say, its light and heat—were visible and apparent in this mirror. If we look into the mirror, we see the sun, and we say, "It is the sun." Therefore, the Word and the Holy Spirit, which signify the perfections of God, are the divine appearance. This is the meaning of the verse in the Gospel which says: "The Word was with God, and the Word was God";[1] for the divine perfections are not different from the Essence of Oneness. The perfections of Christ are called the Word because all the beings are in the condition of letters, and one letter has not a complete meaning, while the perfections of Christ have the power of the word because a com-

1. John 1:1.

plete meaning can be inferred from a word. As the Reality of Christ was the manifestation of the divine perfections, therefore, it was like the word. Why? because He is the sum of perfect meanings. This is why He is called the Word.

And know that the proceeding of the Word and the Holy Spirit from God, which is the proceeding and appearance of manifestation, must not be understood to mean that the Reality of Divinity had been divided into parts, or multiplied, or that it had descended from the exaltation of holiness and purity. God forbid! If a pure, fine mirror faces the sun, the light and heat, the form and the image of the sun will be resplendent in it with such manifestation that if a beholder says of the sun, which is brilliant and visible in the mirror, "This is the sun," it is true. Nevertheless, the mirror is the mirror, and the sun is the sun. The One Sun, even if it appears in numerous mirrors, is one. This state is neither abiding nor entering, neither commingling nor descending; for entering, abiding, descending, issuing forth and commingling are the necessities and characteristics of bodies, not of spirits; then how much less do they belong to the sanctified and pure Reality of God. God is exempt from all that is not in accordance with His purity and His exalted and sublime sanctity.

The Sun of Reality, as we have said, has always been in one condition; it has no change, no alteration, no transformation and no vicissitude. It is eternal and everlasting. But the Holy Reality of the Word of God is in the condition of the pure, fine and shining mirror; the heat, the light, the image and likeness—that is to say, the perfections of the Sun of Reality—appear in it. That is why Christ says in the Gospel, "The Father is in the Son"—that is to say, the Sun of Reality appears in the mirror.[1] Praise be to the One Who shone upon this Holy Reality, Who is sanctified among the beings!

1. Cf. John 14:11; 17:21.

55

SOUL, SPIRIT AND MIND

Question.—What is the difference between the mind, spirit and soul?

Answer.—It has been before explained that spirit is universally divided into five categories: the vegetable spirit, the animal spirit, the human spirit, the spirit of faith, and the Holy Spirit.

The vegetable spirit is the power of growth which is brought about in the seed through the influence of other existences.

The animal spirit is the power of all the senses, which is realized from the composition and mingling of elements; when this composition decomposes, the power also perishes and becomes annihilated. It may be likened to this lamp: when the oil, wick and fire are combined, it is lighted; and when this combination is dissolved—that is to say, when the combined parts are separated from one another—the lamp also is extinguished.

The human spirit which distinguishes man from the animal is the rational soul, and these two names—the human spirit and the rational soul—designate one thing. This spirit, which in the terminology of the philosophers is the rational soul, embraces all beings, and as far as human ability permits discovers the realities of things and becomes cognizant of their peculiarities and effects, and of the qualities and properties of beings. But the human spirit, unless assisted by the spirit of faith, does not become acquainted with the divine secrets and the heavenly realities. It is like a mirror which, although clear, polished and brilliant, is still in need of light. Until a ray of the sun reflects upon it, it cannot discover the heavenly secrets.

But the mind is the power of the human spirit. Spirit is the lamp; mind is the light which shines from the lamp. Spirit is the tree, and the mind is the fruit. Mind is the perfection of the spirit and is its essential quality, as the sun's rays are the essential necessity of the sun.

This explanation, though short, is complete; therefore, reflect upon it, and if God wills, you may become acquainted with the details.

56

THE PHYSICAL POWERS AND THE
INTELLECTUAL POWERS

IN man five outer powers exist, which are the agents of perception—that is to say, through these five powers man perceives material beings. These are sight, which perceives visible forms; hearing, which perceives audible sounds; smell, which perceives odors; taste, which perceives foods; and feeling, which is in all parts of the body and perceives tangible things. These five powers perceive outward existences.

Man has also spiritual powers: imagination, which conceives things; thought, which reflects upon realities; comprehension, which comprehends realities; memory, which retains whatever man imagines, thinks and comprehends. The intermediary between the five outward powers and the inward powers is the sense which they possess in common—that is to say, the sense which acts between the outer and inner powers, conveys to the inward powers whatever the outer powers discern. It is termed the common faculty, because it communicates between the outward and inward powers and thus is common to the outward and inward powers.

For instance, sight is one of the outer powers; it sees and perceives this flower, and conveys this perception to the inner power—the common faculty—which transmits this perception to the power of imagination, which in its turn conceives and forms this image and transmits it to the power of thought; the power of thought reflects and, having grasped the reality, conveys it to the power of com-

prehension; the comprehension, when it has comprehended it, delivers the image of the object perceived to
the memory, and the memory keeps it in its repository.

The outward powers are five: the power of sight, of
hearing, of taste, of smell and of feeling.

The inner powers are also five: the common faculty,
and the powers of imagination, thought, comprehension
and memory.

57

THE CAUSES OF THE DIFFERENCES
IN THE CHARACTERS OF MEN

Question.—How many kinds of character has man, and what is the cause of the differences and varieties in men?

Answer.—He has the innate character, the inherited character, and the acquired character which is gained by education.

With regard to the innate character, although the divine creation is purely good, yet the varieties of natural qualities in man come from the difference of degree; all are excellent, but they are more or less so, according to the degree. So all mankind possess intelligence and capacities, but the intelligence, the capacity and the worthiness of men differ. This is evident.

For example, take a number of children of one family, of one place, of one school, instructed by one teacher, reared on the same food, in the same climate, with the same clothing, and studying the same lessons—it is certain that among these children some will be clever in the sciences, some will be of average ability, and some dull. Hence it is clear that in the original nature there exists a difference of degree and varieties of worthiness and capacity. This difference does not imply good or evil but is simply a difference of degree. One has the highest degree, another the medium degree, and another the lowest degree. So man exists; the animal, the plant and the mineral exist also—but the degrees of these four existences vary. What a difference between the existence of man and of the

212

animal! Yet both are existences. It is evident that in existence there are differences of degrees.

The variety of inherited qualities comes from strength and weakness of constitution—that is to say, when the two parents are weak, the children will be weak; if they are strong, the children will be robust. In the same way, purity of blood has a great effect; for the pure germ is like the superior stock which exists in plants and animals. For example, you see that children born from a weak and feeble father and mother will naturally have a feeble constitution and weak nerves; they will be afflicted and will have neither patience, nor endurance, nor resolution, nor perseverance, and will be hasty; for the children inherit the weakness and debility of their parents.

Besides this, an especial blessing is conferred on some families and some generations. Thus it is an especial blessing that from among the descendants of Abraham should have come all the Prophets of the children of Israel. This is a blessing that God has granted to this descent: to Moses from His father and mother, to Christ from His mother's line; also to Muḥammad and the Báb, and to all the Prophets and the Holy Manifestations of Israel. The Blessed Beauty[1] is also a lineal descendant of Abraham, for Abraham had other sons besides Ishmael and Isaac who in those days migrated to the lands of Persia and Afghanistan, and the Blessed Beauty is one of their descendants.

Hence it is evident that inherited character also exists, and to such a degree that if the characters are not in conformity with their origin, although they belong physically to that lineage, spiritually they are not considered members of the family, like Canaan,[2] who is not reckoned as being of the race of Noah.

1. Bahá'u'lláh.
2. Cf. Gen. 9:25.

But the difference of the qualities with regard to culture is very great, for education has great influence. Through education the ignorant become learned; the cowardly become valiant. Through cultivation the crooked branch becomes straight; the acid, bitter fruit of the mountains and woods becomes sweet and delicious; and the five-petaled flower becomes hundred petaled. Through education savage nations become civilized, and even the animals become domesticated. Education must be considered as most important, for as diseases in the world of bodies are extremely contagious, so, in the same way, qualities of spirit and heart are extremely contagious. Education has a universal influence, and the differences caused by it are very great.

Perhaps someone will say that, since the capacity and worthiness of men differ, therefore, the difference of capacity certainly causes the difference of characters.[1]

But this is not so, for capacity is of two kinds: natural capacity and acquired capacity. The first, which is the creation of God, is purely good—in the creation of God there is no evil; but the acquired capacity has become the cause of the appearance of evil. For example, God has created all men in such a manner and has given them such a constitution and such capacities that they are benefited by sugar and honey and harmed and destroyed by poison. This nature and constitution is innate, and God has given it equally to all mankind. But man begins little by little to accustom himself to poison by taking a small quantity each day, and gradually increasing it, until he reaches such a point that he cannot live without a gram of opium every day. The natural capacities are thus completely perverted. Observe how much the natural capacity and constitution can be changed, until by different habits and training they become entirely perverted. One does not criticize vicious

1. i.e., therefore people cannot be blamed for their character.

people because of their innate capacities and nature, but rather for their acquired capacities and nature.

In creation there is no evil; all is good. Certain qualities and natures innate in some men and apparently blameworthy are not so in reality. For example, from the beginning of his life you can see in a nursing child the signs of greed, of anger and of temper. Then, it may be said, good and evil are innate in the reality of man, and this is contrary to the pure goodness of nature and creation. The answer to this is that greed, which is to ask for something more, is a praiseworthy quality provided that it is used suitably. So if a man is greedy to acquire science and knowledge, or to become compassionate, generous and just, it is most praiseworthy. If he exercises his anger and wrath against the bloodthirsty tyrants who are like ferocious beasts, it is very praiseworthy; but if he does not use these qualities in a right way, they are blameworthy.

Then it is evident that in creation and nature evil does not exist at all; but when the natural qualities of man are used in an unlawful way, they are blameworthy. So if a rich and generous person gives a sum of money to a poor man for his own necessities, and if the poor man spends that sum of money on unlawful things, that will be blameworthy. It is the same with all the natural qualities of man, which constitute the capital of life; if they be used and displayed in an unlawful way, they become blameworthy. Therefore, it is clear that creation is purely good. Consider that the worst of qualities and most odious of attributes, which is the foundation of all evil, is lying. No worse or more blameworthy quality than this can be imagined to exist; it is the destroyer of all human perfections and the cause of innumerable vices. There is no worse characteristic than this; it is the foundation of all evils. Notwithstanding all this, if a doctor consoles a sick man by saying, "Thank God you are better, and there is hope of your recovery," though these words are contrary to the truth, yet they may become the consolation of the patient and the turning point of the illness. This is not blameworthy.

This question is now clearly elucidated. Salutations!

58

THE DEGREE OF KNOWLEDGE POSSESSED
BY MAN AND THE
DIVINE MANIFESTATIONS

Question. —Of what degree is the perception of the human world, and what are its limitations?

Answer. —Know that perception varies. The lowest degree of perception is that of the animals—that is to say, the natural feeling which appears through the powers of the senses, and which is called sensation. In this, men and animals are sharers; moreover, some animals with regard to the senses are more powerful than man. But in humanity, perception differs and varies in accordance with the different conditions of man.

The first condition of perception in the world of nature is the perception of the rational soul. In this perception and in this power all men are sharers, whether they be neglectful or vigilant, believers or deniers. This human rational soul is God's creation; it encompasses and excels other creatures; as it is more noble and distinguished, it encompasses things. The power of the rational soul can discover the realities of things, comprehend the peculiarities of beings, and penetrate the mysteries of existence. All sciences, knowledge, arts, wonders, institutions, discoveries and enterprises come from the exercised intelligence of the rational soul. There was a time when they were unknown, preserved mysteries and hidden secrets; the rational soul gradually discovered them and brought them out from the plane of the invisible and the hidden into the realm of the visible. This is the greatest power of perception in the world of nature, which in its highest flight and soaring comprehends the realities, the properties and the effects of the contingent beings.

But the universal divine mind, which is beyond nature, is the bounty of the Preexistent Power. This universal mind is divine; it embraces existing realities, and it receives the light of the mysteries of God. It is a conscious power, not a power of investigation and of research. The intellectual power of the world of nature is a power of investigation, and by its researches it discovers the realities of beings and the properties of existences; but the heavenly intellectual power, which is beyond nature, embraces things and is cognizant of things, knows them, understands them, is aware of mysteries, realities and divine significations, and is the discoverer of the concealed verities of the Kingdom. This divine intellectual power is the special attribute of the Holy Manifestations and the Dawning-places of prophethood; a ray of this light falls upon the mirrors of the hearts of the righteous, and a portion and a share of this power comes to them through the Holy Manifestations.

The Holy Manifestations have three conditions: one, the physical condition; one, that of the rational soul; and one, that of the manifestation of perfection and of the lordly splendor. The body comprehends things according to the degree of its ability in the physical world; therefore, in certain cases it shows physical weakness. For example: "I was sleeping and unconscious; the breeze of God passed over Me and awoke Me, and commanded Me to proclaim the Word"; or when Christ in His thirtieth year was baptized, and the Holy Spirit descended upon Him; before this the Holy Spirit did not manifest itself in Him. All these things refer to the bodily condition of the Manifestations; but Their heavenly condition embraces all things, knows all mysteries, discovers all signs, and rules over all things; before as well as after Their mission, it is the same. That is why Christ has said: "I am Alpha and Omega, the first and the last"[1]—that is to say, there has never been and never shall be any change and alteration in Me.

1. Cf. Rev. 22:13.

59

MAN'S KNOWLEDGE OF GOD

Question.—To what extent can the understanding of man comprehend God?

Answer.—This subject requires ample time, and to explain it thus at table is not easy; nevertheless, we will speak of it briefly.

Know that there are two kinds of knowledge: the knowledge of the essence of a thing and the knowledge of its qualities. The essence of a thing is known through its qualities; otherwise, it is unknown and hidden.

As our knowledge of things, even of created and limited things, is knowledge of their qualities and not of their essence, how is it possible to comprehend in its essence the Divine Reality, which is unlimited? For the inner essence of anything is not comprehended, but only its qualities. For example, the inner essence of the sun is unknown, but is understood by its qualities, which are heat and light. The inner essence of man is unknown and not evident, but by its qualities it is characterized and known. Thus everything is known by its qualities and not by its essence. Although the mind encompasses all things, and the outward beings are comprehended by it, nevertheless these beings with regard to their essence are unknown; they are only known with regard to their qualities.

Then how can the eternal everlasting Lord, Who is held sanctified from comprehension and conception, be known by His essence? That is to say, as things can only be known by their qualities and not by their essence, it is certain that the Divine Reality is unknown with regard to its essence and is known with regard to its attributes. Besides, how can the phenomenal reality embrace the Preexistent Reality? For comprehension is the result of encompassing—embracing must be, so that comprehension may be—and the Essence of Unity surrounds all and is not surrounded.

Also the difference of conditions in the world of beings is an obstacle to comprehension. For example, this mineral belongs to the mineral kingdom; however far it may rise, it can never comprehend the power of growth. The plants, the trees, whatever progress they may make, cannot conceive of the power of sight or the powers of the other senses; and the animal cannot imagine the condition of man—that is to say, his spiritual powers. Difference of condition is an obstacle to knowledge; the inferior degree cannot comprehend the superior degree. How then can the phenomenal reality comprehend the Preexistent Reality? Knowing God, therefore, means the comprehension and the knowledge of His attributes, and not of His Reality. This knowledge of the attributes is also proportioned to the capacity and power of man; it is not absolute. Philosophy consists in comprehending the reality of things as they exist, according to the capacity and the power of man. For the phenomenal reality can comprehend the Preexistent attributes only to the extent of the human capacity. The mystery of Divinity is sanctified and purified from the comprehension of the beings, for all that comes to the imagination is that which man understands, and the power of the understanding of man does not embrace the Reality of the Divine Essence. All that man is able to understand are the attributes of Divinity, the radiance of which appears and is visible in the world and within men's souls.

When we look at the world and within men's souls, we see wonderful signs of the divine perfections, which are clear and apparent; for the reality of things proves the

Universal Reality. The Reality of Divinity may be compared to the sun, which from the height of its magnificence shines upon all the horizons; and each horizon, and each soul, receives a share of its radiance. If this light and these rays did not exist, beings would not exist; all beings express something and partake of some ray and portion of this light. The splendors of the perfections, bounties and attributes of God shine forth and radiate from the reality of the Perfect Man—that is to say, the Unique One, the supreme Manifestation of God. Other beings receive only one ray, but the supreme Manifestation is the mirror for this Sun, which appears and becomes manifest in it, with all its perfections, attributes, signs and wonders.

The knowledge of the Reality of the Divinity is impossible and unattainable, but the knowledge of the Manifestations of God is the knowledge of God, for the bounties, splendors and divine attributes are apparent in Them. Therefore, if man attains to the knowledge of the Manifestations of God, he will attain to the knowledge of God; and if he be neglectful of the knowledge of the Holy Manifestations, he will be bereft of the knowledge of God. It is then ascertained and proved that the Holy Manifestations are the center of the bounty, signs and perfections of God. Blessed are those who receive the light of the divine bounties from the enlightened Dawning-points!

We hope that the Friends of God, like an attractive force, will draw these bounties from the source itself, and that they will arise with such illumination and signs that they will be evident proofs of the Sun of Reality.

60

THE IMMORTALITY OF THE SPIRIT (1)

HAVING shown that the spirit of man exists,[1] we must prove its immortality.

The immortality of the spirit is mentioned in the Holy Books; it is the fundamental basis of the divine religions. Now punishments and rewards are said to be of two kinds: first, the rewards and punishments of this life; second, those of the other world. But the paradise and hell of existence are found in all the worlds of God, whether in this world or in the spiritual heavenly worlds. Gaining these rewards is the gaining of eternal life. That is why Christ said, "Act in such a way that you may find eternal life, and that you may be born of water and the spirit, so that you may enter into the Kingdom."[2]

The rewards of this life are the virtues and perfections which adorn the reality of man. For example, he was dark and becomes luminous; he was ignorant and becomes wise; he was neglectful and becomes vigilant; he was asleep and becomes awakened; he was dead and becomes living; he was blind and becomes a seer; he was deaf and becomes a hearer; he was earthly and becomes heavenly; he was material and becomes spiritual. Through these rewards he gains spiritual birth and becomes a new creature. He becomes the manifestation of the verse in the Gospel where it is said of the disciples that they "were born, not of blood, nor of the will of the flesh, nor of the will of man,

1. Cf. "The Difference between Man and the Animal," p. 185.
2. Cf. John 3:5.

but of God"[1]—that is to say, they were delivered from the
animal characteristics and qualities which are the characteristics of human nature, and they became qualified
with the divine characteristics, which are the bounty of
God. This is the meaning of the second birth. For such
people there is no greater torture than being veiled from
God, and no more severe punishment than sensual vices,
dark qualities, lowness of nature, engrossment in carnal
desires. When they are delivered through the light of faith
from the darkness of these vices, and become illuminated
with the radiance of the sun of reality, and ennobled with
all the virtues, they esteem this the greatest reward, and
they know it to be the true paradise. In the same way they
consider that the spiritual punishment—that is to say, the
torture and punishment of existence—is to be subjected to
the world of nature; to be veiled from God; to be brutal
and ignorant; to fall into carnal lusts; to be absorbed in
animal frailties; to be characterized with dark qualities,
such as falsehood, tyranny, cruelty, attachment to the affairs of the world, and being immersed in satanic ideas.
For them, these are the greatest punishments and tortures.

Likewise, the rewards of the other world are the eternal
life which is clearly mentioned in all the Holy Books, the
divine perfections, the eternal bounties and everlasting
felicity. The rewards of the other world are the perfections and the peace obtained in the spiritual worlds after
leaving this world, while the rewards of this life are the
real luminous perfections which are realized in this world,
and which are the cause of eternal life, for they are the very
progress of existence. It is like the man who passes from
the embryonic world to the state of maturity and becomes
the manifestation of these words: "Blessed, therefore, be
God, the most excellent of Makers."[2] The rewards of the

1. John 1:13.
2. Qur'án 23:14.

other world are peace, the spiritual graces, the various
spiritual gifts in the Kingdom of God, the gaining of the
desires of the heart and the soul, and the meeting of God in
the world of eternity. In the same way the punishments of
the other world—that is to say, the torments of the other
world—consist in being deprived of the special divine
blessings and the absolute bounties, and falling into the
lowest degrees of existence. He who is deprived of these
divine favors, although he continues after death, is considered as dead by the people of truth.

The logical proof of the immortality of the spirit is this,
that no sign can come from a nonexisting thing—that is to
say, it is impossible that from absolute nonexistence signs
should appear—for the signs are the consequence of an
existence, and the consequence depends upon the existence of the principle. So from a nonexisting sun no light
can radiate; from a nonexisting sea no waves appear; from
a nonexisting cloud no rain falls; a nonexisting tree yields
no fruit; a nonexisting man neither manifests nor produces
anything. Therefore, as long as signs of existence appear,
they are a proof that the possessor of the sign is existent.

Consider that today the Kingdom of Christ exists.
From a nonexisting king how could such a great kingdom
be manifested? How, from a nonexisting sea, can the
waves mount so high? From a nonexisting garden, how
can such fragrant breezes be wafted? Reflect that no effect,
no trace, no influence remains of any being after its members are dispersed and its elements are decomposed,
whether it be a mineral, a vegetable or an animal. There is
only the human reality and the spirit of man which, after
the disintegration of the members, dispersing of the particles, and the destruction of the composition, persists and
continues to act and to have power.

This question is extremely subtle: consider it attentively. This is a rational proof which we are giving, so that

the wise may weigh it in the balance of reason and justice. But if the human spirit will rejoice and be attracted to the Kingdom of God, if the inner sight becomes opened, and the spiritual hearing strengthened, and the spiritual feelings predominant, he will see the immortality of the spirit as clearly as he sees the sun, and the glad tidings and signs of God will encompass him.

Tomorrow we will give other proofs.

61

THE IMMORTALITY OF THE SPIRIT (2)

YESTERDAY we were occupied in discussing the immortality of the spirit. Know that the power and the comprehension of the human spirit are of two kinds—that is to say, they perceive and act in two different modes. One way is through instruments and organs: thus with this eye it sees; with this ear it hears; with this tongue it talks. Such is the action of the spirit, and the perception of the reality of man, by means of organs—that is to say, that the spirit is the seer, through the eyes; the spirit is the hearer, through the ear; the spirit is the speaker, through the tongue.

The other manifestation of the powers and actions of the spirit is without instruments and organs. For example, in the state of sleep without eyes it sees; without an ear it hears; without a tongue it speaks; without feet it runs. Briefly, these actions are beyond the means of instruments and organs. How often it happens that it sees a dream in the world of sleep, and its signification becomes apparent two years afterward in corresponding events. In the same way, how many times it happens that a question which one cannot solve in the world of wakefulness is solved in the world of dreams. In wakefulness the eye sees only for a short distance, but in dreams he who is in the East sees the West. Awake he sees the present; in sleep he sees the future. In wakefulness, by means of rapid transit, at the most he can travel only twenty farsakhs[1] an hour; in sleep, in the twinkling of an eye, he traverses the East and West. For the spirit travels in two different ways: without

1. One *farsakh* is equivalent to about four miles.

means, which is spiritual traveling; and with means, which is material traveling: as birds which fly, and those which are carried.

In the time of sleep this body is as though dead; it does not see nor hear; it does not feel; it has no consciousness, no perception—that is to say, the powers of man have become inactive, but the spirit lives and subsists. Nay, its penetration is increased, its flight is higher, and its intelligence is greater. To consider that after the death of the body the spirit perishes is like imagining that a bird in a cage will be destroyed if the cage is broken, though the bird has nothing to fear from the destruction of the cage. Our body is like the cage, and the spirit is like the bird. We see that without the cage this bird flies in the world of sleep; therefore, if the cage becomes broken, the bird will continue and exist. Its feelings will be even more powerful, its perceptions greater, and its happiness increased. In truth, from hell it reaches a paradise of delights because for the thankful birds there is no paradise greater than freedom from the cage. That is why with utmost joy and happiness the martyrs hasten to the plain of sacrifice.

In wakefulness the eye of man sees at the utmost as far as one hour of distance[1] because through the instrumentality of the body the power of the spirit is thus determined; but with the inner sight and the mental eye it sees America, and it can perceive that which is there, and discover the conditions of things and organize affairs. If, then, the spirit were the same as the body, it would be necessary that the power of the inner sight should also be in the same proportion. Therefore, it is evident that this spirit is different from the body, and that the bird is different from the cage, and that the power and penetration of the spirit is stronger without the intermediary of the body. Now, if the instrument is abandoned, the possessor of the instrument continues to act. For example, if the pen is

1. It is a Persian custom to reckon distance by time.

abandoned or broken, the writer remains living and present; if a house is ruined, the owner is alive and existing. This is one of the logical evidences for the immortality of the soul.

There is another: this body becomes weak or heavy or sick, or it finds health; it becomes tired or rested; sometimes the hand or leg is amputated, or its physical power is crippled; it becomes blind or deaf or dumb; its limbs may become paralyzed; briefly, the body may have all the imperfections. Nevertheless, the spirit in its original state, in its own spiritual perception, will be eternal and perpetual; it neither finds any imperfection, nor will it become crippled. But when the body is wholly subjected to disease and misfortune, it is deprived of the bounty of the spirit, like a mirror which, when it becomes broken or dirty or dusty, cannot reflect the rays of the sun nor any longer show its bounties.

We have already explained that the spirit of man is not in the body because it is freed and sanctified from entrance and exit, which are bodily conditions. The connection of the spirit with the body is like that of the sun with the mirror. Briefly, the human spirit is in one condition. It neither becomes ill from the diseases of the body nor cured by its health; it does not become sick, nor weak, nor miserable, nor poor, nor light, nor small—that is to say, it will not be injured because of the infirmities of the body, and no effect will be visible even if the body becomes weak, or if the hands and feet and tongue be cut off, or if it loses the power of hearing or sight. Therefore, it is evident and certain that the spirit is different from the body, and that its duration is independent of that of the body; on the contrary, the spirit with the utmost greatness rules in the world of the body; and its power and influence, like the bounty of the sun in the mirror, are apparent and visible. But when the mirror becomes dusty or breaks, it will cease to reflect the rays of the sun.

62

PERFECTIONS ARE WITHOUT LIMIT

KNOW that the conditions of existence are limited to the conditions of servitude, of prophethood and of Deity, but the divine and the contingent perfections are unlimited. When you reflect deeply, you discover that also outwardly the perfections of existence are also unlimited, for you cannot find a being so perfect that you cannot imagine a superior one. For example, you cannot see a ruby in the mineral kingdom, a rose in the vegetable kingdom, or a nightingale in the animal kingdom, without imagining that there might be better specimens. As the divine bounties are endless, so human perfections are endless. If it were possible to reach a limit of perfection, then one of the realities of the beings might reach the condition of being independent of God, and the contingent might attain to the condition of the absolute. But for every being there is a point which it cannot overpass—that is to say, he who is in the condition of servitude, however far he may progress in gaining limitless perfections, will never reach the condition of Deity. It is the same with the other beings. A mineral, however far it may progress in the mineral kingdom, cannot gain the vegetable power. Also in a flower, however far it may progress in the vegetable kingdom, no power of the senses will appear. So this silver mineral cannot gain hearing or sight; it can only improve in its own condition and become a perfect mineral, but it cannot acquire the power of growth, or the power of sensation, or attain to life; it can only progress in its own condition.

For example, Peter cannot become Christ. All that he can do is, in the condition of servitude, to attain endless perfections; for every existing reality is capable of making progress. As the spirit of man after putting off this material form has an everlasting life, certainly any existing being is capable of making progress; therefore, it is permitted to ask for advancement, forgiveness, mercy, beneficence and blessings for a man after his death because existence is capable of progression. That is why in the prayers of Bahá'u'lláh forgiveness and remission of sins are asked for those who have died. Moreover, as people in this world are in need of God, they will also need Him in the other world. The creatures are always in need, and God is absolutely independent, whether in this world or in the world to come.

The wealth of the other world is nearness to God. Consequently, it is certain that those who are near the Divine Court are allowed to intercede, and this intercession is approved by God. But intercession in the other world is not like intercession in this world. It is another thing, another reality, which cannot be expressed in words.

If a wealthy man at the time of his death bequeaths a gift to the poor and miserable, and gives a part of his wealth to be spent for them, perhaps this action may be the cause of his pardon and forgiveness, and of his progress in the Divine Kingdom.

Also a father and mother endure the greatest troubles and hardships for their children; and often when the children have reached the age of maturity, the parents pass on to the other world. Rarely does it happen that a father and mother in this world see the reward of the care and trouble they have undergone for their children. Therefore, children, in return for this care and trouble, must show forth charity and beneficence, and must implore pardon and forgiveness for their parents. So you ought, in return for the love and kindness shown you by your father, to give to the poor for his sake, with greatest submission and humility implore pardon and remission of sins, and ask for the supreme mercy.

It is even possible that the condition of those who have died in sin and unbelief may become changed—that is to say, they may become the object of pardon through the bounty of God, not through His justice—for bounty is giving without desert, and justice is giving what is deserved. As we have power to pray for these souls here, so likewise we shall possess the same power in the other world, which is the Kingdom of God. Are not all the people in that world the creatures of God? Therefore, in that world also they can make progress. As here they can receive light by their supplications, there also they can plead for forgiveness and receive light through entreaties and supplications. Thus as souls in this world, through the help of the supplications, the entreaties and the prayers of the holy ones, can acquire development, so is it the same after death. Through their own prayers and supplications they can also progress, more especially when they are the object of the intercession of the Holy Manifestations.

63

THE PROGRESS OF MAN IN THE OTHER WORLD

KNOW that nothing which exists remains in a state of repose—that is to say, all things are in motion. Everything is either growing or declining; all things are either coming from nonexistence into being, or going from existence into nonexistence. So this flower, this hyacinth, during a certain period of time was coming from the world of nonexistence into being, and now it is going from being into nonexistence. This state of motion is said to be essential—that is, natural; it cannot be separated from beings because it is their essential requirement, as it is the essential requirement of fire to burn.

Thus it is established that this movement is necessary to existence, which is either growing or declining. Now, as the spirit continues to exist after death, it necessarily progresses or declines; and in the other world to cease to progress is the same as to decline; but it never leaves its own condition, in which it continues to develop. For example, the reality of the spirit of Peter, however far it may progress, will not reach to the condition of the Reality of Christ; it progresses only in its own environment.

Look at this mineral. However far it may evolve, it only evolves in its own condition; you cannot bring the crystal to a state where it can attain to sight. This is impossible. So the moon which is in the heavens, however far it might evolve, could never become a luminous sun, but in its own condition it has apogee and perigee. However far the disciples might progress, they could never become Christ. It is true that coal could become a diamond, but both are in the mineral condition, and their component elements are the same.

64

THE STATE OF MAN AND HIS PROGRESS AFTER DEATH

WHEN we consider beings with the seeing eye, we observe that they are limited to three sorts—that is to say, as a whole they are either mineral, vegetable or animal, each of these three classes containing species. Man is the highest species because he is the possessor of the perfections of all the classes—that is, he has a body which grows and which feels. As well as having the perfections of the mineral, of the vegetable and of the animal, he also possesses an especial excellence which the other beings are without—that is, the intellectual perfections. Therefore, man is the most noble of beings.

Man is in the highest degree of materiality, and at the beginning of spirituality—that is to say, he is the end of imperfection and the beginning of perfection. He is at the last degree of darkness, and at the beginning of light; that is why it has been said that the condition of man is the end of the night and the beginning of day, meaning that he is the sum of all the degrees of imperfection, and that he possesses the degrees of perfection. He has the animal side as well as the angelic side, and the aim of an educator is to so train human souls that their angelic aspect may overcome their animal side. Then if the divine power in man, which is his essential perfection, overcomes the satanic power, which is absolute imperfection, he becomes the most excellent among the creatures; but if the satanic power overcomes the divine power, he becomes the lowest of the creatures. That is why he is the end of imperfection and the beginning of perfection. Not in any other of the species in the world of existence is there such a difference, contrast, contradiction and opposition as in the species of man. Thus the reflection of the Divine Light was in man, as in Christ, and see how loved and honored He is! At the same time we see man worshiping a stone, a clod of earth or a tree. How vile he is, in that his object of worship should be the lowest existence—that is, a stone or clay, without spirit; a mountain, a forest or a tree. What shame is greater for man than to worship the lowest existences? In the same way, knowledge is a quality of man, and so is ignorance; truthfulness is a quality of man; so is falsehood; trustworthiness and treachery, justice and injustice, are qualities of man, and so forth. Briefly, all the perfections and virtues, and all the vices, are qualities of man.

Consider equally the differences between individual men. The Christ was in the form of man, and Caiaphas was in the form of man; Moses and Pharaoh, Abel and Cain, Bahá'u'lláh and Yaḥyá,[1] were men.

Man is said to be the greatest representative of God, and he is the Book of Creation because all the mysteries of beings exist in him. If he comes under the shadow of the True Educator and is rightly trained, he becomes the essence of essences, the light of lights, the spirit of spirits; he becomes the center of the divine appearances, the source of spiritual qualities, the rising-place of heavenly lights, and the receptacle of divine inspirations. If he is deprived of this education, he becomes the manifestation of satanic qualities, the sum of animal vices, and the source of all dark conditions.

The reason of the mission of the Prophets is to educate men, so that this piece of coal may become a diamond, and

1. Mírzá Yaḥyá Ṣubḥ-i-Azal, half-brother of Bahá'u'lláh, and His irreconcilable enemy.

this fruitless tree may be engrafted and yield the sweetest, most delicious fruits. When man reaches the noblest state in the world of humanity, then he can make further progress in the conditions of perfection, but not in state; for such states are limited, but the divine perfections are endless.

Both before and after putting off this material form, there is progress in perfection but not in state. So beings are consummated in perfect man. There is no other being higher than a perfect man. But man when he has reached this state can still make progress in perfections but not in state because there is no state higher than that of a perfect man to which he can transfer himself. He only progresses in the state of humanity, for the human perfections are infinite. Thus, however learned a man may be, we can imagine one more learned.

Hence, as the perfections of humanity are endless, man can also make progress in perfections after leaving this world.

65

EXPLANATION OF A VERSE IN
THE KITÁB-I-AQDAS

Question.—It is said in the Kitáb-i-Aqdas ". . . whoso is deprived thereof, hath gone astray, though he be the author of every righteous deed." What is the meaning of this verse?

Answer.—This blessed verse means that the foundation of success and salvation is the knowledge of God, and that the results of the knowledge of God are the good actions which are the fruits of faith.

If man has not this knowledge, he will be separated from God, and when this separation exists, good actions have not complete effect. This verse does not mean that the souls separated from God are equal, whether they perform good or bad actions. It signifies only that the foundation is to know God, and the good actions result from this knowledge. Nevertheless, it is certain that between the good, the sinners and the wicked who are veiled from God there is a difference. For the veiled one who has good principles and character deserves the pardon of God, while he who is a sinner, and has bad qualities and character, is deprived of the bounties and blessings of God. Herein lies the difference.

Therefore, the blessed verse means that good actions alone, without the knowledge of God, cannot be the cause of eternal salvation, everlasting success, and prosperity, and entrance into the Kingdom of God.

66

THE EXISTENCE OF THE RATIONAL SOUL
AFTER THE DEATH OF THE BODY

Question.—After the body is put aside and the spirit has obtained freedom, in what way will the rational soul exist? Let us suppose that the souls who are assisted by the bounty of the Holy Spirit attain to true existence and eternal life. But what becomes of the rational souls—that is to say, the veiled spirits?[1]

Answer.—Some think that the body is the substance and exists by itself, and that the spirit is accidental and depends upon the substance of the body, although, on the contrary, the rational soul is the substance, and the body depends upon it. If the accident—that is to say, the body—be destroyed, the substance, the spirit, remains.

Second, the rational soul, meaning the human spirit, does not descend into the body—that is to say, it does not enter it, for descent and entrance are characteristics of bodies, and the rational soul is exempt from this. The spirit never entered this body, so in quitting it, it will not be in need of an abiding-place: no, the spirit is connected with the body, as this light is with this mirror. When the mirror is clear and perfect, the light of the lamp will be apparent in it, and when the mirror becomes covered with dust or breaks, the light will disappear.

The rational soul—that is to say, the human spirit—has neither entered this body nor existed through it; so

1. "Veiled spirits" here signify rational souls, souls not possessing the spirit of faith. Cf. "Soul, Spirit and Mind," p. 208.

after the disintegration of the composition of the body, how should it be in need of a substance through which it may exist? On the contrary, the rational soul is the substance through which the body exists. The personality of the rational soul is from its beginning; it is not due to the instrumentality of the body, but the state and the personality of the rational soul may be strengthened in this world; it will make progress and will attain to the degrees of perfection, or it will remain in the lowest abyss of ignorance, veiled and deprived from beholding the signs of God.

Question.—Through what means will the spirit of man—that is to say, the rational soul—after departing from this mortal world, make progress?

Answer.—The progress of man's spirit in the divine world, after the severance of its connection with the body of dust, is through the bounty and grace of the Lord alone, or through the intercession and the sincere prayers of other human souls, or through the charities and important good works which are performed in its name.

THE IMMORTALITY OF CHILDREN

Question.—What is the condition of children who die before attaining the age of discretion or before the appointed time of birth?

Answer.—These infants are under the shadow of the favor of God; and as they have not committed any sin and are not soiled with the impurities of the world of nature, they are the centers of the manifestation of bounty, and the Eye of Compassion will be turned upon them.

67

ETERNAL LIFE AND ENTRANCE INTO THE KINGDOM OF GOD

You question about eternal life and the entrance into the Kingdom. The outer expression used for the Kingdom is heaven; but this is a comparison and similitude, not a reality or fact, for the Kingdom is not a material place; it is sanctified from time and place. It is a spiritual world, a divine world, and the center of the Sovereignty of God; it is freed from body and that which is corporeal, and it is purified and sanctified from the imaginations of the human world. To be limited to place is a property of bodies and not of spirits. Place and time surround the body, not the mind and spirit. Observe that the body of man is confined to a small place; it covers only two spans of earth. But the spirit and mind of man travel to all countries and regions—even through the limitless space of the heavens—surround all that exists, and make discoveries in the exalted spheres and infinite distances. This is because the spirit has no place; it is placeless; and for the spirit the earth and the heaven are as one since it makes discoveries in both. But the body is limited to a place and does not know that which is beyond it.

For life is of two kinds: that of the body and that of the spirit. The life of the body is material life, but the life of the spirit expresses the existence of the Kingdom, which consists in receiving the Spirit of God and becoming vivified by the breath of the Holy Spirit. Although the material life has existence, it is pure nonexistence and absolute death for the holy saints. So man exists, and this

241

stone also exists, but what a difference between the existence of man and that of the stone! Though the stone exists, in relation to the existence of man it is nonexistent.

The meaning of eternal life is the gift of the Holy Spirit, as the flower receives the gift of the season, the air, and the breezes of spring. Consider: this flower had life in the beginning like the life of the mineral; but by the coming of the season of spring, of the bounty of the clouds of the springtime, and of the heat of the glowing sun, it attained to another life of the utmost freshness, delicacy and fragrance. The first life of the flower, in comparison to the second life, is death.

The meaning is that the life of the Kingdom is the life of the spirit, the eternal life, and that it is purified from place, like the spirit of man which has no place. For if you examine the human body, you will not find a special spot or locality for the spirit, for it has never had a place; it is immaterial. It has a connection with the body like that of the sun with this mirror. The sun is not within the mirror, but it has a connection with the mirror.

In the same way the world of the Kingdom is sanctified from everything that can be perceived by the eye or by the other senses—hearing, smell, taste or touch. The mind which is in man, the existence of which is recognized—where is it in him? If you examine the body with the eye, the ear or the other senses, you will not find it; nevertheless, it exists. Therefore, the mind has no place, but it is connected with the brain. The Kingdom is also like this. In the same way love has no place, but it is connected with the heart; so the Kingdom has no place, but is connected with man.

Entrance into the Kingdom is through the love of God, through detachment, through holiness and chastity, through truthfulness, purity, steadfastness, faithfulness and the sacrifice of life.

These explanations show that man is immortal and lives

eternally. For those who believe in God, who have love of God, and faith, life is excellent—that is, it is eternal; but to those souls who are veiled from God, although they have life, it is dark, and in comparison with the life of believers it is nonexistence.

For example, the eye and the nail are living; but the life of the nail in relation to the life of the eye is nonexistent. This stone and this man both exist; but the stone in relation to the existence of man is nonexistent; it has no being; for when man dies, and his body is destroyed and annihilated, it becomes like stone and earth. Therefore, it is clear that although the mineral exists, in relation to man it is nonexistent.

In the same way, the souls who are veiled from God, although they exist in this world and in the world after death, are, in comparison with the holy existence of the children of the Kingdom of God, nonexisting and separated from God.

68

FATE

Question. —Is the predestination which is mentioned in the Holy Books a decreed thing? If so, is not the effort to avoid it useless?

Answer. —Fate is of two kinds: one is decreed, and the other is conditional or impending. The decreed fate is that which cannot change or be altered, and conditional fate is that which may occur. So, for this lamp, the decreed fate is that the oil burns and will be consumed; therefore, its eventual extinction is a decree which it is impossible to alter or to change because it is a decreed fate. In the same way, in the body of man a power of life has been created, and as soon as it is destroyed and ended, the body will certainly be decomposed, so when the oil in this lamp is burnt and finished, the lamp will undoubtedly become extinguished.

But conditional fate may be likened to this: while there is still oil, a violent wind blows on the lamp, which extinguishes it. This is a conditional fate. It is wise to avoid it, to protect oneself from it, to be cautious and circumspect. But the decreed fate, which is like the finishing of the oil in the lamp, cannot be altered, changed nor delayed. It must happen; it is inevitable that the lamp will become extinguished.

69

THE INFLUENCE OF THE STARS

Question.—Have the stars of the heavens any influence upon the human soul, or have they not?

Answer.—Some of the celestial stars have a clear and apparent material effect upon the terrestrial globe and the earthly beings, which needs no explanation. Consider the sun, which through the aid and the providence of God develops the earth and all earthly beings. Without the light and heat of the sun, all the earthly creatures would be entirely nonexistent.

With regard to the spiritual influence of stars, though this influence of stars in the human world may appear strange, still, if you reflect deeply upon this subject, you will not be so much surprised at it. My meaning is not, however, that the decrees which the astrologers of former times inferred from the movements of the stars corresponded to occurrences; for the decrees of those former astrologers were forms of imagination which were originated by Egyptian, Assyrian and Chaldean priests; nay, rather, they were due to the fancies of Hindus, to the myths of the Greeks, Romans and other star worshipers. But I mean that this limitless universe is like the human body, all the members of which are connected and linked with one another with the greatest strength. How much the organs, the members and the parts of the body of man are intermingled and connected for mutual aid and help, and how much they influence one another! In the same way, the parts of this infinite universe have their members and elements connected with one another, and influence one another spiritually and materially.

For example, the eye sees, and all the body is affected; the ear hears, and all the members of the body are moved. Of this there is no doubt; and the universe is like a living person. Moreover, the connection which exists between the members of beings must necessarily have an effect and impression, whether it be material or spiritual.

For those who deny spiritual influence upon material things we mention this brief example: wonderful sounds and tones, melodies and charming voices, are accidents which affect the air—for sound is the term for vibrations of the air—and by these vibrations the nerves of the tympanum of the ear are affected, and hearing results. Now reflect that the vibration of the air, which is an accident of no importance, attracts and exhilarates the spirit of man and has great effect upon him: it makes him weep or laugh; perhaps it will influence him to such a degree that he will throw himself into danger. Therefore, see the connection which exists between the spirit of man and the atmospheric vibration, so that the movement of the air becomes the cause of transporting him from one state to another, and of entirely overpowering him; it will deprive him of patience and tranquillity. Consider how strange this is, for nothing comes forth from the singer which enters into the listener; nevertheless, a great spiritual effect is produced. Therefore, surely so great a connection between beings must have spiritual effect and influence.

It has been mentioned that the members and parts of man affect and influence one another. For example, the eye sees; the heart is affected. The ear hears; and the spirit is influenced. The heart is at rest; the thoughts become serene, and for all the members of man's body a pleasant condition is realized. What a connection and what an agreement is this! Since this connection, this spiritual effect and this influence, exists between the members of the body of man, who is only one of many finite beings, certainly between these universal and infinite beings there will also be a spiritual and material connection. Although by existing rules and actual science these connections cannot be discovered, nevertheless, their existence between all beings is certain and absolute.

To conclude: the beings, whether great or small, are connected with one another by the perfect wisdom of God, and affect and influence one another. If it were not so, in the universal system and the general arrangement of existence, there would be disorder and imperfection. But as beings are connected one with another with the greatest strength, they are in order in their places and perfect.

This subject is worthy of examination.

70

FREE WILL

Question.—Is man a free agent in all his actions, or is he compelled and constrained?

Answer.—This question is one of the most important and abstruse of divine problems. If God wills, another day, at the beginning of dinner, we will undertake the explanation of this subject in detail; now we will explain it briefly, in a few words, as follows. Some things are subject to the free will of man, such as justice, equity, tyranny and injustice, in other words, good and evil actions; it is evident and clear that these actions are, for the most part, left to the will of man. But there are certain things to which man is forced and compelled, such as sleep, death, sickness, decline of power, injuries and misfortunes; these are not subject to the will of man, and he is not responsible for them, for he is compelled to endure them. But in the choice of good and bad actions he is free, and he commits them according to his own will.

For example, if he wishes, he can pass his time in praising God, or he can be occupied with other thoughts. He can be an enkindled light through the fire of the love of God, and a philanthropist loving the world, or he can be a hater of mankind, and engrossed with material things. He can be just or cruel. These actions and these deeds are subject to the control of the will of man himself; consequently, he is responsible for them.

Now another question arises. Man is absolutely helpless and dependent, since might and power belong especially to God. Both exaltation and humiliation depend upon the good pleasure and the will of the Most High.

It is said in the New Testament that God is like a potter who makes "one vessel unto honour, and another unto dishonour."[1] Now the dishonored vessel has no right to find fault with the potter saying, "Why did you not make me a precious cup, which is passed from hand to hand?" The meaning of this verse is that the states of beings are different. That which is in the lowest state of existence, like the mineral, has no right to complain, saying, "O God, why have You not given me the vegetable perfections?" In the same way, the plant has no right to complain that it has been deprived of the perfections of the animal world. Also it is not befitting for the animal to complain of the want of the human perfections. No, all these things are perfect in their own degree, and they must strive after the perfections of their own degree. The inferior beings, as we have said, have neither the right to, nor the fitness for, the states of the superior perfections. No, their progress must be in their own state.

Also the inaction or the movement of man depend upon the assistance of God. If he is not aided, he is not able to do either good or evil. But when the help of existence comes from the Generous Lord, he is able to do both good and evil; but if the help is cut off, he remains absolutely helpless. This is why in the Holy Books they speak of the help and assistance of God. So this condition is like that of a ship which is moved by the power of the wind or steam; if this power ceases, the ship cannot move at all. Nevertheless, the rudder of the ship turns it to either side, and the power of the steam moves it in the desired direction. If it is directed to the east, it goes to the east; or if it is directed to the west, it goes to the west. This motion does not come from the ship; no, it comes from the wind or the steam.

1. Rom. 9:21.

In the same way, in all the action or inaction of man, he receives power from the help of God; but the choice of good or evil belongs to the man himself. So if a king should appoint someone to be the governor of a city, and should grant him the power of authority, and should show him the paths of justice and injustice according to the laws—if then this governor should commit injustice, although he should act by the authority and power of the king, the latter would be absolved from injustice. But if he should act with justice, he would do it also through the authority of the king, who would be pleased and satisfied.

That is to say, though the choice of good and evil belongs to man, under all circumstances he is dependent upon the sustaining help of life, which comes from the Omnipotent. The Kingdom of God is very great, and all are captives in the grasp of His Power. The servant cannot do anything by his own will; God is powerful, omnipotent, and the Helper of all beings.

This question has become clearly explained. Salutations!

71

VISIONS AND COMMUNICATION
WITH SPIRITS

Question. —Some people believe that they achieve spiritual discoveries—that is to say, that they converse with spirits. What kind of communion is this?

Answer. —Spiritual discoveries are of two kinds: one kind is of the imagination and is only the assertion of a few people; the other kind resembles inspiration, and this is real—such are the revelations of Isaiah, of Jeremiah and of St. John, which are real.

Reflect that man's power of thought consists of two kinds. One kind is true, when it agrees with a determined truth. Such conceptions find realization in the exterior world; such are accurate opinions, correct theories, scientific discoveries and inventions.

The other kind of conceptions is made up of vain thoughts and useless ideas which yield neither fruit nor result, and which have no reality. No, they surge like the waves of the sea of imaginations, and they pass away like idle dreams.

In the same way, there are two sorts of spiritual discoveries. One is the revelations of the Prophets, and the spiritual discoveries of the elect. The visions of the Prophets are not dreams; no, they are spiritual discoveries and have reality. They say, for example, "I saw a person in a certain form, and I said such a thing, and he gave such an answer." This vision is in the world of wakefulness, and not in that of sleep. Nay, it is a spiritual discovery which is expressed as if it were the appearance of a vision.

The other kind of spiritual discoveries is made up of
pure imaginations, but these imaginations become embodied in such a way that many simple-hearted people believe that they have a reality. That which proves it clearly
is that from this controlling of spirits no result or fruit has
ever been produced. No, they are but narratives and
stories.

Know that the reality of man embraces the realities of
things, and discovers the verities, properties and secrets of
things. So all these arts, wonders, sciences and knowledge
have been discovered by the human reality. At one time
these sciences, knowledge, wonders and arts were hidden
and concealed secrets; then gradually the human reality
discovered them and brought them from the realm of the
invisible to the plane of the visible. Therefore, it is evident
that the reality of man embraces things. Thus it is in
Europe and discovers America; it is on the earth, and it
makes discoveries in the heavens. It is the revealer of the
secrets of things, and it is the knower of the realities of that
which exists. These discoveries corresponding to the
reality are similar to revelation, which is spiritual comprehension, divine inspiration and the association of
human spirits. For instance, the Prophet says, "I saw, I
said, I heard such a thing." It is, therefore, evident that the
spirit has great perception without the intermediary of
any of the five senses, such as the eyes or ears. Among
spiritual souls there are spiritual understandings, discoveries, a communion which is purified from imagination
and fancy, an association which is sanctified from time and
place. So it is written in the Gospel that, on Mount Tabor,
Moses and Elias came to Christ, and it is evident that this
was not a material meeting. It was a spiritual condition
which is expressed as a physical meeting.

The other sort of converse, presence and communications of spirits is but imagination and fancy, which only
appears to have reality.

The mind and the thought of man sometimes discover truths, and from this thought and discovery signs and results are produced. This thought has a foundation. But many things come to the mind of man which are like the waves of the sea of imaginations; they have no fruit, and no result comes from them. In the same way, man sees in the world of sleep a vision which becomes exactly realized; at another time, he sees a dream which has absolutely no result.

What we mean is that this state, which we call the converse and communications of spirits, is of two kinds: one is simply imaginary, and the other is like the visions which are mentioned in the Holy Book, such as the revelations of St. John and Isaiah and the meeting of Christ with Moses and Elias. These are real, and produce wonderful effects in the minds and thoughts of men, and cause their hearts to be attracted.

72

HEALING BY SPIRITUAL MEANS

Question.—Some people heal the sick by spiritual means—that is to say, without medicine. How is this?

Answer.—Know that there are four kinds of curing and healing without medicine. Two are due to material causes, and two to spiritual causes.

Of the two kinds of material healing, one is due to the fact that in man both health and sickness are contagious. The contagion of disease is violent and rapid, while that of health is extremely weak and slow. If two bodies are brought into contact with each other, it is certain that microbic particles will pass from one to the other. In the same way that disease is transferred from one body to another with rapid and strong contagion, it may be that the strong health of a healthy man will alleviate a very slight malady in a sick person. That is to say, the contagion of disease is violent and has a rapid effect, while that of health is very slow and has a small effect, and it is only in very slight diseases that it has even this small effect. The strong power of a healthy body can overcome a slight weakness of a sick body, and health results. This is one kind of healing.

The other kind of healing without medicine is through the magnetic force which acts from one body on another and becomes the cause of cure. This force also has only a slight effect. Sometimes one can benefit a sick person by placing one's hand upon his head or upon his heart. Why? Because of the effect of the magnetism, and of the mental impression made upon the sick person, which causes the disease to vanish. But this effect is also very slight and weak.

Of the two other kinds of healing which are spiritual—that is to say, where the means of cure is a spiritual power—one results from the entire concentration of the mind of a strong person upon a sick person, when the latter expects with all his concentrated faith that a cure will be effected from the spiritual power of the strong person, to such an extent that there will be a cordial connection between the strong person and the invalid. The strong person makes every effort to cure the sick patient, and the sick patient is then sure of receiving a cure. From the effect of these mental impressions an excitement of the nerves is produced, and this impression and this excitement of the nerves will become the cause of the recovery of the sick person. So when a sick person has a strong desire and intense hope for something and hears suddenly the tidings of its realization, a nervous excitement is produced which will make the malady entirely disappear. In the same way, if a cause of terror suddenly occurs, perhaps an excitement may be produced in the nerves of a strong person which will immediately cause a malady. The cause of the sickness will be no material thing, for that person has not eaten anything, and nothing harmful has touched him; the excitement of the nerves is then the only cause of the illness. In the same way the sudden realization of a chief desire will give such joy that the nerves will be excited by it, and this excitement may produce health.

To conclude, the complete and perfect connection between the spiritual doctor and the sick person—that is, a connection of such a kind that the spiritual doctor entirely concentrates himself, and all the attention of the sick person is given to the spiritual doctor from whom he expects to realize health—causes an excitement of the nerves, and health is produced. But all this has effect only to a certain extent, and that not always. For if someone is afflicted with a very violent disease, or is wounded, these means will not remove the disease nor close and heal the wound—that is to say, these means have no power in severe maladies, unless the constitution helps, because a strong constitution often overcomes disease. This is the third kind of healing.

But the fourth kind of healing is produced through the power of the Holy Spirit. This does not depend on contact, nor on sight, nor upon presence; it is not dependent upon any condition. Whether the disease be light or severe, whether there be a contact of bodies or not, whether a personal connection be established between the sick person and the healer or not, this healing takes place through the power of the Holy Spirit.

73

HEALING BY MATERIAL MEANS

YESTERDAY at table we spoke of curative treatment and spiritual healing, which consists in treating maladies through the spiritual powers.

Now let us speak of material healing. The science of medicine is still in a condition of infancy; it has not reached maturity. But when it has reached this point, cures will be performed by things which are not repulsive to the smell and taste of man—that is to say, by aliments, fruits and vegetables which are agreeable to the taste and have an agreeable smell. For the provoking cause of disease—that is to say, the cause of the entrance of disease into the human body—is either a physical one or is the effect of excitement of the nerves.

But the principal causes of disease are physical, for the human body is composed of numerous elements, but in the measure of an especial equilibrium. As long as this equilibrium is maintained, man is preserved from disease; but if this essential balance, which is the pivot of the constitution, is disturbed, the constitution is disordered, and disease will supervene.

For instance, there is a decrease in one of the constituent ingredients of the body of man, and in another there is an increase; so the proportion of the equilibrium is disturbed, and disease occurs. For example, one ingredient must be one thousand grams in weight, and another five grams, in order that the equilibrium be maintained. The part which is one thousand grams diminishes to seven hundred grams, and that which is five grams augments until the measure of the equilibrium is disturbed; then disease occurs. When by remedies and treatments the equilibrium is reestablished, the disease is banished. So if the sugar constituent increases, the health is impaired; and when the doctor forbids sweet and starchy foods, the sugar constituent diminishes, the equilibrium is reestablished, and the disease is driven off. Now the readjustment of these constituents of the human body is obtained by two means—either by medicines or by aliments; and when the constitution has recovered its equilibrium, disease is banished. All the elements that are combined in man exist also in vegetables; therefore, if one of the constituents which compose the body of man diminishes, and he partakes of foods in which there is much of that diminished constituent, then the equilibrium will be established, and a cure will be obtained. So long as the aim is the readjustment of the constituents of the body, it can be effected either by medicine or by food.

The majority of the diseases which overtake man also overtake the animal, but the animal is not cured by drugs. In the mountains, as in the wilderness, the animal's physician is the power of taste and smell. The sick animal smells the plants that grow in the wilderness; he eats those that are sweet and fragrant to his smell and taste, and is cured. The cause of his healing is this. When the sugar ingredient has become diminished in his constitution, he begins to long for sweet things; therefore, he eats an herb with a sweet taste, for nature urges and guides him; its smell and taste please him, and he eats it. The sugar ingredient in his nature will be increased, and health will be restored.

It is, therefore, evident that it is possible to cure by foods, aliments and fruits; but as today the science of medicine is imperfect, this fact is not yet fully grasped. When the science of medicine reaches perfection, treatment will be given by foods, aliments, fragrant fruits and vegetables, and by various waters, hot and cold in temperature.

This discourse is brief; but, if God wills, at another time, when the occasion is suitable, this question will be more fully explained.

Part Five

MISCELLANEOUS SUBJECTS

74

THE NONEXISTENCE OF EVIL

THE true explanation of this subject is very difficult. Know that beings are of two kinds: material and spiritual, those perceptible to the senses and those intellectual.

Things which are sensible are those which are perceived by the five exterior senses; thus those outward existences which the eyes see are called sensible. Intellectual things are those which have no outward existence but are conceptions of the mind. For example, mind itself is an intellectual thing which has no outward existence. All man's characteristics and qualities form an intellectual existence and are not sensible.

Briefly, the intellectual realities, such as all the qualities and admirable perfections of man, are purely good, and exist. Evil is simply their nonexistence. So ignorance is the want of knowledge; error is the want of guidance; forgetfulness is the want of memory; stupidity is the want of good sense. All these things have no real existence.

In the same way, the sensible realities are absolutely good, and evil is due to their nonexistence—that is to say, blindness is the want of sight, deafness is the want of hearing, poverty is the want of wealth, illness is the want of health, death is the want of life, and weakness is the want of strength.

Nevertheless a doubt occurs to the mind—that is, scorpions and serpents are poisonous. Are they good or evil, for they are existing beings? Yes, a scorpion is evil in relation to man; a serpent is evil in relation to man; but in relation to themselves they are not evil, for their poison is their weapon, and by their sting they defend themselves. But as the elements of their poison do not agree with our elements—that is to say, as there is antagonism between these different elements, therefore, this antagonism is evil; but in reality as regards themselves they are good.

The epitome of this discourse is that it is possible that one thing in relation to another may be evil, and at the same time within the limits of its proper being it may not be evil. Then it is proved that there is no evil in existence; all that God created He created good. This evil is nothingness; so death is the absence of life. When man no longer receives life, he dies. Darkness is the absence of light: when there is no light, there is darkness. Light is an existing thing, but darkness is nonexistent. Wealth is an existing thing, but poverty is nonexisting.

Then it is evident that all evils return to nonexistence. Good exists; evil is nonexistent.

75

TWO KINDS OF TORMENT

KNOW that there are two kinds of torment: subtile and gross. For example, ignorance itself is a torment, but it is a subtile torment; indifference to God is itself a torment; so also are falsehood, cruelty and treachery. All the imperfections are torments, but they are subtile torments. Certainly for an intelligent man death is better than sin, and a cut tongue is better than lying or calumny.

The other kind of torment is gross—such as penalties, imprisonment, beating, expulsion and banishment. But for the people of God separation from God is the greatest torment of all.

76

THE JUSTICE AND MERCY OF GOD

Know that to do justice is to give to everyone according to his deserts. For example, when a workman labors from morning until evening, justice requires that he shall be paid his wages; but when he has done no work and taken no trouble, he is given a gift: this is bounty. If you give alms and gifts to a poor man although he has taken no trouble for you, nor done anything to deserve it, this is bounty. So Christ besought forgiveness for his murderers: this is called bounty.

Now the question of the good or evil of things is determined by reason or by law. Some believe that it is determined by law; such are the Jews, who, believing all the commandments of the Pentateuch to be absolutely obligatory, regard them as matters of law, not of reason. Thus they say that one of the commandments of the Pentateuch is that it is unlawful to partake of meat and butter together because it is *taref*, and *taref* in Hebrew means unclean, as *kosher* means clean. This, they say, is a question of law and not of reason.

But the theologians think that the good and evil of things depend upon both reason and law. The chief foundation of the prohibition of murder, theft, treachery, falsehood, hypocrisy and cruelty, is reason. Every intelligent man comprehends that murder, theft, treachery, falsehood, hypocrisy and cruelty are evil and reprehensible; for if you prick a man with a thorn, he will cry out, complain and groan; so it is evident that he will understand that murder according to reason is evil and reprehensible. If he commits a murder, he will be responsible, whether the renown of the Prophet has reached him or not; for it is reason that formulates the reprehensible character of the action. When a man commits this bad action, he will surely be responsible.

But in a place where the commands of a Prophet are not known, and where the people do not act in conformity with the divine instructions, such as the command of Christ to return good for evil, but act according to the desires of nature—that is, if they torment those who torment them—from the point of view of religion they are excused because the divine command has not been delivered to them. Though they do not deserve mercy and beneficence, nevertheless, God treats them with mercy and forgives them.

Now vengeance, according to reason, is also blameworthy, because through vengeance no good result is gained by the avenger. So if a man strikes another, and he who is struck takes revenge by returning the blow, what advantage will he gain? Will this be a balm for his wound or a remedy for his pain? No, God forbid! In truth the two actions are the same: both are injuries; the only difference is that one occurred first, and the other afterward. Therefore, if he who is struck forgives, nay, if he acts in a manner contrary to that which has been used toward him, this is laudable. The law of the community will punish the aggressor but will not take revenge. This punishment has for its end to warn, to protect and to oppose cruelty and transgression so that other men may not be tyrannical.

But if he who has been struck pardons and forgives, he shows the greatest mercy. This is worthy of admiration.

77

THE RIGHT METHOD OF TREATING CRIMINALS

Question. —Should a criminal be punished, or forgiven and his crime overlooked?

Answer. —There are two sorts of retributory punishments. One is vengeance, the other, chastisement. Man has not the right to take vengeance, but the community has the right to punish the criminal; and this punishment is intended to warn and to prevent so that no other person will dare to commit a like crime. This punishment is for the protection of man's rights, but it is not vengeance; vengeance appeases the anger of the heart by opposing one evil to another. This is not allowable, for man has not the right to take vengeance. But if criminals were entirely forgiven, the order of the world would be upset. So punishment is one of the essential necessities for the safety of communities, but he who is oppressed by a transgressor has not the right to take vengeance. On the contrary, he should forgive and pardon, for this is worthy of the world of man.

The communities must punish the oppressor, the murderer, the malefactor, so as to warn and restrain others from committing like crimes. But the most essential thing is that the people must be educated in such a way that no crimes will be committed; for it is possible to educate the masses so effectively that they will avoid and shrink from perpetrating crimes, so that the crime itself will appear to them as the greatest chastisement, the utmost condemnation and torment. Therefore, no crimes which require punishment will be committed.

We must speak of things that are possible of performance in this world. There are many theories and high ideas on this subject, but they are not practicable; consequently, we must speak of things that are feasible.

For example, if someone oppresses, injures and wrongs another, and the wronged man retaliates, this is vengeance and is censurable. If the son of 'Amr kills the son of Zayd, Zayd has not the right to kill the son of 'Amr; if he does so, this is vengeance. If 'Amr dishonors Zayd, the latter has not the right to dishonor 'Amr; if he does so, this is vengeance, and it is very reprehensible. No, rather he must return good for evil, and not only forgive, but also, if possible, be of service to his oppressor. This conduct is worthy of man: for what advantage does he gain by vengeance? The two actions are equivalent; if one action is reprehensible, both are reprehensible. The only difference is that one was committed first, the other later.

But the community has the right of defense and of self-protection; moreover, the community has no hatred nor animosity for the murderer: it imprisons or punishes him merely for the protection and security of others. It is not for the purpose of taking vengeance upon the murderer, but for the purpose of inflicting a punishment by which the community will be protected. If the community and the inheritors of the murdered one were to forgive and return good for evil, the cruel would be continually ill-treating others, and assassinations would continually occur. Vicious people, like wolves, would destroy the sheep of God. The community has no ill-will and rancor in the infliction of punishment, and it does not desire to appease the anger of the heart; its purpose is by punishment to protect others so that no atrocious actions may be committed.

Thus when Christ said: "Whosoever shall smite thee on the right cheek, turn to him the left one also,"[1] it was for the purpose of teaching men not to take personal revenge. He did not mean that, if a wolf should fall upon a flock of sheep and wish to destroy it, the wolf should be encouraged to do so. No, if Christ had known that a wolf had entered the fold and was about to destroy the sheep, most certainly He would have prevented it.

As forgiveness is one of the attributes of the Merciful One, so also justice is one of the attributes of the Lord. The tent of existence is upheld upon the pillar of justice and not upon forgiveness. The continuance of mankind depends upon justice and not upon forgiveness. So if, at present, the law of pardon were practiced in all countries, in a short time the world would be disordered, and the foundations of human life would crumble. For example, if the governments of Europe had not withstood the notorious Attila, he would not have left a single living man.

Some people are like bloodthirsty wolves: if they see no punishment forthcoming, they will kill men merely for pleasure and diversion. One of the tyrants of Persia killed his tutor merely for the sake of making merry, for mere fun and sport. The famous Mutavakkil, the Abbasid, having summoned his ministers, councillors and functionaries to his presence, let loose a box full of scorpions in the assembly and forbade anyone to move. When the scorpions stung those present, he burst forth into boisterous laughter.

To recapitulate: the constitution of the communities depends upon justice, not upon forgiveness. Then what Christ meant by forgiveness and pardon is not that, when nations attack you, burn your homes, plunder your goods, assault your wives, children and relatives, and violate your honor, you should be submissive in the presence of these tyrannical foes and allow them to perform all their

1. Cf. Matt. 5:39.

cruelties and oppressions. No, the words of Christ refer to the conduct of two individuals toward each other: if one person assaults another, the injured one should forgive him. But the communities must protect the rights of man. So if someone assaults, injures, oppresses and wounds me, I will offer no resistance, and I will forgive him. But if a person wishes to assault Siyyid Manshadí,[1] certainly I will prevent him. Although for the malefactor noninterference is apparently a kindness, it would be an oppression to Manshadí. If at this moment a wild Arab were to enter this place with a drawn sword, wishing to assault, wound and kill you, most assuredly I would prevent him. If I abandoned you to the Arab, that would not be justice but injustice. But if he injure me personally, I would forgive him.

One thing remains to be said: it is that the communities are day and night occupied in making penal laws, and in preparing and organizing instruments and means of punishment. They build prisons, make chains and fetters, arrange places of exile and banishment, and different kinds of hardships and tortures, and think by these means to discipline criminals, whereas, in reality, they are causing destruction of morals and perversion of characters. The community, on the contrary, ought day and night to strive and endeavor with the utmost zeal and effort to accomplish the education of men, to cause them day by day to progress and to increase in science and knowledge, to acquire virtues, to gain good morals and to avoid vices, so that crimes may not occur. At the present time the contrary prevails; the community is always thinking of enforcing the penal laws, and of preparing means of punishment, instruments of death and chastisement, places for imprisonment and banishment; and they expect crimes to be committed. This has a demoralizing effect.

But if the community would endeavor to educate the

1. A Bahá'í sitting with us at table.

masses, day by day knowledge and sciences would increase, the understanding would be broadened, the sensibilities developed, customs would become good, and morals normal; in one word, in all these classes of perfections there would be progress, and there would be fewer crimes.

It has been ascertained that among civilized peoples crime is less frequent than among uncivilized—that is to say, among those who have acquired the true civilization, which is divine civilization—the civilization of those who unite all the spiritual and material perfections. As ignorance is the cause of crimes, the more knowledge and science increases, the more crimes will diminish. Consider how often murder occurs among the barbarians of Africa; they even kill one another in order to eat each other's flesh and blood! Why do not such savageries occur in Switzerland? The reason is evident: it is because education and virtues prevent them.

Therefore, the communities must think of preventing crimes, rather than of rigorously punishing them.

78

STRIKES

You have questioned me about strikes. This question is and will be for a long time the subject of great difficulties. Strikes are due to two causes. One is the extreme greed and rapacity of the manufacturers and industrialists; the other, the excesses, the avidity and intransigence of the workmen and artisans. It is, therefore, necessary to remedy these two causes.

But the principal cause of these difficulties lies in the laws of the present civilization; for they lead to a small number of individuals accumulating incomparable fortunes, beyond their needs, while the greater number remain destitute, stripped and in the greatest misery. This is contrary to justice, to humanity, to equity; it is the height of iniquity, the opposite to what causes divine satisfaction.

This contrast is peculiar to the world of man: with other creatures—that is to say, with nearly all animals—there is a kind of justice and equality. Thus equality exists in a shepherd's flock and in a herd of deer in the country. Likewise, among the birds of the prairie, of the plain, of the hills or of the orchard, and among every kind of animal some kind of equality prevails. With them such a difference in the means of existence is not to be found; so they live in the most complete peace and joy.

It is quite otherwise with the human species, which persists in the greatest error, and in absolute iniquity. Consider an individual who has amassed treasures by colonizing a country for his profit: he has obtained an incomparable fortune and has secured profits and incomes which flow like a river, while a hundred thousand unfortunate people, weak and powerless, are in need of a mouthful of bread. There is neither equality nor benevolence. So you see that general peace and joy are destroyed, and the welfare of humanity is negated to such an extent as to make fruitless the lives of many. For fortune, honors, commerce, industry are in the hands of some industrialists, while other people are submitted to quite a series of difficulties and to limitless troubles: they have neither advantages, nor profits, nor comforts, nor peace.

Then rules and laws should be established to regulate the excessive fortunes of certain private individuals and meet the needs of millions of the poor masses; thus a certain moderation would be obtained. However, absolute equality is just as impossible, for absolute equality in fortunes, honors, commerce, agriculture, industry would end in disorderliness, in chaos, in disorganization of the means of existence, and in universal disappointment: the order of the community would be quite destroyed. Thus difficulties will also arise when unjustified equality is imposed. It is, therefore, preferable for moderation to be established by means of laws and regulations to hinder the constitution of the excessive fortunes of certain individuals, and to protect the essential needs of the masses. For instance, the manufacturers and the industrialists heap up a treasure each day, and the poor artisans do not gain their daily sustenance: that is the height of iniquity, and no just man can accept it. Therefore, laws and regulations should be established which would permit the workmen to receive from the factory owner their wages and a share in the fourth or the fifth part of the profits, according to the capacity of the factory; or in some other way the body of workmen and the manufacturers should share equitably the profits and advantages. Indeed, the capital and management come from the owner of the factory, and the work and labor, from the body of the workmen. Either the workmen should receive wages which assure them an adequate support and, when they cease work, becoming feeble or helpless, they should have sufficient benefits from the income of the industry; or the wages should be high enough to satisfy the workmen with the amount they receive so that they may themselves be able to put a little aside for days of want and helplessness.

When matters will be thus fixed, the owner of the factory will no longer put aside daily a treasure which he has absolutely no need of (for, if the fortune is disproportionate, the capitalist succumbs under a formidable burden and gets into the greatest difficulties and troubles; the administration of an excessive fortune is very difficult and exhausts man's natural strength). And the workmen and artisans will no longer be in the greatest misery and want; they will no longer be submitted to the worst privations at the end of their life.

It is, then, clear and evident that the repartition of excessive fortunes among a small number of individuals, while the masses are in need, is an iniquity and an injustice. In the same way, absolute equality would be an obstacle to life, to welfare, to order and to the peace of humanity. In such a question moderation is preferable. It lies in the capitalists' being moderate in the acquisition of their profits, and in their having a consideration for the welfare of the poor and needy—that is to say, that the workmen and artisans receive a fixed and established daily wage—and have a share in the general profits of the factory.

It would be well, with regard to the common rights of manufacturers, workmen and artisans, that laws be established, giving moderate profits to manufacturers, and to workmen the necessary means of existence and security for the future. Thus when they become feeble and cease working, get old and helpless, or leave behind children under age, they and their children will not be annihilated by excess of poverty. And it is from the income of the factory itself, to which they have a right, that they will derive a share, however small, toward their livelihood.

In the same way, the workmen should no longer make excessive claims and revolt, nor demand beyond their rights; they should no longer go out on strike; they should be obedient and submissive and not ask for exorbitant wages. But the mutual and reasonable rights of both associated parties will be legally fixed and established according to custom by just and impartial laws. In case one of the two parties should transgress, the court of justice should condemn the transgressor, and the executive branch should enforce the verdict; thus order will be reestablished, and the difficulties, settled. The interference of courts of justice and of the government in difficulties pending between manufacturers and workmen is legal, for the reason that current affairs between workmen and manufacturers cannot be compared with ordinary affairs between private persons, which do not concern the public, and with which the government should not occupy itself. In reality, although they appear to be private matters, these difficulties between the two parties produce a detriment to the public; for commerce, industry, agriculture and the general affairs of the country are all intimately linked together. If one of these suffers an abuse, the detriment affects the mass. Thus the difficulties between workmen and manufacturers become a cause of general detriment.

The court of justice and the government have, therefore, the right of interference. When a difficulty occurs between two individuals with reference to private rights, it is necessary for a third to settle the question. This is the part of the government. Then the problem of strikes— which cause troubles in the country and are often connected with the excessive vexations of the workmen, as well as with the rapacity of manufacturers—how could it remain neglected?

Good God! Is it possible that, seeing one of his fellow-creatures starving, destitute of everything, a man can rest and live comfortably in his luxurious mansion? He who meets another in the greatest misery, can he enjoy his fortune? That is why, in the Religion of God, it is prescribed and established that wealthy men each year give over a certain part of their fortune for the maintenance of the poor and unfortunate. That is the foundation of the Religion of God and is binding upon all.

And as man in this way is not forced nor obliged by the government, but is by the natural tendency of his good heart voluntarily and radiantly showing benevolence toward the poor, such a deed is much praised, approved and pleasing.

Such is the meaning of the good works in the Divine Books and Tablets.

79

THE REALITY OF THE EXTERIOR WORLD

CERTAIN sophists think that existence is an illusion, that each being is an absolute illusion which has no existence—in other words, that the existence of beings is like a mirage, or like the reflection of an image in water or in a mirror, which is only an appearance having in itself no principle, foundation or reality.

This theory is erroneous; for though the existence of beings in relation to the existence of God is an illusion, nevertheless, in the condition of being it has a real and certain existence. It is futile to deny this. For example, the existence of the mineral in comparison with that of man is nonexistence, for when man is apparently annihilated, his body becomes mineral; but the mineral has existence in the mineral world. Therefore, it is evident that earth, in relation to the existence of man, is nonexistent, and its existence is illusory; but in relation to the mineral it exists.

In the same manner the existence of beings in comparison with the existence of God is but illusion and nothingness; it is an appearance, like the image reflected in a mirror. But though an image which is seen in a mirror is an illusion, the source and the reality of that illusory image is the person reflected, whose face appears in the mirror. Briefly, the reflection in relation to the person reflected is an illusion.

Then it is evident that although beings in relation to the existence of God have no existence, but are like the mirage or the reflections in the mirror, yet in their own degree they exist.

That is why those who were heedless and denied God were said by Christ to be dead, although they were apparently living; in relation to the people of faith they were dead, blind, deaf and dumb. This is what Christ meant when He said, "Let the dead bury their dead."[1]

1. Matt. 8:22.

80

REAL PREEXISTENCE

Question.—How many kinds of preexistence and of phenomena are there?

Answer.—Some sages and philosophers believe that there are two kinds of preexistence: essential preexistence and preexistence of time. Phenomena are also of two kinds, essential phenomena and that of time.

Essential preexistence is an existence which is not preceded by a cause, but essential phenomena are preceded by causes. Preexistence of time is without beginning, but the phenomena of time have beginnings and endings; for the existence of everything depends upon four causes— the efficient cause, the matter, the form and the final cause. For example, this chair has a maker who is a carpenter, a substance which is wood, a form which is that of a chair, and a purpose which is that it is to be used as a seat. Therefore, this chair is essentially phenomenal, for it is preceded by a cause, and its existence depends upon causes. This is called the essential and really phenomenal.

Now this world of existence in relation to its maker is a real phenomenon. As the body is sustained by the spirit, it is in relation to the spirit an essential phenomenon. The spirit is independent of the body, and in relation to it the spirit is an essential preexistence. Though the rays are always inseparable from the sun, nevertheless, the sun is preexistent and the rays are phenomenal, for the existence of the rays depends upon that of the sun. But the existence of the sun does not depend upon that of the rays, for the sun is the giver and the rays are the gift.

The second proposition is that existence and nonexistence are both relative. If it be said that such a thing came into existence from nonexistence, this does not refer to absolute nonexistence, but means that its former condition in relation to its actual condition was nothingness. For absolute nothingness cannot find existence, as it has not the capacity of existence. Man, like the mineral, is existing; but the existence of the mineral in relation to that of man is nothingness, for when the body of man is annihilated it becomes dust and mineral. But when dust progresses into the human world, and this dead body becomes living, man becomes existing. Though the dust—that is to say, the mineral—has existence in its own condition, in relation to man it is nothingness. Both exist, but the existence of dust and mineral, in relation to man, is nonexistence and nothingness; for when man becomes nonexistent, he returns to dust and mineral.

Therefore, though the world of contingency exists, in relation to the existence of God it is nonexistent and nothingness. Man and dust both exist, but how great the difference between the existence of the mineral and that of man! The one in relation to the other is nonexistence. In the same way, the existence of creation in relation to the existence of God is nonexistence. Thus it is evident and clear that although the beings exist, in relation to God and to the Word of God they are nonexistent. This is the beginning and the end of the Word of God, Who says: "I am Alpha and Omega"; for He is the beginning and the end of Bounty. The Creator always had a creation; the rays have always shone and gleamed from the reality of the sun, for without the rays the sun would be opaque darkness. The names and attributes of God require the existence of beings, and the Eternal Bounty does not cease. If it were to, it would be contrary to the perfections of God.

81

REINCARNATION

Question.—What is the truth of the question of reincarnation, which is believed by some people?

Answer.—The object of what we are about to say is to explain the reality—not to deride the beliefs of other people; it is only to explain the facts; that is all. We do not oppose anyone's ideas, nor do we approve of criticism.

Know, then, that those who believe in reincarnation are of two classes: one class does not believe in the spiritual punishments and rewards of the other world, and they suppose that man by reincarnation and return to this world gains rewards and recompenses; they consider heaven and hell to be restricted to this world and do not speak of the existence of the other world. Among these there are two further divisions. One division thinks that man sometimes returns to this world in the form of an animal in order to undergo severe punishment and that, after enduring this painful torment, he will be released from the animal world and will come again into the human world; this is called transmigration. The other division thinks that from the human world one again returns to the human world, and that by this return rewards and punishments for a former life are obtained; this is called reincarnation. Neither of these classes speak of any other world besides this one.

The second sort of believers in reincarnation affirm the existence of the other world, and they consider reincarnation the means of becoming perfect—that is, they think that man, by going from and coming again to this world, will gradually acquire perfections, until he reaches the inmost perfection. In other words, that men are composed of matter and force: matter in the beginning—that is to say, in the first cycle—is imperfect, but on coming repeatedly to this world it progresses and acquires refinement and delicacy, until it becomes like a polished mirror; and force, which is no other than spirit, is realized in it with all the perfections.

This is the presentation of the subject by those who believe in reincarnation and transmigration. We have condensed it; if we entered into the details, it would take much time. This summary is sufficient. No logical arguments and proofs of this question are brought forward; they are only suppositions and inferences from conjectures, and not conclusive arguments. Proofs must be asked for from the believers in reincarnation, and not conjectures, suppositions and imaginations.

But you have asked for arguments of the impossibility of reincarnation. This is what we must now explain. The first argument for its impossibility is that the outward is the expression of the inward; the earth is the mirror of the Kingdom; the material world corresponds to the spiritual world. Now observe that in the sensible world appearances are not repeated, for no being in any respect is identical with, nor the same as, another being. The sign of singleness is visible and apparent in all things. If all the granaries of the world were full of grain, you would not find two grains absolutely alike, the same and identical without any distinction. It is certain that there will be differences and distinctions between them. As the proof of uniqueness exists in all things, and the Oneness and Unity of God is apparent in the reality of all things, the repetition of the same appearance is absolutely impossible. Therefore, reincarnation, which is the repeated appearance of the same spirit with its former essence and condition in this same world of appearance, is impossible and unrealizable. As the repetition of the same appearance is impossible and interdicted for each of the material beings, so for spiritual beings also, a return to the same condition, whether in the arc of descent or in the arc of ascent, is interdicted and impossible, for the material corresponds to the spiritual.

Nevertheless, the return of material beings with regard to species is evident; so the trees which during former years brought forth leaves, blossoms and fruits in the coming years will bring forth exactly the same leaves, blossoms and fruits. This is called the repetition of species. If anyone makes an objection saying that the leaf, the blossom and the fruit have been decomposed, and have descended from the vegetable world to the mineral world, and again have come back from the mineral world to the vegetable world, and, therefore, there has been a repetition—the answer is that the blossom, the leaf and the fruit of last year were decomposed, and these combined elements were disintegrated and were dispersed in space, and that the particles of the leaf and fruit of last year, after decomposition, have not again become combined, and have not returned. On the contrary, by the composition of new elements, the species has returned. It is the same with the human body, which after decomposition becomes disintegrated, and the elements which composed it are dispersed. If, in like manner, this body should again return from the mineral or vegetable world, it would not have exactly the same composition of elements as the former man. Those elements have been decomposed and dispersed; they are dissipated in this vast space. Afterward, other particles of elements have been combined, and a second body has been formed; it may be that one of the particles of the former individual has entered into the composition of the succeeding individual, but these particles have not been conserved and kept, exactly and completely, without addition or diminution, so that they may be combined again, and from that composition and mingling another individual may come into existence. So it cannot be proved that this body with all its particles has returned; that the former man has become the latter; and that, consequently, there has been repetition; that the spirit also, like the body, has returned; and that after death its essence has come back to this world.

If we say that this reincarnation is for acquiring perfections so that matter may become refined and delicate, and that the light of the spirit may be manifest in it with the greatest perfection, this also is mere imagination. For, even supposing we believe in this argument, still change of nature is impossible through renewal and return. The essence of imperfection, by returning, does not become the reality of perfection; complete darkness, by returning, does not become the source of light; the essence of weakness is not transformed into power and might by returning, and an earthly nature does not become a heavenly reality. The tree of Zaqqúm,[1] no matter how frequently it may come back, will not bring forth sweet fruit, and the good tree, no matter how often it may return, will not bear a bitter fruit. Therefore, it is evident that returning and coming back to the material world does not become the cause of perfection. This theory has no proofs nor evidences; it is simply an idea. No, in reality the cause of acquiring perfections is the bounty of God.

The Theosophists believe that man on the arc of ascent[2] will return many times until he reaches the Supreme Center; in that condition matter becomes a clear mirror, the light of the spirit will shine upon it with its full power, and essential perfection will be acquired. Now, this is an established and deep theological proposition, that the material worlds are terminated at the end of the arc of descent, and that the condition of man is at the end of the arc

1. The infernal tree mentioned in the Qur'án.
2. i.e., of the Circle of Existence.

of descent, and at the beginning of the arc of ascent, which is opposite to the Supreme Center. Also, from the beginning to the end of the arc of ascent, there are numerous spiritual degrees. The arc of descent is called beginning,[1] and that of ascent is called progress.[2] The arc of descent ends in materialities, and the arc of ascent ends in spiritualities. The point of the compass in describing a circle makes no retrograde motion, for this would be contrary to the natural movement and the divine order; otherwise, the symmetry of the circle would be spoiled.

Moreover, this material world has not such value or such excellence that man, after having escaped from this cage, will desire a second time to fall into this snare. No, through the Eternal Bounty the worth and true ability of man becomes apparent and visible by traversing the degrees of existence, and not by returning. When the shell is once opened, it will be apparent and evident whether it contains a pearl or worthless matter. When once the plant has grown it will bring forth either thorns or flowers; there is no need for it to grow up again. Besides, advancing and moving in the worlds in a direct order according to the natural law is the cause of existence, and a movement contrary to the system and law of nature is the cause of nonexistence. The return of the soul after death is contrary to the natural movement, and opposed to the divine system.

Therefore, by returning, it is absolutely impossible to obtain existence; it is as if man, after being freed from the womb, should return to it a second time. Consider what a puerile imagination this is which is implied by the belief in reincarnation and transmigration. Believers in it consider the body as a vessel in which the spirit is contained, as water is contained in a cup; this water has been taken from one cup and poured into another. This is child's play.

1. Lit., bringing forth.
2. Lit., producing something new.

They do not realize that the spirit is an incorporeal being, and does not enter and come forth, but is only connected with the body as the sun is with the mirror. If it were thus, and the spirit by returning to this material world could pass through the degrees and attain to essential perfection, it would be better if God prolonged the life of the spirit in the material world until it had acquired perfections and graces; it then would not be necessary for it to taste of the cup of death, or to acquire a second life.

The idea that existence is restricted to this perishable world, and the denial of the existence of divine worlds, originally proceeded from the imaginations of certain believers in reincarnation; but the divine worlds are infinite. If the divine worlds culminated in this material world, creation would be futile: nay, existence would be pure child's play. The result of these endless beings, which is the noble existence of man, would come and go for a few days in this perishable dwelling, and after receiving punishments and rewards, at last all would become perfect. The divine creation and the infinite existing beings would be perfected and completed, and then the Divinity of the Lord, and the names and qualities of God, on behalf of these spiritual beings, would, as regards their effect, result in laziness and inaction! "Glory to thy Lord, the Lord Who is sanctified from all their descriptions."[1]

Such were the limited minds of the former philosophers, like Ptolemy and the others who believed and imagined that the world, life and existence were restricted to this terrestrial globe, and that this boundless space was confined within the nine spheres of heaven, and that all were empty and void. Consider how greatly their thoughts were limited and how weak their minds. Those who believe in reincarnation think that the spiritual worlds are restricted to the worlds of human imagination. Moreover, some of them, like the Druzes and the

1. Cf. Qur'án 37:180.

Nusayris, think that existence is restricted to this physical world. What an ignorant supposition! For in this universe of God, which appears in the most complete perfection, beauty and grandeur, the luminous stars of the material universe are innumerable! Then we must reflect how limitless and infinite are the spiritual worlds, which are the essential foundation. "Take heed ye who are endued with discernment."[1]

But let us return to our subject. In the Divine Scriptures and Holy Books "return" is spoken of, but the ignorant have not understood the meaning, and those who believed in reincarnation have made conjectures on the subject. For what the divine Prophets meant by "return" is not the return of the essence, but that of the qualities; it is not the return of the Manifestation, but that of the perfections. In the Gospel it says that John, the son of Zacharias, is Elias. These words do not mean the return of the rational soul and personality of Elias in the body of John, but rather that the perfections and qualities of Elias were manifested and appeared in John.

A lamp shone in this room last night, and when tonight another lamp shines, we say the light of last night is again shining. Water flows from a fountain; then it ceases; and when it begins to flow a second time, we say this water is the same water flowing again; or we say this light is identical with the former light. It is the same with the spring of last year, when blossoms, flowers and sweet-scented herbs bloomed, and delicious fruits were brought forth; next year we say that those delicious fruits have come back, and those blossoms, flowers and blooms have returned and come again. This does not mean that exactly the same particles composing the flowers of last year have, after decomposition, been again combined and have then come back and returned. On the contrary, the meaning is that the delicacy, freshness, delicious perfume and won-

1. Qur'án 59:2.

derful color of the flowers of last year are visible and apparent in exactly the same manner in the flowers of this year. Briefly, this expression refers only to the resemblance and likeness which exist between the former and latter flowers. The "return" which is mentioned in the Divine Scriptures is this: it is fully explained by the Supreme Pen[1] in the Kitáb-i-Íqán. Refer to it, so that you may be informed of the truth of the divine mysteries.

Upon you be greetings and praise.

---

1. Bahá'u'lláh.

82

PANTHEISM

Question. —How do the Theosophists and the Ṣúfís understand the question of pantheism?[1] What does it mean, and how nearly does it approximate to the truth?

Answer. —Know that the subject of pantheism is ancient. It is a belief not restricted to the Theosophists and the Ṣúfís; on the contrary, some of the sages of Greece believed in it, like Aristotle, who said, "The simple truth is all things, but it is not any one of them." In this case, "simple" is the opposite of "composed"; it is the isolated Reality, which is purified and sanctified from composition and division, and which resolves Itself into innumerable forms. Therefore, Real Existence is all things, but It is not one of the things.

Briefly, the believers in pantheism think that Real Existence can be compared to the sea, and that beings are like the waves of the sea. These waves, which signify the beings, are innumerable forms of that Real Existence; therefore, the Holy Reality is the Sea of Preexistence,[2] and the innumerable forms of the creatures are the waves which appear.

Likewise, they compare this theory to real unity and the infinitude of numbers; the real unity reflects itself in the degrees of infinite numbers, for numbers are the repetition of the real unity. So the number two is the repetition of one, and it is the same with the other numbers.

1. Lit., the unity of existence.
2. God.

One of their proofs is this: all beings are things known of God; and knowledge without things known does not exist, for knowledge is related to that which exists, and not to nothingness. Pure nonexistence can have no specification or individualization in the degrees of knowledge. Therefore, the realities of beings, which are the things known of God the Most High, have the existence which knowledge has,[1] since they have the form of the Divine Knowledge, and they are preexistent, as the Divine Knowledge is preexistent. As knowledge is preexistent, the things known are equally so, and the individualizations and the specifications of beings, which are the preexistent knowledges of the Essence of Unity, are the Divine Knowledge itself. For the realities of the Essence of Unity, knowledge, and the things known, have an absolute unity which is real and established. Otherwise, the Essence of Unity would become the place of multiple phenomena, and the multiplicity of preexistences[2] would become necessary, which is absurd.

So it is proved that the things known constitute knowledge itself, and knowledge the Essence itself—that is to say, that the Knower, the knowledge and the things known are one single reality. And if one imagines anything outside of this, it necessitates coming back to the multiplicity of preexistences and to enchainment;[3] and preexistences end by becoming innumerable. As the individualization and the specification of beings in the knowledge of God were the Essence of Unity itself, and as there was not any difference between them, there was but one veritable Unity, and all the things known were diffused and included in the reality of the one Essence—that is to say, that, according to the mode of simplicity and of unity,

1. i.e., an intellectual existence.
2. gods.
3. i.e., infinite continuation of causes and effects.

they constitute the knowledge of God the Most High, and the Essence of the Reality. When God manifested His glory, these individualizations and these specifications of beings which had a virtual existence—that is to say, which were a form of the Divine Knowledge—found their existence substantiated in the external world; and this Real Existence resolved Itself into infinite forms. Such is the foundation of their argument.

The Theosophists and the Ṣúfís are divided into two branches: one, comprising the mass, who, simply in the spirit of imitation, believe pantheism without comprehending the meaning of their renowned savants; for the mass of the Ṣúfís believe that the signification of Being is general existence, taken substantively, which is comprehended by the reason and the intelligence—that is to say, that man comprehends it. Instead of that, this general existence is one of the accidents which penetrate the reality of beings, and the qualities of beings are the essence. This accidental existence, which is dependent on beings, is like other properties of things which depend on them. It is an accident among accidents, and certainly that which is the essence is superior to that which is the accident. For the essence is the origin, and the accident is the consequence; the essence is dependent on itself, and the accident is dependent on something else—that is to say, it needs an essence upon which to depend. In this case, God would be the consequence of the creature. He would have need of it, and it would be independent of Him.

For example, each time that the isolated elements combine conformably to the divine universal system, one being among beings comes into the world. That is to say, that when certain elements combine, a vegetable existence is produced; when others combine, it is an animal; again others combine, and they produce different creatures. In this case, the existence of things is the consequence of their reality: how could it be that this existence, which is an accident among accidents, and necessitates another essence upon which it depends, should be the Preexistent Essence, the Author of all things?

But the initiated savants of the Theosophists and Ṣúfís, who have studied this question, think there are two categories of existence. One is general existence, which is understood by the human intelligence; this is a phenomenon, an accident among accidents, and the reality of the things is the essence. But pantheism does not apply to this general and imaginary existence, but only to the Veritable Existence, freed and sanctified from all other interpretation; through It all things exist, and It is the Unity through which all things have come into the world, such as matter, energy and this general existence which is comprehended by the human mind. Such is the truth of this question according to the Theosophists and the Ṣúfís.

Briefly, with regard to this theory that all things exist by the Unity, all are agreed—that is to say, the philosophers and the Prophets. But there is a difference between them. The Prophets say, The Knowledge of God has no need of the existence of beings, but the knowledge of the creature needs the existence of things known; if the Knowledge of God had need of any other thing, then it would be the knowledge of the creature, and not that of God. For the Preexistent is different from the phenomenal, and the phenomenal is opposed to the Preexistent; that which we attribute to the creature—that is, the necessities of the contingent beings—we deny for God; for purification, or sanctification from imperfections, is one of His necessary properties. So in the phenomenal we see ignorance; in the Preexistent we recognize knowledge. In the phenomenal we see weakness; in the Preexistent we recognize power. In the phenomenal we see poverty; in the Preexistent we recognize wealth. So the phenomenal is

the source of imperfections, and the Preexistent is the sum
of perfections. The phenomenal knowledge has need of
things known; the Preexistent Knowledge is independent
of their existence. So the preexistence of the specification
and of the individualization of beings which are the things
known of God the Most High does not exist; and these divine and perfect attributes are not so understood by the
intelligence that we can decide if the Divine Knowledge
has need of things known or not.

Briefly, this is the principal argument of the Ṣúfís; and
if we wished to mention all their proofs and explain their
answers, it would take a very long time. This is their decisive proof and their plain argument—at least, of the savants of the Ṣúfís and the Theosophists.

But the question of the Real Existence by which all
things exist—that is to say, the reality of the Essence of
Unity through which all creatures have come into the
world—is admitted by everyone. The difference resides
in that which the Ṣúfís say, "The reality of the things is the
manifestation of the Real Unity." But the Prophets say, "it
emanates from the Real Unity"; and great is the difference
between manifestation and emanation. The appearance in
manifestation means that a single thing appears in infinite
forms. For example, the seed, which is a single thing possessing the vegetative perfections, which it manifests in
infinite forms, resolving itself into branches, leaves,
flowers and fruits: this is called appearance in manifestation; whereas in the appearance through emanation this
Real Unity remains and continues in the exaltation of Its
sanctity, but the existence of creatures emanates from It
and is not manifested by It. It can be compared to the sun
from which emanates the light which pours forth on all the
creatures; but the sun remains in the exaltation of its sanctity. It does not descend, and it does not resolve itself into
luminous forms; it does not appear in the substance of

things through the specification and the individualization of things; the Preexistent does not become the phenomenal; independent wealth does not become enchained poverty; pure perfection does not become absolute imperfection.

To recapitulate: the Ṣúfís admit God and the creature, and say that God resolves Himself into the infinite forms of the creatures, and manifests like the sea, which appears in the infinite forms of the waves. These phenomenal and imperfect waves are the same thing as the Preexistent Sea, which is the sum of all the divine perfections. The Prophets, on the contrary, believe that there is the world of God, the world of the Kingdom, and the world of Creation: three things. The first emanation from God is the bounty of the Kingdom, which emanates and is reflected in the reality of the creatures, like the light which emanates from the sun and is resplendent in creatures; and this bounty, which is the light, is reflected in infinite forms in the reality of all things, and specifies and individualizes itself according to the capacity, the worthiness and the intrinsic value of things. But the affirmation of the Ṣúfís requires that the Independent Wealth should descend to the degree of poverty, that the Preexistent should confine itself to phenomenal forms, and that Pure Power should be restricted to the state of weakness, according to the limitations of contingent beings. And this is an evident error. Observe that the reality of man, who is the most noble of creatures, does not descend to the reality of the animal, that the essence of the animal, which is endowed with the powers of sensation, does not abase itself to the degree of the vegetable, and that the reality of the vegetable, which is the power of growth, does not descend to the reality of the mineral.

Briefly, the superior reality does not descend nor abase itself to inferior states; then how could it be that the Uni-

versal Reality of God, which is freed from all descriptions
and qualifications, notwithstanding Its absolute sanctity
and purity, should resolve Itself into the forms of the
realities of the creatures, which are the source of imperfections? This is a pure imagination which one cannot
conceive.

On the contrary, this Holy Essence is the sum of the
divine perfections; and all creatures are favored by the
bounty of resplendency through emanation, and receive
the lights, the perfection and the beauty of Its Kingdom, in
the same way that all earthly creatures obtain the bounty
of the light of the rays of the sun, but the sun does not descend and does not abase itself to the favored realities of
earthly beings.

After dinner, and considering the lateness of the hour,
there is no time to explain further.

Salutations.

83

THE FOUR METHODS OF ACQUIRING KNOWLEDGE

THERE are only four accepted methods of comprehension—that is to say, the realities of things are understood by these four methods.

The first method is by the senses—that is to say, all that the eye, the ear, the taste, the smell, the touch perceive is understood by this method. Today this method is considered the most perfect by all the European philosophers: they say that the principal method of gaining knowledge is through the senses; they consider it supreme, although it is imperfect, for it commits errors. For example, the greatest of the senses is the power of sight. The sight sees the mirage as water, and it sees images reflected in mirrors as real and existent; large bodies which are distant appear to be small, and a whirling point appears as a circle. The sight believes the earth to be motionless and sees the sun in motion, and in many similar cases it makes mistakes. Therefore, we cannot trust it.

The second is the method of reason, which was that of the ancient philosophers, the pillars of wisdom; this is the method of the understanding. They proved things by reason and held firmly to logical proofs; all their arguments are arguments of reason. Notwithstanding this, they differed greatly, and their opinions were contradictory. They even changed their views—that is to say, during twenty years they would prove the existence of a thing by logical arguments, and afterward they would deny it by logical arguments—so much so that Plato at first logically

proved the immobility of the earth and the movement of
the sun; later by logical arguments he proved that the sun
was the stationary center, and that the earth was moving.
Afterward the Ptolemaic theory was spread abroad, and
the idea of Plato was entirely forgotten, until at last a new
observer again called it to life. Thus all the mathematicians disagreed, although they relied upon arguments of
reason. In the same way, by logical arguments, they
would prove a problem at a certain time, then afterward
by arguments of the same nature they would deny it. So
one of the philosophers would firmly uphold a theory for a
time with strong arguments and proofs to support it,
which afterward he would retract and contradict by
arguments of reason. Therefore, it is evident that the
method of reason is not perfect, for the differences of the
ancient philosophers, the want of stability and the varia-
tions of their opinions, prove this. For if it were perfect, all
ought to be united in their ideas and agreed in their opinions.

The third method of understanding is by tradition—
that is, through the text of the Holy Scriptures—for
people say, "In the Old and New Testaments, God spoke
thus." This method equally is not perfect, because the
traditions are understood by the reason. As the reason itself is liable to err, how can it be said that in interpreting
the meaning of the traditions it will not err, for it is possible for it to make mistakes, and certainty cannot be attained. This is the method of the religious leaders; whatever they understand and comprehend from the text of the
books is that which their reason understands from the
text, and not necessarily the real truth; for the reason is
like a balance, and the meanings contained in the text of
the Holy Books are like the thing which is weighed. If the
balance is untrue, how can the weight be ascertained?

Know then: that which is in the hands of people, that
which they believe, is liable to error. For, in proving or

disproving a thing, if a proof is brought forward which is taken from the evidence of our senses, this method, as has become evident, is not perfect; if the proofs are intellectual, the same is true; or if they are traditional, such proofs also are not perfect. Therefore, there is no standard in the hands of people upon which we can rely.

But the bounty of the Holy Spirit gives the true method of comprehension which is infallible and indubitable. This is through the help of the Holy Spirit which comes to man, and this is the condition in which certainty can alone be attained.

84

THE NECESSITY OF
FOLLOWING THE TEACHINGS
OF THE DIVINE MANIFESTATIONS

Question. —Those who are blessed with good actions and universal benevolence, who have praiseworthy characteristics, who act with love and kindness toward all creatures, who care for the poor, and who strive to establish universal peace—what need have they of the divine teachings, of which they think indeed that they are independent? What is the condition of these people?

Answer. —Know that such actions, such efforts and such words are praiseworthy and approved, and are the glory of humanity. But these actions alone are not sufficient; they are a body of the greatest loveliness, but without spirit. No, that which is the cause of everlasting life, eternal honor, universal enlightenment, real salvation and prosperity is, first of all, the knowledge of God. It is known that the knowledge of God is beyond all knowledge, and it is the greatest glory of the human world. For in the existing knowledge of the reality of things there is material advantage, and through it outward civilization progresses; but the knowledge of God is the cause of spiritual progress and attraction, and through it the perception of truth, the exaltation of humanity, divine civilization, rightness of morals and illumination are obtained.

Second, comes the love of God, the light of which shines in the lamp of the hearts of those who know God; its brilliant rays illuminate the horizon and give to man the life of the Kingdom. In truth, the fruit of human existence is the love of God, for this love is the spirit of life, and the eternal bounty. If the love of God did not exist, the contingent world would be in darkness; if the love of God did not exist, the hearts of men would be dead, and deprived of the sensations of existence; if the love of God did not exist, spiritual union would be lost; if the love of God did not exist, the light of unity would not illuminate humanity; if the love of God did not exist, the East and West, like two lovers, would not embrace each other; if the love of God did not exist, division and disunion would not be changed into fraternity; if the love of God did not exist, indifference would not end in affection; if the love of God did not exist, the stranger would not become the friend. The love of the human world has shone forth from the love of God and has appeared by the bounty and grace of God.

It is clear that the reality of mankind is diverse, that opinions are various and sentiments different; and this difference of opinions, of thoughts, of intelligence, of sentiments among the human species arises from essential necessity; for the differences in the degrees of existence of creatures is one of the necessities of existence, which unfolds itself in infinite forms. Therefore, we have need of a general power which may dominate the sentiments, the opinions and the thoughts of all, thanks to which these divisions may no longer have effect, and all individuals may be brought under the influence of the unity of the world of humanity. It is clear and evident that this greatest power in the human world is the love of God. It brings the different peoples under the shadow of the tent of affection; it gives to the antagonistic and hostile nations and families the greatest love and union.

See, after the time of Christ, through the power of the love of God, how many nations, races, families and tribes came under the shadow of the Word of God. The divisions and differences of a thousand years were entirely destroyed and annihilated. The thoughts of race and of fatherland completely disappeared. The union of souls and of existences took place; all became true spiritual Christians.

The third virtue of humanity is the goodwill which is the basis of good actions. Certain philosophers have considered intention superior to action, for the goodwill is absolute light; it is purified and sanctified from the impurities of selfishness, of enmity, of deception. Now it may be that a man performs an action which in appearance is righteous, but which is dictated by covetousness. For example, a butcher rears a sheep and protects it; but this righteous action of the butcher is dictated by desire to derive profit, and the result of this care is the slaughter of the poor sheep. How many righteous actions are dictated by covetousness! But the goodwill is sanctified from such impurities.

Briefly, if to the knowledge of God is joined the love of God, and attraction, ecstasy and goodwill, a righteous action is then perfect and complete. Otherwise, though a good action is praiseworthy, yet if it is not sustained by the knowledge of God, the love of God, and a sincere intention, it is imperfect. For example, the being of man must unite all perfections to be perfect. Sight is extremely precious and appreciated, but it must be aided by hearing; the hearing is much appreciated, but it must be aided by the power of speech; the faculty of speech is very acceptable, but it must be aided by the power of reason, and so forth. The same is true of the other powers, organs and members of man; when all these powers, these senses, these organs, these members exist together, he is perfect.

Now, today, we meet with people in the world who, in truth, desire the universal good, and who according to their power occupy themselves in protecting the oppressed and in aiding the poor: they are enthusiastic for peace and the universal well-being. Although from this point of view they may be perfect, if they are deprived of the knowledge and love of God, they are imperfect.

Galen, the physician, in his book in which he comments on the treatise of Plato on the art of government,[1] says that the fundamental principles of religion have a great influence upon a perfect civilization because "the multitude cannot understand the connection of explanatory words; so it has need of symbolical words announcing the rewards and punishments of the other world; and that which proves the truth of this affirmation," he says, "is that today we see a people called Christians who believe in rewards and punishments; and this sect show forth beautiful actions like those which a true philosopher performs. So we all see clearly that they do not fear death, that they expect and desire nothing from the multitude but justice and equity, and they are considered as true philosophers."

Now observe what was the degree of the sincerity, the zeal, the spiritual feeling, the obligation of friendship, and the good actions of a believer in Christ, so that Galen, the philosophical physician, although he was not of the Christian religion, should yet bear witness to the good morals and the perfections of these people, to the point of saying that they were true philosophers. These virtues, these morals, were obtained not only through good actions, for if virtue were only a matter of obtaining and giving forth good, as this lamp is lighted and illuminates the house—without doubt this illumination is a benefit—then why do we not praise the lamp? The sun causes all the beings of the earth to increase, and by its heat and light gives growth and development: is there a greater benefit than that? Nevertheless, as this good does not

1. Cf. Ibn Abí Uṣaybiʻa, *ʻUyūn al-anbā fī ṭabaqāt al-aṭibbā* (Cairo: 1882) tom. i., pp. 76–77.

come from goodwill and from the love and knowledge of God, it is imperfect.

When, on the contrary, a man gives to another a cup of water, the latter is grateful and thanks him. A man, without reflecting, will say, "This sun which gives light to the world, this supreme bounty which is apparent in it, must be adored and praised. Why should we not be grateful and thankful to the sun for its bounty, when we praise a man who performs a simple act of kindness?" But if we look for the truth, we see that this insignificant kindness of the man is due to conscious feelings which exist; therefore, it is worthy of praise, whereas the light and heat of the sun are not due to the feelings and consciousness; therefore, they are not worthy of eulogy or of praise and do not deserve gratitude or thanks.

In the same way, when a person performs a good action, although it is praiseworthy, if it is not caused by the love and knowledge of God, it is imperfect. Moreover, if you reflect justly, you will see that these good actions of other men who do not know God are also fundamentally caused by the teachings of God—that is to say, that the former Prophets led men to perform these actions, explained their beauty to them, and declared their splendid effects; then these teachings were diffused among men and reached them successively, one after the other, and turned their hearts toward these perfections. When men saw that these actions were considered beautiful, and became the cause of joy and happiness for mankind, they conformed to them.

Wherefore these actions also come from the teachings of God. But justice is needed to see this, and not controversy and discussion. Praise be to God, you have been to Persia, and you have seen how the Persians, through the holy breezes of Bahá'u'lláh, have become benevolent toward humanity. Formerly, if they met anyone of another race, they tormented him and were filled with the utmost enmity, hatred and malevolence; they went so far as to throw dirt at him. They burned the Gospel and the Old Testament, and if their hands were polluted by touching these books, they washed them. Today the greater number of them recite and chant, as is suitable, the contents of these two Books in their reunions and assemblies, and they expound their esoteric teaching. They show hospitality to their enemies. They treat the bloodthirsty wolves with gentleness, like gazelles in the plains of the love of God. You have seen their customs and habits, and you have heard of the manners of former Persians. This transformation of morals, this improvement of conduct and of words, are they possible otherwise than through the love of God? No, in the name of God. If, by the help of science and knowledge, we wished to introduce these morals and customs, truly it would take a thousand years, and then they would not be spread throughout the masses.

Today, thanks to the love of God, they are arrived at with the greatest facility.

Be admonished, O possessors of intelligence!

INDEX

INDEX